Introduction

This book is not meant to show distain for the position of President of the United States. In this book I do not make reference to Donald Trump as President. I have great respect for the institution of U.S. President and our government. This book will evolve as time goes on and more indictments come forth. The most damaging being the results of the investigations coming from New York State. There will be another book with another version and volume # 2

Donald Trump likes to use words usually saved for organized crime figures such as Mafia Dons(is this a coincidence Mafia Dons-Donald Trump) however when they are being investigated or arrested. He has surrounded himself with individuals who have used their political associations or positions in the White house to obtain financial gain. Donald Trump's business method of operation with his businesses has bled over to his time in the White house. He avoids offending the Ku Klux Klan and Nazi Organizations.

Trump has miscalculated and underestimated the investigative branch of our government. He has ignored the incredible reputation of Special Counsel Robert

Mueller and the Justice Department.  Like many others who look to bypass laws and norms disputes the FBI. Like John Gotti also found out when sentenced to prison who was also a flamboyant, outspoken figure in public. Trumps association with the underbelly/gutter of our society, and his untruthfulness will come back to haunt him.  Uses the fraise "witch hunt" of the Justice Department investigation of him, his associates, his business practices and into his organization has produced many witches, and the biggest witch is him. There seems to be indicators Donald Trump is a racist, however regardless if he is or not people and organizations which are racist believe he is and support him.

Dedication

To those Who Do Not believe In Alternative Facts And Do Not Believe In Circumventing the Truth.

About Your Author

Retired Police Officer/Detective
B.S. Interdisciplinary Studies-2006
M.S. Criminal Justice/Behavioral Tract-2009
P.H.D. (abd) Public Policy Administration/Homeland
Security.-2013

Married to Doris Derrig

Contents Page

**Conclusion Repeated For effect of Issues to Bring the Truth Home.**

Chap 1-Results of Special Council Robert Mueller Investigation

# Trump Administration (so far in 2yrs)

191 charges
75 indictments
26 Russian nationals
6 indicted Trump officials
5 guilty pleas
5 convictions
3 Russian companies

SIX WITCHES FOUND ABOVE

Trump did not drain the swamp he added to it.
Remember the old saying you can judge a person by the

company he keeps.  Another way to look at this is the lives destroyed as a result of their association with Donald Trump.  Like people having their children torn from them at the border as a result of his policies, associates of his are being separated from their love ones/families as a result of going to prison. Trump's behavior and method of operation draws/attracts people to him who are unethical with a propensity to break the law.

## Chap. 2 Biological Profile of Donald Trump-Witch # 7

It is helpful to look at the biological profile of Donald Trump.  His Grandfather & father Fred Trump also displayed great abilities to mass a fortune.  The difference in them and Donald Trump is their fortunes were not given to them they had to earn them.  Some of this earning did come by way of illegal activity and vices.  Donald Trump did not have the experience of working at the bottom on one's way up.  His father gave him millions of dollars.  When Donald's business dealing started to fail his father would bail him out with millions of dollars to pour into his ventures.

Donald Trumps personal traits can not all be as a result of his environment and upbringing.  His environment and family tree gene interactions of course played a role.  However, where Donald breaks from the norm is his method of over running or verbally using the same tactics he used in his private businesses while in elected office.  Those who do not agree with him in business he just over powered with his and his father wealth.  In the White House and on the campaign trail he resorts to bullying, and name calling.

Trump resorts to lying often which includes rationalizing that made it less dishonest.  He relies on social deception and his ability create a false effect.

Trump has proven to be a compulsive liar.  He is a person who habitually fails to resist the temptation of lying. He like other who habitually lie are good at it. (and typically have high verbal IQs); he takes morality out of the equation.  Where Trump runs into trouble is the media listens to his every word and does fact checking.  The minute he lies a news outlet picks up on it.  When his lying and incorrect statement is discovered by a news outlet, he uses his favorite fall back word- "Fake News".  He ran his businesses in real-estate on deception, false business records and untruthfulness.  The differences there were very few checks and balances of his business actions before he entered the Whitehouse. When he applied for his casino license there wasn't even a check of his financial records. He got buy with his and his fathers associations and known wealth. He had a unchecked pathological pursuit of profit and power.

Donald Trump has stepped outside the norm of people we expect to show virtue and leadership. People tend to emulate those who are at a higher stage of moral development. Because of this tendency, placing virtuous persons in leadership roles can have a positive moral impact on an entire organization. Donald Trump has repeatedly throughout his business career circumvented correct honorable actions. Do we want our children to grow up and be like Donald Trump, I would hope not.

In Conclusion:

I agree with those that we at times have to break from tribal politics. The voting a strict political line regardless of the candidate's history and moral aptitude is a mistake. Voters who support Donald Trump generally do not believe in climate change, have a stronger need for closer, dislike novelty, are more comforted by structure and hierarchy.

perceive circumstances as threatening, and are more parochial in their empathy. As a result of system justification allows Trump followers to rationalize and be less discomfited by inequality.

Many of Donald Trump's followers view our best days are behind us, in familiar circumstances that should be returned to, to "Makes Things Great Again "or "Make America Great Again".  Your author believes America was great before, now & will be great going forward, despite Donald Trump. Donald Trump has persuaded impoverished white Americans to so often vote against their own economic self-interest.  Donald Trump depends on the psychological issues of needing structured familiarity show that for poor whites, voting Trump constitutes an implicit act of system justification and risk aversion. Better to resist change and deal with the devil you know.  Another words Donald Trump takes advantage of those who do not do their research and are attracted to a side show.  It is your authors contention that the lower and middle class are more likely to win a million dollars in the lottery than obtain help from Donald Trump's policies and tax breaks.  Donald Trump has a long history of looking out for the upper class, and corporations.

Timelines

Personnel

Direct
indictments
(list of
charges)

Frederick Trump & Family

**Donald Trumps Grand Father Frederick** In summation, Donald Trump's grandfather Frederick Trump was a German immigrant who made his fortune by opening several restaurants and hotels in Seattle and British Columbia during the Yukon Gold Rush. While some of these hotels may have been used for prostitution, gambling, or other seedy activities common on the trail, it is incorrect to say that Trump built his fortune on illegal activities.

Sources

- Grier, Peter. "Donald Trump: The Son of an Immigrant."
  *The Christian Science Monitor*. 24 August 2015.
- Blair, Gwenda. "The Trumps: Three Generations of Builders and a Presidential Candidate."
  *Simon and Schuster*, 2000. ISBN 0-684-80849-8.

His grandfather, **Friedrich Trump**, a German, lived a migrant life in the US on the edge of illegality and rejection. During the World War I, he belonged to an immigrant group which was sweepingly labelled the "enemy within" or – in his grandson's parlance – a Trojan horse.

## Chap. 3 Donald Trumps Family Tree

## Donald Trump's grandfather was an illegal migrant and 'Trojan horse'

February 26, 2016 4.32am EST

**Author Stefan Manz**

1.  **Stefan Manz**
Reader in German, Aston University

Stefan Manz receives funding from the Arts and Humanities Research Council and the Gerda Henkel Foundation.

**Partners**

Beware Trojan horses.

During New Year celebrations in Cologne, there were more than 500 reported attacks against women, including robbery and sexual assault. Most of the suspects are of **North African origin**, and some are thought to have entered the country illegally or as asylum seekers.

The news was welcome campaign fodder for US presidential hopeful Donald Trump. Referring to German chancellor Angela Merkel's open door policy on refugees from Syria, he commented in his usual rhetoric: "I don't know what the hell she is thinking".

Trump went on to say that he did not want to have "people coming in from migration from Syria (sic)" as these were aggressive young men who "look like they should be on the wrestling team". More dangerously still, Trump believed such people could act as terrorist **"Trojan horses"**.

Trump's comments are in line with his vicious verbal attacks on **Mexicans and other immigrant groups** in the United States. But they betray his own family background. His grandfather, **Friedrich Trump**, a German, lived a migrant life in the US on the edge of illegality and rejection. During the World War I, he belonged to an immigrant group which was sweepingly labelled the "enemy within" or — in his grandson's parlance — a Trojan horse.

## The great wave

Friedrich Trump was swept to the United States in one of the biggest waves of **mass migration in history. During the 1880s and early 1890s, 1.8m Germans emigrated** to various European and overseas destinations. When young Friedrich arrived in New York in 1885 he joined around 200,000 of his compatriots who had already settled in the metropolis, forming a distinct "Little Germany". After working for six years as a barber, he was caught by the Gold Rush, moved west and opened up a chain of restaurants and hotels in Washington State and British Columbia. Hospitality did not only include food and lodging, but also **alcohol and prostitution**. Friedrich anglicised his name to Frederick and became a US citizen.

By 1901, Frederick had made a small fortune and decided to return to his hometown of **Kallstadt** in south-west Germany. (Incidentally, the Heinz family of Ketchup fame has its origins in the same town.) Frederick married his childhood sweetheart, Elisabeth, and planned to settle down.

Frederick Trump.

The Bavarian Palatinate authorities, however, would not let him. They claimed he had left Germany as an illegal emigrant, evading taxes and the compulsory two-year military service. Frederick pleaded that he and Elisabeth were **"loyal Germans and stand behind the high Kaiser and the mighty German Reich"**. It was all to no avail. The Trumps were evicted and resettled to New York.

**Wartime spy fever**

World War I was not a happy time for German-Americans. They were summarily labelled as "alien enemies" whose true allegiance lay with the Fatherland. Nativist spokesmen agitated against "hyphenated Americans" as potential spies and saboteurs. Use of the German language was seen with suspicion. In contrast to many of their compatriots, the Trumps did not need to anglicize their surname as it worked perfectly in English.

The most notorious case of public violence was the lynching of German immigrant **Robert Prager** in Illinois. He was tarred and feathered, forced by an agitated crowd to kiss the American flag and sing patriotic songs, and finally hanged from a tree in front of 200 onlookers.

Frederick Trump evaded the fate of Prager, but not the other deadly weapon which swept the world once the war was nearing its end. In 1918 and 1919, **Spanish influenza** killed between 20m and 50m people worldwide. On a summer's day in 1918, Frederick returned home from a stroll through New York with his son Fred (Donald's father), went to bed feeling sick, and passed away the next day.

## Paranoid nation

The dangerous mix of paranoia and xenophobia directed against German-Americans during World War I had profound and long-lasting effects. The Alien Enemy Bureau was established in the early days of the war with a brief to identify and arrest disloyal foreigners. It was headed by J. Edgar Hoover, then a young civil servant in the Justice Department. Here he picked up the tools he would use later as all-powerful director of the FBI.

In 1940, the notorious House Un-American Affairs Committee published **The Trojan Horse in America**, a compendium of domestic organizations believed to work for foreign powers. Chapter titles included "Mussolini's Trojan Horse in America" and "A Trojan Horse of German War Veterans".

All this was reason enough for the business-minded Trumps to deny their German heritage, claiming they hailed from Sweden instead. Donald's father Fred invested heavily in New York real estate, laying the foundations for today's business empire. It was only from the 1980s that Donald Trump started to **stand by his German roots.**

Trump's own grandfather was an illegal emigrant whose income stream included alcohol and prostitution at a time when these were legally contested. He was an unwanted returnee to Germany, and then a potential "enemy alien" within the United States who had declared his loyalty to the German Kaiser – but ultimately made an immense economic contribution spanning generations.

Today, his grandson lambastes Mexicans as criminals, intends to erect a wall to keep them out, and warns of Syrian refugees as Trojan horses. If Donald Trump wins his party's nomination again, historians will have many a field day digging out the contradictions between his anti-immigrant rhetoric and his family background.

# Donald Trump's Father

## Fred Trump Biography

Frederick Christ Trump Sr., better known as Fred Trump, was an American real-estate developer and the father of the 45th president of the US, Donald Trump. Let's have a look at his family, personal life, career, etc.

**Quick Facts**

**Birthday:** October 11, 1905

**Nationality:**  American

**Famous: Real Estate Entrepreneurs American Men**

**Died At Age:** 93

**Sun Sign:** Libra

**Also Known As:** Frederick Christ Trump Sr., Frederick Christ Trump
**Born In:** The Bronx, New York City, New York
**Famous As:** Real Estate Developer
**Family:**
**Spouse/Ex-:** Mary Anne MacLeod (M. 1936)
**Father:** Frederick Trump
**Mother:** Elizabeth Christ Trump

**Siblings:** John G. Trump

**Children:** Donald Trump, Elizabeth Trump Grau, Frederick Jr., Maryanne Trump Barry, Robert Trump

**Died On:** June 25, 1999

**Place Of Death:** Long Island Jewish Medical Center, New York City, New York

**City: New York City**

**U.S. State:** New Yorkers

Frederick Christ Trump Sr., better known as Fred Trump, was an American real-estate developer and the father of the 45th president of the US, Donald Trump. He was born and raised in New York, US. After his father's death, Fred Trump started a house construction company, in partnership with his mother. He was just 15 years old then. He began with building car garages and progressed to construct apartment houses. He built barracks and apartments near shipyards for 'US Navy' staff, during World War II. He also constructed single-family apartment complexes for returning servicemen and middle-income group people. He built more than 27 thousand apartments in and around New York City. He was investigated for wartime profiteering from public contracts and was called before a 'US Senate' committee. He was a hard-working and ambitious man. Fred Trump and his company faced a racial discrimination suit filed by the 'Civil Rights Division' of the 'US Department of Justice' for violation of the 'Fair Housing Act.' He was married to Mary Anne MacLeod, and they had five children. He suffered from Alzheimer's disease during the later years and died at the age of 93.

Fred Trump

Image credit:
https;//www.youtube.com/watch?y=V6QMY-BTZh0

## Childhood & Early Life

- Fred Trump was born on October 11, 1905, in The Bronx, New York City. His parents, Elizabeth (née Christ) and Frederick Trump, were German Lutheran immigrants. His father was from Kallstadt, Germany, and was a barber who later earned a small fortune in the 'Klondike Gold Rush.' He died of flu when Trump was 13.

- Trump was the second of the three children of his parents. He grew up with his elder sister, Elizabeth Trump Walters, and younger brother, John George Trump. His middle name, "Christ," was taken from his mother's maiden name. Their family shifted to Woodhaven, Queens, after Fred's birth. He studied at the 'Richmond Hill High School.'

- He was only 15 years old when he founded his own construction business, in partnership with his mother, Elizabeth, in the 1920s. He named the venture 'E. Trump & Son.' As he was underage, his mother handled the official work till he was 21. Trump began by building garages for the newly invented and marketed automobiles.

- He learnt carpentry and studied how to read blueprints. He built his first house two years after graduating.

## Career

- Trump had already completed 20 buildings in Queens by 1926. He built a supermarket, 'Trump Market,' in Woodhaven, during the 'Great Depression' of the 1930s. His market, which used the tagline "Serve Yourself and Save!," became successful, and the next year, he sold it to the supermarket chain 'King Kullen.'
- On 'Memorial Day' in 1927, he was one of the seven people arrested in Queens for "...refusing to disperse from a parade when ordered to do so." It was a 'Ku Klux Klan' (KKK) rally of about a thousand people. The rally was held as a protest against the assault on the "Native-born Protestant Americans" by the 'Roman Catholic Police' of New York City. It was not clear whether Trump was an innocent bystander, was arrested due to mistaken identity, or was actually a participant of the rally. It was later reported that he was released without any charges. While answering a press question in 2015, Donald Trump said that his father had not been arrested and that he had never been a member of the 'KKK.'

- Fred Trump's company constructed barracks and apartments for the 'US Navy' officers during World War II. These were built near shipyards of various places, including Newport News, Pennsylvania, Chester, and Norfolk, all along the East Coast. He built more than two thousand middle-income group apartments for war veterans and their families. He built 'Shore Haven' in Bensonhurst (in 1949) and 'Beach Haven' near Coney Island (in 1950). He raised a housing complex of more than three thousand apartments called 'Trump Village' in Coney Island, between 1963 and 1964. The cost of this complex was estimated at $70 million.
- A 'US Senate' committee scrutinized Trump's company in 1954, for profiteering from public contracts and for overstating 'Beach Haven' construction charges. Trump and his partner, William Tomasello, were charged for obtaining loans amounting to $3.5 million more than the apartment cost. During federal investigations, it was found that Trump had collected $1.7 million in excess, as rent, before beginning to pay his low-cost government loan. Real-estate developers often paid bureaucrats to approve their paperwork. Apart from collecting the extra rent, Trump had paid a generous architect fee to himself. The estimated construction costs that

he had indicated were much more than the actual amount he had spent. However, everything was legal on the papers.

- He used his political contacts to access government programs such as subsidized financing for apartment building developers. He admitted his manipulations of the government program before the 'US Senate' committee that investigated the housing abuse. However, he believed there was nothing wrong with what he had done, as everything was done within legal boundaries. He, in fact, complained that the investigating committee had caused damage to his reputation. Other builders refused to answer, but he publicly took a self-justifying stand.

- Trump built large apartment complexes and row houses around Sheepshead Bay, Flatbush, Coney Island, Brighton Beach, and Bensonhurst in Brooklyn; and Flushing and Jamaica Estates in Queens. He retained the ownership, and the apartments were given on affordable rent. His constructions were marked with sturdy brick towers, with neat and presentable parks around them.

- Donald Trump joined 'Trump Management' in 1968, and in 1980, he changed the name to 'The Trump Organization.' During the mid-1970s, he took a loan of $ 1 million from his father to start his own real-estate business in Manhattan. Reportedly, there were a number of loans, which amounted to much more than what was stated.

- Fred Trump was often compared to car magnate Henry Ford. He hated borrowing money and was very frugal by nature. It is said that he would visit the construction sites after a day's work and collect the nails that he found lying around. He would then hand them over to the carpenters the following day. For quite some time, he did not have an office and operated from home. He did all his bookkeeping in a small pocketbook. Around 1940, he got a small place as his office. Amy Luerssen worked as his secretary for 59 years.

- There were charges of racial discrimination against his real-estate company. Reportedly, potential tenants of African–American descent were denied houses in the complexes. In 1973, a case was filed by the 'Civil Rights Division' of the 'US Department of Justice' against 'The Trump Organization' for violating the 'Fair Housing Act' of 1968. The case continued for two years. A consent decree was signed on June 10, 1975, between the 'Department of Justice' and 'The Trump Organization,' and it prohibited the organization from discriminating against people while selling or renting out an apartment. Folk artist Woody Guthrie was one of the tenants at Trump's apartment complex in Brooklyn, in 1950. He wrote a song that clearly suggested that African–American people were not welcome as tenants in Trump's housing complexes.

- During the post-World War II years, Trump claimed to be of Swedish descent and concealed his German ancestry. Those were the peak years of his career. As many of his tenants were Jewish, he was afraid that the German lineage would hurt the business.

## Personal Life

- Trump married Mary Anne MacLeod in January 1936. They lived in Jamaica, Queens, and had five children: Maryanne Trump Barry (born 1937), who later became a federal appeals court judge; Frederick Christ Trump Jr. (born 1938), who later became an airline pilot; Elizabeth Trump Grau (born 1942), a 'Chase Manhattan Bank' executive; Donald Trump (born 1946), the 45th president of the US; and Robert Trump (born 1948), president of 'Trump Management.' Frederick Trump Jr. died in 1981, following alcoholism-related complications.
- Trump supported various charity houses, including various Jewish and Israeli institutions, the 'Salvation Army,' the 'Boy Scouts of America,' and the 'Kew-

Forest School,' where his children studied. He
donated buildings to organizations such as the
'Jamaica Hospital Medical Center,' the 'National
Kidney Foundation,' the 'Cerebral Palsy Foundation,'
and the 'Community Mainstreaming Associates of
Great Neck.'

- Trump suffered from Alzheimer's disease for the last
six years of his life. In June 1999, he fell ill with
pneumonia and was admitted to the 'Long Island
Jewish Medical Center.' He died on June 25, 1999, at
the age of 93.

Author
- Editors, TheFamousPeople.com
Website
- TheFamousPeople.com
URL
- https://www.thefamouspeople.com/profiles/fred-trump-11975.php
Last Updated
- July 17, 2018

**Fred Trump**

Donald Trump's Immigrant Mother
By Mary Pilon
June 24, 2016

*Donald Trump's mother, Mary, was an immigrant. But Trump doesn't often bring up his Scottish ancestry on the campaign trail.*
Photograph by Marina Garnier / NYP Holdings, Inc. via Getty

In November of 1929, a seventeen-year-old Scotswoman, Mary Anne MacLeod, boarded the S.S. Transylvania in Glasgow, bound for New York City. With a high arching brow and deep, round eyes, MacLeod hailed from Tong, a remote fishing community in the parish of Stornoway, in the Outer Hebrides of Scotland. Although the American stock market was in a freefall, Europe, in the shadow of war, was in no better shape. Scots had been emigrating for years, trying to find better opportunities.

In New York, MacLeod would find a well-established community of countrymen and women, including two of her sisters. She took more than one transatlantic trip before settling in New York, in the thirties. On at least two ship manifests and in the 1930 census, her occupation is listed as "maid" or "domestic."

Mary MacLeod would eventually become Mary Trump, the mother of Donald Trump, the presumptive Republican nominee for President. She died in 2000, long before her son's political ascent but not before he became a business celebrity. This week, Trump visited his mother's homeland, attending the official opening of a renovated Trump Turnberry, a golf course he owns in South Ayrshire. As global markets dropped precipitously in response to the Brexit referendum, just the day before, in which British citizens voted to break from the European Union, Trump praised the sprinkler systems on the course—"the highest level"—and Turnberry's "incredible suites." His Turnberry speech was almost entirely about his golf course, but he did talk about his mother, and how she had enjoyed eating dinner at Turnberry when she returned to Scotland to visit. "Her loyalty to Scotland was incredible," he said. "She respected and loved the Queen."

Get the best of *The New Yorker* every day, in your in-box. Sign me up

Like Barack Obama's father, Trump's mother was an immigrant. But Trump doesn't often bring up his Scottish ancestry on the campaign trail. The "about" section of the Trump campaign's Web site makes no mention of the Scottish-born matriarch, nor have his opponents reached much for the chance at a dig, given Trump's campaign-defining comments about immigrants, at least those from Mexico or who are Muslims. Only Ted Cruz brought up Mrs. Trump's Scottish birth, in a Republican Presidential debate in January.

A request for comment from representatives with the Trump campaign went unanswered.

Mary Anne MacLeod was born on May 10, 1912. Her father, Malcolm, was a fisherman on the remote Isle of Lewis, and he and his wife, Mary Smith, raised a large brood of children. Tong is still dominated by fishing and, increasingly, tourism, and many extended MacLeod relatives live in the area. None of Trump's cousins wish to speak to the press, William Foulger, the secretary of the Stornoway Historical Society, said, nor does the owner of the family home.

In the thirties, MacLeod reportedly met Frederick Christ Trump at a dance, and the two fell in love, according to a 2005 profile of the Trump family in *Real Estate Weekly*, although it has been disputed whether she was living in the United States at the time or just visiting. Fred Trump was a builder, having started a construction business while he was still in high school. By the late twenties, he was selling single-family houses in Queens for $3,990 each. Fred Trump and Mary MacLeod married in 1936 and settled in Jamaica, Queens, at the time a haven for Western European immigrants. By 1940, the couple lived with their two children and a Scottish maid, according to census records. The value of their home was twelve thousand and five hundred dollars, or two hundred and fourteen thousand dollars today. Fred made five thousand dollars a year, or about eighty-six thousand in 2016 dollars. As the Second World War raged in Europe, on March 10, 1942, the U.S. District Court in Brooklyn made Mary Trump a naturalized citizen.

Fred Trump's fortunes would rise with the postwar real-estate boom, as throngs of middle-class dwellings sprouted in Brooklyn and Queens. A review of ship manifests reflects the changing nature of Mary Trump's travel, from immigrant steamship to cruises and flights with her family to the Bahamas, Puerto Rico, and Cuba, in the fifties. As the wife of a wealthy developer, Mary Trump became a regular on the New York social circuit and worked on a number of philanthropic causes, including organizations for cerebral palsy and intellectually disabled adults.

This was not the life a fisherman's daughter from the Hebrides might have expected. Among Scots, "she would have been considered a bit of a hick," said Richard Zumkhawala-Cook, an English professor with a focus on Scotland at Shippensburg University of Pennsylvania. "Americans wouldn't have cared," he said, but "most Scots wouldn't have gone there because it's so remote from cosmopolitan ideas, attitudes, and access. Scots Gaelic was not always something they wanted to speak proudly."

In his 1997 book, "The Art of the Comeback," Trump praised his mother—and indirectly criticized other women in his life. "Part of the problem I've had with women has been in having to compare them to my incredible mother, Mary Trump," Trump wrote. "My mother is smart as hell." Trump named a room after his mother at Mar-a-Lago.

Both mother and son shared a penchant for dynamic hair sculpting, as for years Mary Trump appeared in photos with a dramatic orange swirl. Slight in frame, she took to New York City's streets draped in furs and jewelry, a far cry from the teen-age girl who set sail during the Great Depression. "Looking back, I realize now that I got some of my sense of showmanship from my mother," Trump wrote in his 1987 book, "The Art of the Deal." He recounted his mother "being enthralled by the pomp and circumstance" of watching Queen Elizabeth's coronation on television. "She always had a flair for the dramatic and grand. She was a very traditional housewife, but she also had a sense of the world beyond her."

Mary Trump died in New York City, in 2000, at the age of eighty-eight, just a year after her husband. In the aftermath of his mother's death, Trump has had a turbulent history with her homeland. Following Trump's comments regarding Muslims, reports have surfaced that organizers of the 2020 British Open have ruled out staging the event at Trump Turnberry. Trump was stripped of an honorary degree from the Robert Gordon University, in Aberdeen, because of campaign statements that were "wholly incompatible with the ethos and values of the university," a spokesman for the school said. In December, Trump was deemed, by representatives of the Scottish government, who also cited his comments regarding Muslims, "no longer fit" to be a business ambassador to the nation.

Today, Mary Anne Trump is buried in a cemetery in New Hyde Park, New York, next to her husband, her son Fred C. Trump, Jr., and her mother- and father-in-law. More than a third of the people who live in the neighborhood surrounding the cemetery are foreign-born.

- *Mary Pilon is the author of "The Monopolists," a book about the board game Monopoly. She previously worked as a staff reporter at the Times and the Wall Street Journal, where she wrote about sports and business.*

# Chap. 4 Witches Found

## Witches Found-Witch # 1

Paul Manafort Biography
Lawyer, Political Consultant (1949–)

- 
- 
- 
- 
- 

Paul Manafort is a political consultant who served as a campaign manager of presidential candidate Donald Trump in 2016. He was later indicted for money laundering and conspiracy against the United States by special counsel Robert Mueller and sentenced to 90 months in prison.

## Who Is Paul Manafort?

Paul J. Manafort Jr. served as one of **Donald J. Trump**'s campaign managers during America's 2016 presidential election. Prior to this Manafort had earned a reputation as a political consultant who offered his lobbying skills to clients around the globe, some of whom were among the world's most corrupt rulers. In October 2017, a federal grand jury indicted Manafort on 12 counts, including money laundering and conspiracy against the United

States — a result from the investigation of special counsel **Robert Mueller**. Following an August 2018 trial, in which he was convicted on eight counts of bank and tax fraud, and an attempted plea deal, he was sentenced to 7 1/2 years behind bars.

Paul Manafort, former campaign manager for Donald Trump, walks out of the U.S. Courthouse after a bond hearing in Washington, D.C., on Monday, Nov. 6, 2017. (Photo: Andrew Harrer/Bloomberg)

**Indictments**

On October 30, 2017, Manafort surrendered to the FBI to face a 12-count indictment. The charges included conspiracy, failing to register as a foreign agent, not reporting foreign income and making false statements. Manafort was also accused of laundering $18 million. In court he pleaded not guilty to the charges and was released on house arrest with a $10 million bond.

The charges were assembled by special counsel Robert Mueller and his team. Mueller's focus was on Russian interference into the 2016 election, but his office also took over earlier investigations of Manafort (so as not to have overlapping federal inquiries). The charges largely stem from events before the campaign, though Manafort had not registered his prior work as a foreign agent while spearheading Trump's election efforts (in 2017, Manafort belatedly submitted this paperwork).

FBI agents with a no-knock warrant searched Manafort's house in Virginia on the morning of July 26, 2017. They were looking for tax documents and records from foreign banks.

On January 3, 2018, Manafort filed a lawsuit against Mueller and the Justice Department, saying prosecutors had overstepped their bounds by investigating "decade-old business dealings" and charging him for conduct unrelated to Russian interference in the 2016 presidential election.

Manafort's legal problems deepened when Mueller unsealed a new, 32-count indictment in late February that charged the former Trump adviser with lying to banks to secure millions of dollars in loans as part of a long-running money laundering scheme, with help from his business associate Rick Gates. Many of the charges were similar to those from the October 2017 indictment, although the new one outlined additional criminal behavior.

In March, a U.S. district judge assigned to the indictment declared that Manafort posed "a substantial risk of flight" and ordered him confined to house arrest, save for medical appointments, court appearances and meetings with his defense attorneys. "Given the nature of the charges against the defendant and the apparent weight of the evidence against him, defendant faces the very real possibility of spending the rest of his life in prison," wrote the judge.

In early June, prosecutors filed a motion with the U.S. District Court for the District of Columbia, saying they had probable cause to believe that Manafort attempted to tamper with potential witnesses while on pretrial release. According to the filing, Manafort and an associate, a Russian citizen named Konstantin Kilimnik, attempted to repeatedly contact two witnesses to "secure materially false testimony." However, one of the witnesses blew a hole in their covert attempts by submitting saved text messages to the government.

Days later, Manafort was indicted on new charges of conspiring to obstruct justice, prompting a federal judge to revoke his bail and send him to jail to await his July 2018 trial. The news drew a sharp response from President Trump, who cited Manafort's work for **Ronald Reagan and Bob Dole while calling the judge's order** "very unfair."

## Trial and Conviction

Manafort's first trial, in which he faced 18 charges of financial fraud, began on July 31, 2018, in Alexandria, Virginia. Calling him a man who "believed the law did not apply to him," prosecutor Uzo Asonye described Manafort's efforts to conceal earnings from his consultancy work in Ukraine and his method of lying to banks on loan applications, while flouting the system by purchasing a $2 million home and a $15,000 ostrich coat.

The defense countered by shifting blame for wrongdoing to Gates, arguing that Manafort was unaware of the illicit activities orchestrated by his associate and only guilty of placing his trust in the wrong person. Gates subsequently took the stand for three days, during which time he recalled the process of setting up overseas shell companies and forging documents to procure loans for his boss.

After Manafort's lawyers rested without calling any witnesses, the jury began lengthy deliberations on August 16, emerging only to ask Judge T.S. Ellis to define "reasonable doubt." On the morning of August 21, the jury sent out a note asking what to do when unable to reach a consensus on one of the counts.

Later that afternoon, Manafort was found guilty of eight of the 18 counts — five charges of tax fraud, one charge of hiding foreign bank accounts and two charges of bank fraud. Judge Ellis declared a mistrial on the other 10 counts.

Manafort stood to receive a maximum of 80 years in prison for the conviction. The judge did not immediately set a sentencing date, noting he would give prosecutors eight days to decide whether to retry the defendant on the undecided counts.

"Mr. Manafort is disappointed of not getting acquittals all the way through or a complete hung jury on all counts," his attorney told reporters afterward. "However, he would like to thank Judge Ellis for granting him a fair trial, thank the jury for their very long and hard-fought deliberations. He is evaluating all of his options at this point."

Afterward, it was reported that Manafort had explored the possibility of a plea deal prior to the start of his second trial in Washington, D.C., though those discussions stalled over issues raised by the special counsel.

On September 14, 2018, Manafort pleaded guilty to one count of conspiracy against the U.S. and one count of conspiracy to obstruct justice due to attempts to tamper with witnesses. Prosecutor Andrew Weissmann told the judge that Manafort's plea agreement was a "cooperation agreement" and the remaining charges will be dropped at the sentencing "or at the agreement of successful cooperation."

However, Mueller's office later filed a court order that accused Manafort of repeatedly and deliberately giving false statements after agreeing to cooperate. Despite his attorneys' arguments that the alleged lies were unintentional, a federal judge sided with the prosecutors and ruled in February 2019 that they were no longer bound to terms of the plea deal.

On March 7, 2019, Manafort was sentenced to 47 months in prison by Judge Ellis, a far lighter sentence than the 19-to-24-year term sought by prosecutors for his financial crimes. On March 13 he received an additional sentence of 43 months for the federal conspiracy charges.

Shortly after the announcement of his second sentence, Manafort was charged in New York with a series of state felonies that included mortgage fraud, conspiracy and falsifying business records.

## What Is Paul Manafort's Net Worth?

Manafort's attorneys described his net worth as around $28 million. The special counsel's team countered that in May 2016 financial documents reported Manafort having $136 million in assets.

What is certain is that Manafort possesses extensive real estate holdings, including an apartment in New York City's Trump Tower and properties in the Hamptons, Virginia and Florida that together are worth millions of dollars.

The indictment also revealed that Manafort spent large sums of money on antique rugs, high-end clothing, expensive cars and other luxury purchases.

## Wife and Daughters

Manafort is married to Kathleen, a 1979 graduate of George Washington University who received her law degree from Georgetown in 1988. The couple have two daughters: Jessica (born in 1982) and Andrea (born in 1985).

Jessica filed for divorce from husband Jeffrey Yohai in March 2017, but before that Manafort had spent millions to support some of his son-in-law's real estate deals.

## Manafort and Russia

In 2006, Manafort signed a $10 million-per-year contract with Oleg Deripaska, a Russian oligarch with close ties to Vladimir Putin. With Rick Gates, Manafort started Pericles, a private equity fund, in 2006; Deripaska became an investor.

In 2014, Deripaska filed a petition alleging Manafort owed him millions from an investment, a claim that seems to have been put aside by late 2015. A report by

NBC News in October 2017 stated that Deripaska's known business dealings with Manafort added up to approximately $60 million.

The *Washington Post* reported in September 2017 that while Manafort was working on the Trump campaign he reached out, via an intermediary, to offer Deripaska "private briefings" on the presidential race. There is no evidence such briefings occurred.

**Work in Ukraine**

Manafort began to work for Ukraine's Viktor Yanukovych and his Party of Regions after questions of electoral fraud (and the poisoning of an opponent) led to the country's highest court annulling a Yanukovych victory in the 2004 Ukrainian presidential election. Manafort guided the politician through an image makeover; critics also say the consultant went along with campaign tactics that exacerbated the divide between the country's Russian and Ukrainian speakers.

Yanukovych won the presidency in 2010; this time he successfully took office. But his pro-Russian stance — he decided not to sign a European Union pact in November 2013 — led to massive protests against him. In February 2014, Yanukovych fled to Russia. Manafort continued to offer counsel to Yanukovych's former political party, which renamed itself the Opposition Bloc.

The foreign agent paperwork that Manafort filed in 2017 showed that from 2012 to 2014 his firm received more than $17 million from Ukraine clients. Manafort also brought in other lobbying firms, including the Podesta Group, via a think tank in Belgium.

## Trump Campaign Manager

In March 2016, Manafort became an adviser to Donald Trump's presidential campaign. At the time Trump was facing possible delegate defections at the national convention; as Manafort had forestalled a similar challenge in 1976 by wrangling delegates, his skills were appreciated. Manafort became manager of the campaign in June, putting him in charge during the Republican National Convention in July.

Manafort offered his services for free, which was unusual for him. Though he'd been introduced to Trump by mutual acquaintance Roy Cohn in 1979 or 1980, and had purchased a condominium in New York City's Trump Tower in 2006, Manafort wasn't close to the candidate.

On June 9, Manafort, along with Jared Kushner and Donald Trump Jr., met with a Russian lawyer who supposedly had negative information to share about Hillary Clinton, the Democratic presidential nominee. Manafort later gave investigators notes he'd taken on a smartphone during the meeting.

An article about an alleged $12 million in illegal payments made to Manafort during his time in Ukraine was published by the *New York Times* in August (Manafort denied these payments; in 2017 Ukrainian prosecutors would state they had no proof of them). On August 19, 2016, Manafort left the campaign.

## When and Where Was Paul Manafort Born?

Paul John Manafort Jr. was born in New Britain, Connecticut on April 1, 1949.

## Early Life and Education

Manafort grew up in New Britain, where his father, Paul J. Manafort Sr., served three terms as mayor. He attended St. Thomas Aquinas High School.

In 1971, Manafort graduated with a degree in business administration from Georgetown University; he received his law degree from the same school in 1974.

## Beginning a Career in Politics

During the 1976 Republican National Convention, President **Gerald Ford was facing a challenge from Ronald Reagan. Mana**fort corralled delegates to make sure the incumbent president remained his party's nominee (Ford would lose the general election **to Jimmy Carter).**

Manafort also worked on Ronald Reagan's successful 1980 presidential campaign. That same year he helped found the lobbying firm Black, Manafort & Stone, partnering with Roger Stone.

## Political Consultant and Lobbyist

Manafort lobbied for clients from around the world, including regimes in the Philippines, Kenya and Nigeria. Many of those he served had demonstrated little respect for human rights.

In 1995, Manafort and Rick Davis started the firm Davis Manafort, which also provided lobbying services. In addition, Manafort remained connected to U.S. politics, working **for George H.W. Bush** and Bob Dole's presidential campaigns.

Manafort registered the firm DMP International in 2011. This is the firm that, between 2012 and 2014, received more than $17 million for work in the Ukraine.

Citation Information

Article Title
Paul Manafort Biography

Author
Biography.com Editors

Website Name
The Biography.com website

URL
https://www.biography.com/people/paul-manafort-121417

Access Date  3/15/2019

Publisher
A&E Television Networks

Last Updated
March 14, 2019

Original Published Date
December 14, 2017

Michael Flynn-Witch # 2

Michael Flynn Biography
(1958–)

- 
- 
- 
- 
- 

Michael Flynn rose to the rank of lieutenant general over 33 years in the U.S. Army. He briefly served as President Donald Trump's national security adviser before resigning in February 2017. Later that year he pleaded guilty to lying to the FBI over reports of his contact with the Russian ambassador.

**Who Is Michael Flynn?**

Born in 1958 in Rhode Island, Michael Flynn began his 33-year Army career as a second lieutenant in military intelligence. After three years as intelligence chief of the JSOC in Iran, he returned stateside for top bureaucratic posts, but was forced out as director of the Defense Intelligence Agency in 2014. Flynn emerged as a strong supporter of presidential candidate **Donald Trump** in 2016, and was named Trump's national security adviser in November. He resigned after 24 days in office over the revelation of his contact with the Russian ambassador, and subsequently faced legal problems related to his lobbying interests and failures to disclose information. In December 2017, he pleaded guilty to lying to the FBI about his conversations with the Russian ambassador.

**Early Years**

Michael Thomas Flynn was born in December 1958 in Middletown, Rhode Island. One of nine children, he grew up in a busy, but loving Irish Catholic household, with dad Charles, a former Army sergeant, and mom Helen stressing the importance of education.

Flynn engaged in an array of athletic activities as a child and teenager, from driveway basketball games to surfing. He also excelled in football at Middletown High School, leading the team to a Division B state championship in 1976. He then enrolled at the University of Rhode Island, where he joined the ROTC program and earned a degree in management science in 1981.

## U.S. Army Officer

After graduation, Flynn joined the U.S. Army and was commissioned a second lieutenant in military intelligence. He was assigned to Fort Bragg in North Carolina, from where he was deployed as a platoon leader to Grenada in 1983.

Flynn received a steady string of promotions as he rotated from posts at Schofield Barracks in Hawaii, Fort Polk in Louisiana and Fort Huachuca in Arizona. Additionally, he was named chief of joint war plans for the American invasion of Haiti in 1994.

## Intelligence Director

By the time of the September 11, 2001, terrorist attacks, Flynn was well positioned for top roles in his field. He served as director of intelligence for Joint Task Force 180 in Afghanistan until 2002, and commanded the 111th Military Intelligence Brigade for another two years.

In 2004, Commander **Stanley McChrystal** appointed Flynn director of intelligence for the Joint Special Operations Command (JSOC) in Iran. Taking advantage of technological resources, Flynn mined cell phone data and utilized drones to infiltrate terrorist cells, and was credited with largely disrupting Al Qaeda activity in the area.

Returning stateside after three years, Flynn became director of intelligence for United States Central Command and then the Joint Staff. In 2009, after McChrystal took command of U.S. forces in Afghanistan, he again placed his old colleague in charge of intelligence. Flynn followed with a report that criticized American operations in the region, a move that rankled supervisors.

After a stint in the office of National Intelligence, Flynn became director of the Defense Intelligence Agency in 2012. He attempted to reorganize the agency but instead alienated many subordinates, and was informed he would not remain for the normal three-year term. In

August 2014, he retired after 33 years in the military, with the rank of lieutenant general.

## Private Consultant to Trump Administration

Back in the private sector, Flynn formed the Virginia-based Flynn Intel Group, which offered private intelligence and security services, and he signed on with a speakers' bureau. He also made the rounds as a television analyst, including appearances on the Russian state network RT. In late 2015, he sat next to Russian president **Vladimir Putin** at an RT banquet.

After three decades spent largely behind the scenes, Flynn surprised former colleagues with his sudden outspokenness and turn toward more extreme positions. He tweeted "Fear of Muslims is RATIONAL" in February 2016, and that summer he co-authored a book, *The Field of Fight*, on how to combat radical Islam. At the 2016 Republican National Convention, he whipped the crowd into a frenzy over the transgressions of Democratic candidate **Hillary Clinton**, leading the chant of "lock her up!"

After serving as Republican nominee Donald Trump's go-to man for national security issues over the final months of the campaign, Flynn was rewarded with the post of national security adviser in November 2016.

## Dismissal and Investigations

Flynn came under fire almost immediately after the election, beginning with a report that he had lobbied for Turkish interests during the U.S. presidential campaign. It was soon revealed that, prior to taking office, he had contact with Russian ambassador Sergey Kislyak over **President Barack Obama**'s recently issued sanctions. Flynn subsequently resigned on February 13, 2017, after just 24 days as national security adviser, the shortest tenure in the history of the position.

Flynn's problems continued to mount through various congressional investigations, drawing scrutiny for his failures to register as a foreign agent, disclose compensation and comply with subpoenas. Additionally, he remained a central figure in special counsel **Robert Mueller's probe into ties between the 2016 Trump** presidential campaign and Russian officials.

The wagons seemed to be circling Flynn by November, when news reports revealed that his son, also named Michael, was a subject of investigations. Later that month, lawyers for the elder Flynn told President

Trump's legal team that they were no longer able to share information about their client's cooperation with the Mueller probe.

**Guilty Plea**

On December 1, 2017, Flynn pleaded guilty to lying to the FBI about his conversations with the Russian ambassador during the previous year's presidential transition. Prosecutors said that Flynn had agreed to cooperate with the authorities, and that at least some of his contacts with Russian officials had been coordinated with a "senior official of the presidential transition."

After appearing in federal court in Washington, D.C., Flynn released a statement that said: "I recognize that the actions I acknowledged in court today were wrong, and, through my faith in God, I am working to set things right. My guilty plea and agreement to cooperate with the special counsel's office reflect a decision I made in the best interests of my family and of our country."

**Personal Life**

Flynn has garnered some of the military's top honors, including the Defense Superior Service Medal, the Bronze Star Medal and Legion of Merit. Additionally, he has acquired graduate degrees in telecommunications, military arts and sciences and national security and strategic studies, as well as an Honorary Doctorate of Laws from The Institute of World Politics in Washington, D.C.

Flynn has two sons with his high school sweetheart, Lori. His brother Charlie also became a decorated Army officer, with Michael pinning the general's star on his sibling during a ceremony in September 2011.

Citation Information

Article Title
Michael Flynn Biography

Author
Biography.com Editors

Website Name
The Biography.com website

URL
https://www.biography.com/people/michael-flynn-06072017

January 17, 2018

Original Published Date

June 7, 2017

- 
- 
- 
- 
-

**Michael Dean Cohen** (born August 25, 1966) is an American former attorney who was a lawyer for Donald Trump from 2006 until May 2018.[1][2]

Cohen was a vice-president of The Trump Organization, and the personal counsel to Trump, and was often described by media as Trump's "fixer".[3][4] He previously served as co-president of Trump Entertainment and was a board member of the Eric Trump Foundation, a children's health charity.[5] From 2017 to 2018, Cohen was deputy finance chairman of the Republican National Committee.[6][7]

Trump employed Cohen until May 2018, a year after the Special Counsel investigation into Russian interference in the 2016 United States elections began. The investigation led him to plead guilty on August 21, 2018, to eight counts including campaign finance violations, tax fraud, and bank fraud.[8] Cohen said he violated campaign finance laws at the direction of Trump and "for the principal purpose of influencing" the 2016 presidential election.[9] In November 2018, Cohen entered a second guilty plea for lying to a Senate committee about efforts to build a <u>Trump Tower in Moscow</u>.[10][11]

In December 2018, he was sentenced to three years in <u>federal prison</u> and ordered to pay a $50,000 fine. He is scheduled to report to prison on May 6, 2019.[8][12]

## Contents

## Early life and education

Cohen grew up in the town of Lawrence on Long Island, New York.[5] His mother was a nurse, and his father, who survived the Holocaust, was a surgeon.[5][13] Cohen is Jewish.[14] He attended Woodmere Academy[15] and received his BA from American University in 1988 and his JD from Thomas M. Cooley Law School in 1991.[16]

## Career

### Legal career

Cohen began practicing personal injury law in New York in 1992, working for Melvyn Estrin in Manhattan.[15][17] As of 2003, Cohen was an attorney in private practice and CEO of MLA Cruises, Inc., and of the Atlantic Casino.[18]

In 2006, Cohen was a partner at the law firm Phillips Nizer LLP|Phillips, Nizer, Benjamin, Krim & Ballon.[16] He practiced law at the firm for about a year before joining The Trump Organization.[17] Following his 2018 felony convictions, Cohen was automatically disbarred in New York.[19]

## Business ventures

In 2003, Cohen was a candidate for New York City Council when he provided a biography to the New York City Campaign Finance Board for inclusion in its voters' guide. The guide listed him as co-owner of Taxi Funding Corp. and a fleet of New York City taxicabs numbering over 200.[18][20][21] At the time, Cohen was a business partner in the taxi business with "taxi king" Simon Garber.[21] As of 2017, Cohen was estimated to own at least 34 taxi medallions through 17 limited liability companies (LLCs).[21] Until April 2017, another "taxi king", disbarred attorney and convicted felon Gene Freidman,[22] managed the medallions still held by Cohen; this arrangement ended after the city's Taxi and Limousine Commission decided not to renew Freidman's licenses.[21] Between April and June 2017, the New York State Department of Taxation and Financefiled seven tax warrants against Cohen and his wife for $37,434 in unpaid taxi taxes due to the MTA.[23]

Cohen has been involved in real estate ventures in Manhattan, including the purchase and sale of four apartment buildings between 2011 and 2014. The total purchase price of the four buildings was $11 million and the total sales price was $32 million.[17][24] Cohen sold the four properties at above their assessed values, in all-cash transactions, to LLCs owned by persons whose identities are not public.[25] After this was reported by McClatchy DC in October 2017, Cohen said that all four properties were purchased by an American-owned "New York real estate family fund" that paid cash for the properties in order to obtain a tax deferred (Section 1031) exchange, but did not specifically identify the buyer.[24]

In 2015, Cohen purchased an Upper East Side apartment building for $58 million.[17]

## Politics

Cohen volunteered for the 1988 presidential campaign of Michael Dukakis.[5] He was also an intern for Congressman Joe Moakley[13] and voted for Barack Obama in 2008, although he later became disappointed with Obama.[5]

**Michael Cohen**   via Twitter

@MichaelCohen212

Made the official move today and joined the #RepublicanParty! It took a great man (@POTUS) to get me to make the switch. #MAGA

March 9, 2017[26]

In 2003, he unsuccessfully ran as a Republican for the New York City Council from the Fourth Council District[27] (a Manhattan district).[18] Cohen received 4,205 votes and was defeated by Democratic candidate Eva S. Moskowitz, who received 13,745 votes.[28] In 2010, Cohen briefly campaigned for a seat in the New York State Senate.[13][29] He was a registered Democrat until he officially registered as a Republican on March 9, 2017.[30][26] On October 11, 2018, Cohen re-registered as a Democrat in an effort to distance "himself from the values of the current" administration.[31][32]

## 2006

Cohen joined the Trump Organization in 2006.[33] Trump hired him in part because he was already an admirer of Trump, having read Trump's *Art of the Deal* twice. He had purchased several Trump properties and convinced his own parents and in-laws, as well as a business partner, to buy condominiums in Trump World Tower.[17] Cohen aided Trump in his struggle with the condominium board at the Trump World Tower, which led Trump to obtain control of the board.[17] Cohen became a close confidant to Trump, maintaining an office near Trump at Trump Tower.[17]

## 2008

Cohen was named COO of mixed martial arts promotion company Affliction Entertainment in which Trump held a significant financial stake.[34]

## 2011

While Cohen was an executive at the organization, he was known as Trump's "pit bull". In late 2011, when Trump was publicly speculating about running for the 2012 Republican Party presidential nomination, Cohen co-founded the website "Should Trump Run?" to draft Trump into entering the race.[13]

In an interview with ABC News in 2011, Cohen stated, "If somebody does something Mr. Trump doesn't like, I do everything in my power to resolve it to Mr. Trump's benefit. If you do something wrong, I'm going to come at you, grab you by the neck and I'm not going to let you go until I'm finished."[35]

## 2013

In 2013, Cohen sent an email to the satirical news website *The Onion*, demanding that an article *The Onion* had published that mocked Donald Trump ("When You're Feeling Low, Just Remember I'll Be Dead In About 15 Or 20 Years")[36] be removed with an apology, claiming it was defamatory.[37]

## 2015

In 2015, in response to an inquiry by reporter Tim Mak of *The Daily Beast* concerning rape allegations (later recanted) by Ivana Trump about her then-husband Donald Trump, Cohen said, "I'm warning you, tread very fucking lightly, because what I'm going to do to you is going to be fucking disgusting."[33]

## 2016

A video of an interview of Cohen by CNN's Brianna Keilar went viral, in which Cohen said "Says who?" several times in response to Keilar's statement that Trump was behind in all of the polls.[38][39]

Cohen defended Trump against charges of antisemitism.[14]

In 2016, he was a co-founder, along with Darrell C. Scott, of the National Diversity Coalition for Trump.[40][41] Peter J. Gleason, a lawyer who filed for protection of documents pertaining to two women with sexual abuse allegations against Eric T. Schneiderman, stated—

without offering details or corroborating evidence—that Cohen told him that if Trump had been elected governor of New York in 2013, the latter would have helped bring the accusations to public attention.[42]

## 2017

The Trump–Russia dossier, published in January 2017, alleges that Cohen met with Russian officials in Prague, Czech Republic in 2016 with the objective of paying those who had hacked the DNC and to "cover up all traces of the hacking operation". The dossier contains raw intelligence, and is thought to be a mix of accurate and inaccurate information.[43][44] Cohen denied the allegations against him,[45][46][47] stating that he was in Los Angeles between August 23 and 29, and in New York for the entire month of September.[48] According to a Czech intelligence source, there is no record of him entering Prague by plane, but *Respekt* magazine and *Politico* pointed out that he could have theoretically entered by car or train from a neighboring country within the Schengen Area, for example Italy. In the latter case, a record of Cohen entering the Schengen zone from a non-Schengen country should exist, if it occurred.[49][50]

However, on April 13, 2018, the DC Bureau of McClatchy Newspapers reported that Special Counsel Robert Mueller has evidence that Cohen did travel to Prague during the late summer of 2016, with two sources having confirmed this secret trip. The evidence is said to show that Cohen entered the Czech Republic from Germany, and since both countries are in the European Union's Schengen passport area, Cohen would not have needed to receive a passport stamp to enter Czech territory.[51] The following day, Cohen again denied he has "ever been to Prague".[52] Cohen also said that he didn't travel to the European Union in August 2016.[52] McClatchy reported in December 2018 that a mobile phone traced to Cohen had "pinged" cellphone towers around Prague in late summer 2016. McClatchy also reported that during that time an eastern European intelligence agency had intercepted communications between Russians, one of whom mentioned that Cohen was in Prague.[53]

In late January 2017, Cohen met with Ukrainian opposition politician Andrey Artemenko and Felix Sater at the Loews Regency in Manhattan to discuss a plan to lift sanctions against Russia. The proposed plan would require that Russian forces withdraw from eastern Ukraine and that Ukraine hold a referendum on whether Crimea should be "leased" to Russia for 50 or 100 years. Cohen was given a written proposal in a sealed envelope that he delivered to then-National Security Advisor Michael Flynn in early February.[54]

On April 3, 2017, Cohen was appointed as national deputy finance chairman of the Republican National Committee.[55][56] In April 2017, Cohen also formed an alliance with Squire Patton Boggs for legal and lobbying counsel on behalf of Trump.[57]

In May 2017, amidst expanding inquiries into alleged Russian interference in the 2016 U.S. election, two congressional panels asked Cohen to provide information about any communications he had with people connected to the Russian government.[58][59][17][60][61] He was a subject of the Mueller investigation in 2018.[62][63][64]

## 2018

In May 2018, BBC News reported that Cohen had received a secret payment of between $400,000 and $600,000 from intermediaries for Ukrainian President Petro Poroshenko to arrange a meeting between Poroshenko and Trump, though Cohen was not registered as a foreign agent.[65] Cohen and the Ukrainian president's office denied the allegations.[65]

In May 2018, Rudy Giuliani announced that Cohen was no longer Trump's lawyer.[66] In July, seized tapes secretly recorded by Cohen of his conversations with Trump about hush payments to Karen McDougal were disclosed to *The New York Times*, seemingly contradicting earlier statements by Trump denying knowledge of the payments,[67] and raising questions about campaign finance ethics.[67] Cohen also asserted that then-candidate Trump knew in advance about the June 2016 Trump Tower meeting between his son Donald Jr., and other Trump campaign officials with Russians who claimed to possess information damaging to the Hillary Clinton campaign, contradicting the President's repeated denials that he was aware of the meeting until long after it had taken place.[68]

In June 2018, Cohen resigned as deputy finance chairman of the Republican National Committee. His resignation letter cited the ongoing investigations and also criticized the Trump administration's policy of separating undocumented families at the border.[7]

**Payment to Stormy Daniels**
*Main article: Stormy Daniels–Donald Trump scandal*

In the fall of 2016, adult film actress Stormy Daniels (legal name Stephanie Clifford) was speaking to some reporters and said that she had had a sexual affair with Trump in 2006. In October, Cohen and Daniels' attorney Keith M. Davidson negotiated a non-disclosure agreement under which she was to be paid $130,000 hush money. Cohen created a Delaware LLC called Essential Consultants and used it to pay the $130,000.[69] The arrangement was reported by *The Wall Street Journal* in January 2018.[70][71]

Cohen told *The New York Times* in February 2018 that he paid the $130,000 to Daniels from his own pocket; he also said that the payment was not a campaign contribution and he was not reimbursed by either the Trump Organization or the Trump campaign.[72] *The Washington Post* later noted that, by stating that he used his own money to "facilitate" the payment, Cohen was not ruling out the possibility that Trump, as an individual, reimbursed Cohen for the payment.[73] In April 2018, Trump acknowledged for the first time that Cohen has represented him in the Stormy Daniels case, after previously having denied knowledge of the $130,000 payment.[74]

On March 5, *The Wall Street Journal* cited anonymous sources recounting Cohen as saying he missed two deadlines to pay Daniels because Cohen "couldn't reach Mr. Trump in the hectic final days of the presidential campaign", and that after Trump's election, Cohen had complained that he had not been reimbursed for the payment. Cohen described this report as "fake news".[75]

On March 9, NBC News reported that Cohen had used his Trump Organization email to negotiate with Daniels regarding her nondisclosure agreement, and that Cohen had used the same Trump Organization email to arrange for a transfer for funds that would eventually lead to Daniels' payment.[76] In response, Cohen acknowledged that he had transferred funds from his home equity line of credit to the LLC and from the LLC to Daniels' attorney.[77]

In a March 25, 2018, interview with *60 Minutes*, Daniels said that she and Trump had sex once, and that later she had been threatened in front of her infant daughter and felt pressured to later sign a non-disclosure agreement.[78][79]

On March 26, David Schwarz, a lawyer for Cohen, told ABC's *Good Morning America* that Daniels was lying in the *60 Minutes* interview. Cohen's lawyer sent a cease-and-desist letter claiming Daniels' statements constituted "libel per se and intentional infliction of emotional distress" to Cohen.[80]

Cohen initiated a private arbitration case against Daniels in February 2018, based on an October 2016 non-disclosure agreement signed by Daniels in October 2016, in exchange for $130,000. Cohen obtained an order from an arbitrator barring Daniels from publicly discussing her alleged relationship with Trump.[81][82] Daniels subsequently brought a lawsuit in federal court against Trump and Cohen, arguing that the non-disclosure agreement is legally invalid because Trump never signed it,[83] Cohen responded by seeking to compel arbitration, which would avoid public proceedings.[82] In April 2018, Cohen filed a declaration in the court saying that he would invoke his Fifth Amendment right not to incriminate himself in the Daniels lawsuit.[84][85]

On May 18, lawyers for Cohen filed an objection to Daniel's lawyer Michael Avenatti being allowed to represent her in a case involving Cohen, claiming it (the objection) was based on the violations of ethical rules and local court rules, among other issues.[86] After Cohen's August 2018 conviction, Trump stated that the payment to Daniels came from him personally and not from the campaign during a Fox & Friends interview.[87]

## Recording of discussion regarding Karen McDougal

In 2016, Karen McDougal, a former *Playboy* model, claimed that she and Trump had an affair from 2006 until 2007, a claim that Trump has since denied.[88] The *National Enquirer* paid McDougal $150,000 for her story but never published it, a practice known as catch and kill.[89] On September 30, 2016, Cohen created Resolution Consultants LLC, a Delaware shell company, to purchase the rights to McDougal's story from the *National Enquirer*, though the rights to the story were ultimately never purchased.[90][91]

Cohen had been known to record conversations and phone calls with other people.[92] According to his lawyer Lanny Davis, "Michael Cohen had the habit of using his phone to record conversations instead of taking notes."[93] Altogether the prosecutors have been given more than one hundred audio recordings from the material seized from Cohen in the April raid, after the Trump team withdrew their claims of privilege for those items; reportedly only one of them features a substantive conversation with Trump.[93] The existence of that tape was revealed on July 20 and the actual recording was released on July 25.[88][94]

On July 20, it was revealed that Cohen secretly recorded a conversation between Trump and him. The discussion involved a potential hush payment to the publisher of the *National Enquirer*. The recording had been classified as a privileged attorney-client communication by the Special Master reviewing the Cohen material, but Trump's attorneys waived that claim, meaning that prosecutors can have it and use it. The conversation in that tape occurred in September 2016, two months before the election and weeks after the *Enquirer* paid McDougal the $150,000. In the conversation, Trump and Cohen discuss whether to buy the rights to her story from the *Enquirer*, and Trump appears to approve the idea. Trump's lawyer, Rudy Giuliani, initially claimed that the tape shows Trump saying "make sure it's done correctly, and make sure it's done by check." Giuliani also noted that no payment was ultimately made, and asserted that Trump's team waived privilege and allowed the recording to be revealed because it shows no violation of law.[88] The recording appears to contradict Hope Hicks, then Trump's spokeswoman, who said when the story of the *Enquirer* payment came out a few days before the election that the Trump campaign had "no knowledge of any of this".[95]

On July 25, Cohen's attorney Lanny Davis released the actual recording to CNN, which played it on the air on the *Cuomo Prime Time* program. On it, Trump can be heard concluding a telephone conversation with an unidentified person and then discussing several items of business with Cohen. Cohen mentions that he needs to "open up a company for the transfer of all of that info regarding our friend David", interpreted as meaning David Pecker, the head of American Media, which publishes the *National Enquirer*. Later when they discuss financing, Trump is heard saying something about "pay with cash", to which Cohen responds "no, no, no", but the tape is unclear and it is disputed what is said next; the word "check" can be heard.[94] A transcript provided by Trump's attorneys has Trump saying "Don't pay with cash ... check."[96] The tape cuts off abruptly at that point.[97] A lawyer for the Trump Organization said that any reference to "cash" would not have meant "green currency", but a one-time payment ("cash") vs. extended payments ("financing"), in either case accompanied by documents.[94] According to Aaron Blake at *The Washington Post*, "the tape provides the first evidence that Trump spoke with Cohen about purchasing the rights to women's stories—apparently to silence them—before the 2016 election."[97] He also notes that Cohen speaks in "somewhat coded language", which Trump understands, suggesting that he is already familiar with the issue.[*citation needed*]

Despite the taped conversation, on August 23, in a Fox News interview Trump stated that he was not aware of the hush-money payments until "later on": "Later on I knew. Later on. What he did—and they weren't taken out of the campaign finance, that's the big thing." He added: "In fact, my first question when I heard about it was, did they come out of the campaign, because that could be a little dicey. And they didn't come out of the campaign and that's big. But they weren't ... that's not even a campaign violation."[98] According to U.S. election rules, any payments intended to influence an election vote must be reported.[87]

**Payment to Shera Bechard**
*See also: Keith M. Davidson § Shera Bechard*

In April 2018, *The Wall Street Journal* reported that Shera Bechard, a former *Playboy* Playmate, had an affair with married Republican fundraiser Elliott Broidy. She became pregnant by him, had an abortion, and was to be paid $1.6 million hush money.[99][100] Broidy is a Republican fundraiser and deputy finance chair of the Republican National Committee.

In a 2018 court proceeding, Cohen said he had given legal advice to only three clients in 2017: Donald Trump, Sean Hannity, and Elliott Broidy.[101] In late 2017, Cohen arranged the $1.6 million payment by Broidy to Bechard as part of a nondisclosure agreement requiring Bechard to keep silent about the matter.[102] Cohen was Broidy's attorney and Keith M. Davidson represented Bechard.[102] Davidson had previously been the attorney for Stormy Daniels and Karen McDougal.[102] The Bechard nondisclosure agreement used the same pseudonyms – David Dennison for the man and Peggy Peterson for the woman – as in the Daniels agreement.[103] The payments were to be made in installments.

On July 6, 2018, Bechard filed a lawsuit against Broidy, Davidson, and Daniels' attorney Michael Avenatti, claiming the three had breached the agreement in relation to the cessation of the settlement payments.[104][105][106][107]

## Essential Consultants LLC

Essential Consultants LLC is a Delaware shell company created by Cohen in October 2016 to facilitate payment of hush money to Stormy Daniels.[69] For many months thereafter, Cohen used the LLC[108] for an array of business activities largely unknown to the public, with at least $4.4 million moving through the LLC between Trump's election to the presidency and January 2018.[109] In May 2018, Stormy Daniels' lawyer Michael Avenatti posted a seven-page report to Twitter detailing what he said were financial transactions involving Essential Consultants and Cohen. Avenatti did not reveal the source of his information, which was later largely confirmed by *The New York Times* and other publications.[109] The data showed that hundreds of thousands of dollars were given to Cohen, via Essential Consultants, from Fortune 500 firms such as Novartis and AT&T, which had business before the Trump administration. It was also revealed that Essential Consultants had received at least $500,000 from a New York-based investment firm called Columbus Nova, which is linked to a Russian oligarch. The firm's largest client is a company controlled by Viktor Vekselberg, a Ukrainian-born Russian oligarch.[109][110][111][112] Vekselberg is a business partner of Soviet-born billionaire and major Republican Party donor, Leonard Blavatnik.[113] A spokesperson for Columbus Nova said that the payment was a consulting fee that had nothing to do with Vekselberg.[109]

Questions were raised about many of the payments, such as four totaling $200,000 that AT&T paid to the LLC between October 2017 and January 2018,[114][115] while at the same time the proposed merger between the company and Time Warner was pending before the Justice Department. AT&T claimed that the money was paid to the LLC and other firms that were used to provide insights into understanding the new administration, and that the LLC did no legal or lobbying work for AT&T.[109][116]

On May 11, 2018, the CEO of AT&T stated that in early 2017 it was approached by Cohen to provide "his opinion on the new president and his administration". Cohen was paid $600,000 ($50,000 per month) over the year, which its CEO described as "a big mistake". Novartis was also approached by Cohen and was offered similar services.[117]

Novartis, a Switzerland–based pharmaceutical giant paid the LLC nearly $1.2 million in separate payments.[118] Novartis released a statement May 9, 2018, that it hired the LLC to help the company understand the "health care policy" of the new administration, but it actually did not receive benefit for its investment. The statement continued that Novartis made a decision to not engage Essential Consultants further, but it could not terminate the contract for "cause", raising concerns on why the company did not pursue reimbursement.[119]

Korea Aerospace Industries paid $150,000,[112] ostensibly for advice on "cost accounting standards".[119]

Franklin L. Haney agreed to pay Cohen $10 million if he successfully lobbied for the United States Department of Energy to finance the Bellefonte Nuclear Generating Station, or a reduced fee if the funding targets were only partially met.[120]

## Federal investigations

### Cohen v US – Govt Opposition to TRO Request

As of April 2018, Cohen was under federal criminal investigation by the United States Attorney for the Southern District of New York.[121]

On April 9, 2018, the FBI raided Cohen's office at the law firm of Squire Patton Boggs, as well as his home and his hotel room in the Loews Regency Hotel in New York City, pursuant to a federal search warrant.[122][123] The warrant was obtained by the U.S. Attorney's Office for the

Southern District of New York, whose public corruption unit was conducting an investigation.[20] Seeking the warrant required high-level approval from the Department of Justice.[124] The Interim U.S. Attorney, Geoffrey Berman, was recused.[125] Deputy Attorney General Rod Rosenstein and FBI Director Christopher Wray—both of whom are Trump appointees—had supervisory roles.[126] The FBI obtained the warrant after a referral from Robert Mueller's Special Counsel investigation into Russian interference in the 2016 United States elections, although underlying reasons for the raid were not revealed.[124][127] Following the raid, Squire Patton Boggs law firm ended its formal working relationship with Cohen.[128]

Agents seized emails, tax records, business records, and other matter related to several topics, including payments made by Cohen to Stormy Daniels,[124] and records related to Trump's *Access Hollywood* controversy.[129] Recordings of phone conversations Cohen made were also obtained.[130] According to Stormy Daniels' attorney Michael Avenattiand civil rights attorney Lisa Bloom, some of the recordings may have included participants located in California, which would make the recordings illegal, as California is a "two party consent" state.[131]

Since Cohen is an attorney, the search included the seizure of materials normally protected by attorney-client privilege, which is subject to a crime-fraud exception if a crime is suspected.[132] Some legal scholars opined that Trump's denial that he had knowledge of the Daniels payment, combined with denials by Cohen and his lawyer David Schwartz, meant both sides had effectively said that matter did not involve attorney-client communications.[133] Cohen and his lawyers argued that all of the thousands of items seized during the FBI raid should be protected by attorney-client privilege and thus withheld from the prosecutors. U.S. District Judge Kimba M. Wood, appointed a special master, former federal judge Barbara S. Jones, to review all of the seized materials for attorney-client privilege. She found that only 14 of the 639 paper documents were privileged, and out of the 291,770 electronic files seized, only 148 files were withheld from the prosecution.[134] The search warrant itself has been sealed, making it unavailable to the public.[135] The FBI also sought documents pertaining to Cohen's ownership of taxi medallions.[20][136] Cohen's taxi fleet is operated by Gene Freidman, who is facing legal trouble for alleged tax evasion.[137]

A few days after the raid, McClatchy reported that the Mueller investigation was in possession of evidence that Cohen traveled to Prague in August or September 2016. If true, the report bolsters similar claims in 3 of 17 reports from the Trump–Russia dossier. According to McClatchy's confidential sources, Cohen traveled to Prague via Germany, a passage thtat would not have required use of a passport due to both countries being within the Schengen Area.[138][139][140] In reaction, Cohen denied having ever been to Prague, as he had done in his January 2017 denial following the dossier's release.[141][52] *Mother Jones* reported that Cohen had told them "I was in Prague for one afternoon 14 years ago," contradicting later statements that he had never visited.[142]

In May 2018, NBC reported that Cohen's phone calls had been monitored by pen register, which logs the origins and destinations of calls but not the contents.[143][144]

*The Wall Street Journal* reported on July 26, 2018, that longtime Trump Organization CFO Allen Weisselberg had been subpoenaed to testify before a federal grand jury regarding the Cohen investigation.[145]

## Conviction on campaign finance, tax evasion, and other charges

In August 2018, it was reported that investigators were in the final stages of their investigation.[146] Cohen officially surrendered to the FBI on August 21, 2018.[147] That afternoon, Cohen pleaded guilty to eight criminal[148] charges: five counts of tax evasion, one count of making false statements to a financial institution, one count of willfully causing an unlawful corporate contribution, and one count of making an excessive campaign contribution at the request of a candidate (Trump) for the "principal purpose of influencing [the] election".[149][150][151][150]

After Cohen's conviction, his personal lawyer Lanny Davis stated that Cohen was ready to "tell everything about Donald Trump that he knows".[152] Davis alluded to Cohen's knowledge that could be used against Trump, and hinted that Cohen had knowledge of whether Trump knew in advance about the computer hacking that was detrimental to Hillary Clinton's presidential campaign, as well as knowledge of the meeting at Trump Tower in June 2016.[153] He later added that he believed Cohen would agree to testify before Congress, even without immunity.[154]

Responding to speculation that President Trump might issue a pardon for Cohen, lawyer Davis said on NPR, "I know that Mr. Cohen would never accept a pardon from a man that he considers to be both corrupt and a dangerous person in the oval office. And [Cohen] has flatly authorized me to say under no circumstances would he accept a pardon from Mr. Trump."[155] In his interview to Sky News, Davis said the turning point for his client's attitude toward Trump was the Helsinki summit in July 2018, which caused him to doubt Trump's loyalty to the U.S.[156]

*The New York Times* reported on August 22, 2018, that Cohen court documents revealed that two senior Trump Organization executives were also involved in the hush money payments, and that Cohen "coordinated with one or more members of the campaign, including through meetings and phone calls" about the payments.[157]

By mid-October 2018, Cohen had sat for at least 50 hours of interviews with Mueller's investigators and other investigators, although he had no formal cooperation agreement with prosecutors.[158] Cohen also cooperated in a separate investigation by New York State investigators regarding the Trump Organization and Trump Foundation.[159]

On December 12, 2018, U.S. District Judge William H. Pauley III sentenced Cohen to three years in prison and a $50,000 fine, and additionally ordered Cohen to pay $1.4 million in restitution and to forfeit$500,000.[160][161][162] At his sentencing hearing, Cohen stated: "I take full responsibility for each act that I pled guilty to: The personal ones to me and those involving the president of the United States of

America."[160]Cohen said Trump was "the man that caused me to choose the path of darkness" and do "dirty deeds".[163][162] Before passing sentence, Judge Pauley said, "each of these crimes is a serious offense against the United States. Mr. Cohen pled guilty to a veritable smorgasbord of fraudulent conduct."[160]

## Conviction for perjury in congressional testimony

On November 29, 2018, Cohen pleaded guilty to lying to the Senate Intelligence Committee and House Intelligence Committee in 2017 regarding the proposed Trump Tower Moscow deal that he spearheaded in 2015 and 2016.[11][164] Cohen had told Congress that the deal ceased in January 2016 when it actually ended in June 2016, and that he had not received a response about the deal from the office of a senior Russian official when he actually had.[165][164] Cohen said that he had given the false testimony in order to be consistent with Trump's "repeated disavowals of commercial and political ties between himself and Russia" and out of loyalty to Trump.[164] Cohen received a two-month sentence, to be served concurrently with his three-year sentence for tax fraud, for the false testimony.[8]

This charge was brought directly by Robert Mueller's investigation, rather than the United States Attorney for the Southern District of New York, who brought the previous charges against Cohen.[166] In a sentencing memorandum filed the following day, Cohen's attorneys stated he kept Trump "apprised" of the "substantive conversation" Cohen had in January 2016 with a Russian official, and discussed with Trump traveling to Russia to advance the project during the summer of 2016. The filing also stated Cohen "remained in close and regular contact with White House-based staff and legal counsel" as he prepared to provide false testimony to Congress.[167]

According to a BuzzFeed report on January 17, 2019, President Donald Trump personally directed Cohen to lie to Congress about the Trump Tower Moscow project.[168][169] However, a spokesman for the Special Counsel investigation later said the report was "not accurate".[170]

## State of New York's investigations

On August 22, 2018, it was announced that the New York State Department of Taxation and Finance had subpoenaed Cohen in connection with its investigation into whether the Donald J. Trump Foundation had violated New York tax laws.[171] This investigation is separate from the New York Attorney General's lawsuit alleging that the foundation and its directors violated state and federal laws about the operation of charities.[172]

## Congressional investigations

On January 10, 2019, Cohen agreed to testify publicly before the House Oversight Committee to give a "full and credible account" of his work on behalf of Trump.[173] On January 12, Fox News contributor and legal analyst Jeanine Pirro took a 20-minute, on-air phone call from Trump in which he claimed Cohen had fabricated stories to reduce the length of his expected sentence. Trump suggested that investigations should instead focus on Cohen's father-in-law, saying "that's the one people want to look at."[174] The father-in-law, Fima Shusterman, owned condos both at Trump Tower and in a Trump development near Miami.[175]According to former federal investigators, Shusterman actually introduced Trump to Cohen.[176] On several subsequent occasions Trump hinted publicly that Cohen's father-in-law, or possibly even Cohen's wife, could be tied to criminal activity. On January 20 Trump's attorney Rudy Giuliani suggested on CNN that the father-in-law "may have ties to something called organized crime".[177]

On January 23, Cohen announced through his attorney that he would postpone his testimony to a later date, citing "ongoing threats against his family from President

Trump" and Giuliani.[177] Some legal analysts asserted that these comments by Trump and Giuliani constituted intimidation and witness tampering;[178] House Oversight Committee chairman Elijah Cummings and House Intelligence Committee chairman Adam Schiff said that threatening a witness's family is "textbook mob tactics".[179][180]

After several scheduling delays, Cohen testified before three congressional committees in late February. First was a February 26, 2019, closed-door hearing before the Senate Intelligence Committee. He testified for more than seven hours.[181]

Also on February 26, Florida Republican Congressman Matt Gaetz directly threatened Cohen via Twitter, hinting about unspecified disclosures to Cohen's wife and father-in-law.[182][183] The Florida Bar Associationplans to investigate the incident.[184]

The following day, February 27, Cohen gave 10 hours of public, televised testimony before the House Oversight Committee, during which he described Trump as a "racist," a "con man", and a "cheat", and expressed remorse and shame for the things he had done for Trump. He said the president had reimbursed him for illegal hush money payments, suggested that he should lie to Congress and the public about the Trump Tower

Moscow negotiations, and filed false financial statements with banks and insurance companies. Republicans hammered on his previous false testimony, asking why he should be believed now.[185][186]

On February 28, Cohen testified behind closed doors to the House Intelligence Committee for more than seven hours. Cohen returned to that committee for more questioning on March 6.[187]

## Personal life

Cohen married Ukrainian-born Laura Shusterman in 1994.[17][188][189] Laura Shusterman's father, Fima Shusterman, left Soviet Ukraine for New York in 1975.[189] They have a daughter, Samantha, and a son, Jake.[190] Cohen's father-in-law was the person who introduced him to Trump, according to a Trump biographer.[176][191] Cohen's uncle is a doctor who treated members of the Lucchese crime family.[189] The uncle owned "El Caribe Country Club", known to be frequented by individuals associated with the Russian mafia: Evsei Agron, Marat Balagula, and Boris Nayfeld.[192]

Before joining the Trump Organization, Cohen had purchased several homes in Trump's buildings.[13] A 2017 New York Times article reported that Cohen is known for having "a penchant for luxury"; he was married at The Pierre, drove a Porsche while attending college, and once owned a Bentley.[17]

## In popular culture

As the investigation surrounding Donald Trump was in the daily news headlines, the story became fodder for parody on *Saturday Night Live*, with Trump being portrayed by Alec Baldwin and Cohen by Ben Stiller.[193]

## References and Recommended further reading

1. ^ *Helderman, Rosalind (January 19, 2017). "Michael Cohen will stay Trump's personal attorney—even in the White House". The Washington Post. Archived from the original on January 29, 2017. Retrieved February 1, 2017.*
2. ^ *Samuelsohn, Darren (May 11, 2018). "Giuliani: Cohen is not Trump's lawyer anymore 'as far as we know'". Politico. Archived from the original on January 29, 2019. Retrieved January 29, 2019.*
3. ^ *Durkin, Erin (December 12, 2018). "From fixer to inmate: Michael Cohen reckons with his 'blind loyalty' to Trump". The*

*Guardian*. *Archived* from the original on December 13, 2018. Retrieved December 14, 2018.

4. ^ Stracqualursi, Veronica (December 14, 2018). *"Michael Cohen says Donald Trump knew hush payments were wrong"*. *CNN*. *Archived* from the original on December 14, 2018. Retrieved December 15, 2018.

5. ^ Jump up to:*a b c d e* Nathan-Kazis, Josh (July 20, 2015). *"Meet Michael Cohen, Donald Trump's Jewish Wingman"*. *The Forward*. *Archived* from the original on January 8, 2016. Retrieved January 15, 2016.

6. ^ Sheth, Sonam. *"Trump's personal lawyer will serve as key RNC finance executive"*. *Business Insider*. *Archived* from the original on August 22, 2018. Retrieved August 22, 2018.

7. ^ Jump up to:*a b* Larramendia, Eliana; Zaki, Zunaira (June 20, 2018). *"Michael Cohen resigns from RNC committee post, sources*

say". *ABC News*. *Archived* from the original on August 21, 2018. Retrieved August 22,2018.

8. ^ Jump up to:<u>a</u> <u>b</u> <u>c</u> Mangan, Dan; Breuninger, Kevin (December 12, 2018). *"Trump's ex-lawyer and fixer Michael Cohen sentenced to 3 years"*. *CNBC*. *Archived* from the original on December 12, 2018. Retrieved December 12, 2018.

9. <u>^</u> Rashbaum, William K.; *Haberman, Maggie*; Protess, Ben; *Rutenberg, Jim* (August 21, 2018). *"Michael Cohen Says He Arranged Payments to Women at Trump's Direction"*. *The New York Times*. *Archived* from the original on August 21, 2018. Retrieved August 22, 2018.

10. <u>^</u> *"Michael Cohen pleads guilty to lying to Senate about Trump Tower project in Russia"*. *CBC*. *Associated Press*. November 29, 2018. *Archived* from the original on December 11, 2018. Retrieved December 13, 2018.

11. ^ Jump up to:*a b* Orden, Erica; Scannell, Kara; Brown, Pamela; Collinson, Stephen; Borger, Gloria (November 29, 2018). "Michael Cohen pleads guilty, says he lied about Trump's knowledge of Moscow project". CNN. Archived from the original on November 29, 2018. Retrieved November 29, 2018.

12. ^ "Former Trump lawyer Michael Cohen, sentenced to prison, asked for this lockup". NBC News. Archived from the original on January 16, 2019. Retrieved February 5, 2019.

13. ^ Jump up to:*a b c d e* Falcone, Michael (April 16, 2011). "Donald Trump's Political 'Pit Bull': Meet Michael Cohen". ABC News. Archived from the original on February 27, 2017. Retrieved March 9, 2017.

14. ^ Jump up to:*a b* Rosen, Armin (July 15, 2016). "Trump's Jews". Tablet. Archived from the

original on March 12, 2017. Retrieved March 9,2017.

15. ^ Jump up to:_a b_ Cramer, Meg (April 18, 2018). _"The Company Michael Cohen Kept"_. _New York Public Radio_. _Archived_ from the original on May 2, 2018. Retrieved May 2, 2018.

16. ^ Jump up to:_a b_ _"Michael D. Cohen – Attorney Bio"_. _Phillips Nizer_. Archived from _the original_ on October 23, 2006. Retrieved April 10, 2018.

17. ^ Jump up to:_a b c d e f g h i j_ Schwirtz, Michael (July 2, 2017). _"Trump Foot Soldier Sidelined Under Glare of Russia Inquiry"_. _The New York Times_. _Archived_ from the original on July 3, 2017. Retrieved July 3, 2017.

18. ^ Jump up to:_a b c_ _"4th City Council District, Michael D. Cohen, Republican"_. _2003 Voter Guide_. _New York City Campaign Finance Board_. _Archived_ from the original on April 13, 2018. Retrieved April 10,2018.

19. ^ *"New York law mandates ex-Trump lawyer Michael Cohen be disbarred for felonies"*. *USA Today*. *Archived* from the original on December 27, 2018. *Retrieved December 27, 2018.*

20. ^ Jump up to:*a b c* Shear, Michael D.; Apuzzo, Matt; LaFraniere, Sharon (April 10, 2018). *"Raids on Trump's Lawyer Sought Records of Payments to Women"*. *The New York Times*. *Archived* from the original on April 12, 2018. *Retrieved August 23, 2018.*

21. ^ Jump up to:*a b c d* Brenzel, Kathryn (February 27, 2018). *"Meet Trump attorney Michael Cohen's nemesis: Uber"*. *The Real Deal*. *Archived* from the original on August 25, 2018. *Retrieved August 23, 2018.*

22. ^ *"Michael Cohen's business partner, known as "Taxi King", pleads guilty in deal"*. *CBS News*. *Archived* from the original on November 16, 2018. *Retrieved September 20, 2018.*

23. ^ Dan Rivoli & Reuven Blau, Trump's personal lawyer owes New York State nearly $40G in unpaid taxi taxes Archived April 11, 2018, at the Wayback Machine, *New York Daily News* (August 8, 2017).

24. ^ Jump up to:[a] [b] *Stone, Peter; Gordon, Greg (October 26, 2017). "Michael Cohen says Americans paid cash for NY properties to get tax breaks". McClatchyDC. Archived from the original on April 15, 2018. Retrieved April 14, 2018.*

25. ^ *Stone, Peter; Gordon, Greg (October 25, 2017). "Trump associate Cohen sold four NY buildings for cash to mysterious buyers". McClatchyDC. Archived from the original on October 25, 2017. Retrieved October 25, 2017.*

26. ^ Jump up to:[a] [b] *Cohen, Michael [@MichaelCohen212] (March 9, 2017). "Made the official move today and joined the*

#RepublicanParty! It took a great man (@POTUS ) to get me to make the switch. #MAGA" (Tweet). Retrieved March 9, 2017 – via _Twitter_.

27. ^ _"Archived copy"_. _Archived_ from the original on February 28, 2019. Retrieved February 28, 2019.

28. ^ _"2003 General Election, New York County: Statement and Return of the Votes for the Office of Member of the City Council 4th Council District"_ (PDF). _New York City Board of Elections_. December 5, 2003. p. 9. _Archived_ (PDF) from the original on March 3, 2016. Retrieved April 11, 2018.

29. ^ _"Michael D. Cohen"_. _The Real Deal_. _Archived_ from the original on December 1, 2015. Retrieved January 15, 2016.

30. ^ Howell, Kellan (April 14, 2016). _"Michael Cohen, top Trump surrogate, can't vote for him because he's a registered Democrat"_. _The Washington_

_Times_. _Archived_ from the original on November 11, 2016. Retrieved November 11, 2016.

31. ^ "Michael Cohen re-registers as Democrat as he distances himself from Trump". _The Guardian_. October 11, 2018. _Archived_ from the original on October 12, 2018. Retrieved October 11, 2018.

32. ^ Samuels, Brett (October 11, 2018). "Michael Cohen re-registers as a Democrat, lawyer says". _The Hill_. _Archived_ from the original on October 11, 2018. Retrieved October 11, 2018.

33. ^ Jump up to:_a_ _b_ "Who is Michael Cohen?". _CBS News_. March 26, 2018. _Archived_ from the original on March 28, 2018. Retrieved March 28,2018.

34. ^ "Michael Cohen Named COO of Affliction". sherdog.com. _Archived_ from the original on May 28, 2018. Retrieved May 27, 2018.

35. ^ Slater, Joanna (April 10, 2018). "FBI's probe of presidential lawyer Michael Cohen increases Trump's exposure". *The Globe and Mail*. Archived from the original on April 27, 2018. Retrieved August 23,2018.

36. ^ "When You're Feeling Low, Just Remember I'll Be Dead In About 15 Or 20 Years". *The Onion*. January 23, 2013. Archived from the original on August 31, 2018. Retrieved August 23, 2018.

37. ^ Restuccia, Andrew (May 20, 2018). "How Trump changed everything for The Onion". *Politico*. Archived from the original on July 9, 2018. Retrieved August 23, 2018. Cohen was fuming over a satirical article published under Trump's name with the headline, "When You're Feeling Low, Just Remember I'll Be Dead In About 15 Or 20 Years." On Trump's behalf, Cohen demanded that *The Onion* immediately remove the

article and apologize. "This commentary goes way beyond defamation and, if not immediately removed, I will take all actions necessary to ensure your actions do not go without consequence," Cohen wrote, according to a copy of the email provided to Politico. "Guide yourself accordingly."

38. ^ _"Exchange between Trump attorney, CNN anchor goes viral"_. _CNN_. _Archived_ from the original on November 16, 2016. Retrieved November 15, 2016.

39. ^ _Wemple, Erik_ (November 15, 2016). _"An apology for Trump lawyer Michael Cohen"_. _The Washington Post_. _Archived_ from the original on January 24, 2017. Retrieved January 28, 2017.

40. ^ _Vitali, Ali_ (April 18, 2016). _"Trump 'Diversity Coalition' Holds Hectic First Meeting"_. _NBC News_. _Archived_ from the original on July 22, 2018. Retrieved August 22, 2018.

41. ^ Bernal, Rafael (August 18, 2017). _"Trump diversity council in spotlight after Charlottesville remarks"_. _The Hill_. Archived from the original on July 9, 2018. Retrieved August 23, 2018.

42. ^ Feuer, Alan (May 11, 2018). _"Lawyer for 2 Schneiderman Accusers Brought Their Claims to Michael Cohen"_. _The New York Times_. ISSN 0362-4331. Archived from the original on May 12, 2018. Retrieved May 12, 2018.

43. ^ Borger, Julian (November 15, 2017). _"Christopher Steele believes his dossier on Trump-Russia is 70-90% accurate"_. _The Guardian_. Archived from the original on August 21, 2018. Retrieved August 23,2018.

44. ^ _"Some questions in Trump-Russia dossier now finding answers"_. _CBS News_. June 29, 2018. Archived from the original on August 22, 2018. Retrieved August 22, 2018.

45. ^ *Harding, Luke (May 10, 2017). "What do we know about alleged links between Trump and Russia?". The Guardian. Archived from the original on January 21, 2018. Retrieved December 26, 2017.*

46. ^ *Borger, Julian (April 28, 2017). "UK was given details of alleged contacts between Trump campaign and Moscow". The Guardian. Archived from the original on December 26, 2017. Retrieved December 26, 2017.*

47. ^ *Cormier, Anthony (May 5, 2017). "This Is The Inside of Trump's Lawyer's Passport". BuzzFeed. Archived from the original on December 23, 2017. Retrieved December 24, 2017.*

48. ^ *Gray, Rosie (January 10, 2017). "Michael Cohen: 'It Is Fake News Meant to Malign Mr. Trump'". The Atlantic. Archived from the original on December 12, 2017. Retrieved December 24, 2017. I'm*

telling you emphatically that I've not been to Prague, I've never been to Czech [Republic], I've not been to Russia.

49. ^ RFE/RL (January 11, 2017). "Report: Czech Intelligence Says No Evidence Trump Lawyer Traveled To Prague". Radio Free Europe/Radio Liberty. Archived from the original on February 23, 2018. Retrieved January 19, 2018. According to Radio Free Europe/Radio Liberty, 'A Czech intelligence source told the Respektmagazine that there is no record of Cohen arriving in Prague by plane, although the news weekly pointed out he could have traveled by car or train from a nearby EU country, avoiding passport control under Schengen zone travel rules.'

50. ^ Meyer, Josh (December 6, 2017). "Investigators probe European travel of Trump associates". Politico. Archived from

the original on February 27, 2018. Retrieved February 27, 2018.

51. ^ Stone, Peter; Gordon, Greg (April 13, 2018). *"Sources: Mueller has evidence Cohen was in Prague in 2016"*. *McClatchy DC Bureau*. *Archived* from the original on April 13, 2018. Retrieved April 14,2018.

52. ^ Jump up to:*a b c* *"Trump lawyer Michael Cohen denies traveling to Prague"*. *CBS News*. April 14, 2018. *Archived* from the original on April 15, 2018. Retrieved April 15, 2018.

53. ^ Stone, Peter; Gordon, Greg (December 27, 2018). *"Cell signal puts Cohen outside Prague around time of purported Russian meeting"*. *McClatchyDC*. *Archived* from the original on December 27, 2018. Retrieved February 27, 2019.

54. ^ *Twohey, Megan*; *Shane, Scott* (February 19, 2017). *"A Back-Channel Plan for Ukraine and Russia, Courtesy of Trump*

Associates". *The New York Times*. Archived from the original on August 23, 2018. Retrieved August 23, 2018.

55. ^ *"RNC Announces Additions To RNC Finance Leadership Team"*. Republican National Committee. April 3, 2017. Archived from the original on October 26, 2017. Retrieved October 25, 2017.

56. ^ Sheth, Sonam (April 3, 2017). *"Trump's personal lawyer will serve as key RNC finance executive"*. Business Insider. Archived from the original on October 24, 2017. Retrieved October 25, 2017.

57. ^ Barber, C. Ryan; Polantz, Katelyn (April 4, 2017). *"Trump lawyer salaries revealed as Squire Patton Boggs seals alliance with president's personal adviser"*. Legal Week. Archived from the original on April 12, 2018. Retrieved April 11, 2018.

58. ^ "Russia inquiry expands to Trump lawyer Michael Cohen". BBC. May 30, 2017. Archived from the original on May 31, 2017. Retrieved May 30, 2017.

59. ^ Ross, Brian; Mosk, Matthew (May 30, 2017). "Congress expands Russia investigation to include Trump's personal attorney". ABC News. Archived from the original on May 30, 2017. Retrieved May 30, 2017.

60. ^ "Donald Trump fundraiser June 29, 2017". Soundcloud. Archived from the original on July 3, 2017. Retrieved July 3, 2017.

61. ^ Grim, Ryan; Fang, Lee (June 30, 2017). "Here's the Audio of Donald Trump's Private RNC Fundraiser at His Own Hotel". The Intercept. Archived from the original on July 3, 2017. Retrieved July 3, 2017.

62. ^ Swan, Jonathan (March 4, 2018). "Scoop: Mueller's hit

list". *Axios*. *Archived* from the original on March 5, 2018. Retrieved March 5,2018.

63. ^ *"Mueller probe tracking down Trump business partners, with Cohen a focus of queries"*. *McClatchy*. April 6, 2018. *Archived* from the original on April 6, 2018. Retrieved April 6, 2018.

64. ^ Helderman, Rosalind S.; Hamburger, Tom; *Dawsey, Josh* (March 6, 2018). *"Special counsel has examined episodes involving Michael Cohen, Trump's longtime lawyer"*. *The Washington Post*. *Archived* from the original on March 6, 2018. Retrieved March 6, 2018.

65. ^ Jump up to:*a b* *Wood, Paul* (May 23, 2018). *"Ukraine 'paid Trump lawyer for talks'"*. *BBC News*. *Archived* from the original on July 25, 2018. Retrieved August 21, 2018.

66. ^ *"Rudy Giuliani: Michael Cohen is no longer Trump's attorney"*. *The Washington Examiner*. May 6, 2018. *Archived* from the original on May 22, 2018. Retrieved May 22, 2018.

67. ^ Jump up to:*a b* *"Michael Cohen Secretly Taped Trump Discussing Payment to Playboy Model"*. *The New York Times*. July 20, 2018. *Archived* from the original on July 22, 2018. Retrieved July 22, 2018. *The recording's existence appears to undercut the Trump campaign's denial of any knowledge of payments to the model.*

68. ^ Sciutto, Jim; Bernstein, Carl; Cohen, Marshall. *"Cohen claims Trump knew in advance of 2016 Trump Tower meeting"*. *CNN Politics*. *Archived* from the original on July 27, 2018. Retrieved July 28, 2018.

69. ^ Jump up to:*a b* *Matthews, Dylan* (April 6, 2018). *"The definitive guide to the Stormy Daniels*

*scandal"*. *Vox*. *Vox Media*. Archived from the original on July 26, 2018. Retrieved July 26, 2018.

70. ^ Twohey, Megan; Rutenberg, Jim (January 12, 2018). "Porn Star Was Reportedly Paid to Stay Quiet About Trump". *The New York Times*. Archived from the original on February 14, 2018. Retrieved February 14, 2018.

71. ^ Palazzolo, Joe; Rothfeld, Michael (January 18, 2018). "Trump Lawyer Used Private Company, Pseudonyms to Pay Adult film Star 'Stormy Daniels'; Michael Cohen created limited liability company just before $130,000 payment". *The Wall Street Journal*. Archived from the original on January 24, 2018. Retrieved January 25, 2018.

72. ^ Haberman, Maggie (February 13, 2018). "Trump's Longtime Lawyer Says He Paid Stormy Daniels Out of His Own Pocket". *The New York Times*. Archived from the original on

February 14, 2018.
Retrieved February 14, 2018.

73. ^ Blake, Aaron (February 14, 2018). *"Analysis | Did Trump's lawyer just implicate Trump in the Stormy Daniels payment?"*. *The Washington Post*. ISSN 0190-8286. *Archived* from the original on February 14, 2018.
Retrieved February 15, 2018.

74. ^ Rucker, Philip (April 26, 2018). *"Trump says for first time that Cohen represented him in Stormy Daniels case"*. *The Washington Post*. *Archived* from the original on August 22, 2018.
Retrieved August 23,2018.

75. ^ Palazzolo, Joe; Rothfeld, Michael. *"Trump Lawyer's Payment to Stormy Daniels Was Reported as Suspicious by Bank"*. *The Wall Street Journal*. *Archived* from the original on March 10, 2018. Retrieved March 11, 2018.

76. ^ Fitzpatrick, Sarah; Connor, Tracy. *"Michael Cohen used Trump*

company email in Stormy Daniels arrangements". *NBC News*. Archived from the original on March 10, 2018. Retrieved March 11,2018.

77. ^ Llamas, Tom; Zaki, Zunaira; Faulders, Katherine; Peck, Christina. *"Michael Cohen dismisses claims of email as proof that Trump knew about payment to porn star to buy her silence"*. *ABC News*. Archived from the original on March 10, 2018. Retrieved March 11,2018.

78. ^ *"Stormy Daniels describes her alleged affair with Donald Trump"*. *60 Minutes*. CBS News. March 25, 2018. Archived from the original on March 26, 2018. Retrieved March 26, 2018. Includes video and transcript.

79. ^ Parks, Miles (March 25, 2018). *"Stormy Daniels Shares Graphic Details About Alleged Affair With Trump"*. *NPR*. Archived from

the original on March 26, 2018. Retrieved March 26, 2018.

80. ^ "Lawyers for Trump attorney say Stormy Daniels lied in '60 Minutes' interview". CBS News. Archived from the original on March 26, 2018. Retrieved March 26, 2018.

81. ^ Fitzpatrick, Sarah. "Trump lawyer Michael Cohen tries to silence adult-film star Stormy Daniels". NBC News. Archived from the original on March 8, 2018. Retrieved March 8, 2018.

82. ^ Jump up to:ᵃ ᵇ "Trump attorney seeks to force porn star's lawsuit into arbitration". Reuters. April 2, 2018. Archived from the original on September 14, 2018. Retrieved August 23, 2018.

83. ^ Beech, Eric; Freifeld, Karen (April 2, 2018). "Trump attorney seeks to force porn star's lawsuit into arbitration". Reuters. Archived from the original on August 23, 2018. Retrieved May 9, 2018.

84. ^ Feuer, Alan; Weiser, Benjamin (April 25, 2018). _"Michael Cohen to Take Fifth Amendment in Stormy Daniels Lawsuit"_. _The New York Times_. _Archived_ from the original on August 22, 2018. Retrieved August 23, 2018.

85. ^ Brown, Emma; _Helderman, Rosalind S._ (April 25, 2018). _"Michael Cohen to invoke Fifth Amendment right in Stormy Daniels case"_. _The Washington Post_. _Archived_ from the original on April 27, 2018. Retrieved April 27, 2018.

86. ^ Mangan, Dan; Breuninger, Kevin (May 18, 2018). _"Cohen lawyers object to Stormy Daniels' attorney Michael Avenatti intervening in New York case"_. _CNBC_. _Archived_ from the original on May 19, 2018. Retrieved May 19, 2018.

87. ^ Jump up to:_a_ _b_ _"Trump: Hush money payments came from me"_. _BBC News_. August 23, 2018. _Archived_ from the original on

August 23, 2018. Retrieved August 23, 2018.

88. ^ Jump up to:ᵃ ᵇ ᶜ *Borger, Gloria; Orden, Erica; Bash, Dana; Perez, Evan (July 22, 2018). "Trump attorneys waive privilege on secret recording about ex-Playmate payment". CNN. Archived from the original on August 22, 2018. Retrieved August 23, 2018.*

89. ^ *Shelter, Brian (February 16, 2018). "'Catch and kill': How a tabloid shields Trump from troublesome stories". CNN. Archived from the original on August 23, 2018. Retrieved August 23, 2018.*

90. ^ *Palazzolo, Joe; Rothfeld, Michael; Ballhaus, Rebecca (July 25, 2018). "Trump's Former Lawyer Michael Cohen Formed Delaware Company to Purchase Ex-Playboy Model's Story". The Wall Street Journal. Archived from the original on July 25, 2018. Retrieved August 23, 2018.*

91. ^ Cohen, Michael (September 30, 2016). *"State of Delaware Limited Liability Company Certificate of Formation: Resolution Consultants LLC"* (PDF). *The Wall Street Journal*. *Secretary of State of Delaware*(Jeffrey W. Bullock). *Archived from the original* (PDF) on January 18, 2018.

92. ^ Thomsen, Jacqueline (April 12, 2018). *"Trump allies fear feds seized lawyer's recordings of conversations: report"*. *The Hill*. *Archived*from the original on July 22, 2018. Retrieved July 21, 2018.

93. ^ Jump up to:*a b* Zhou, Li (July 26, 2018). *"Report: federal authorities have seized more than 100 Michael Cohen tapes"*. *Vox*. *Vox Media*. *Archived*from the original on July 26, 2018. Retrieved July 27, 2018.

94. ^ Jump up to:*a b c* *"Exclusive: CNN obtains secret Trump-Cohen tape"*. *CNN*. July 25,

2018. _Archived_ from the original on July 25, 2018. Retrieved July 25, 2018.

95. ^ Tucker, Eric; Peltz, Jennifer (July 20, 2018). _"Trump was taped talking of paying for Playboy model's story"_. _Associated Press_. _Archived_ from the original on July 22, 2018. Retrieved October 19,2018.

96. ^ Faulders, Katherine (July 25, 2018). _"Trump-Cohen secret audio tape made public"_. _ABC News_. _Archived_ from the original on July 25, 2018. Retrieved July 25, 2018.

97. ^ Jump up to:_a_ _b_ Blake, Aaron (July 24, 2018). _"The Trump-Michael Cohen tape transcript, annotated"_. _The Washington Post_. _Archived_ from the original on July 25, 2018. Retrieved July 25, 2018.

98. ^ Singman, Brooke (August 23, 2018). _"Trump rips Cohen for 'flipping,' praises Manafort in_

exclusive FNC interview". *Fox News*. *Archived*from the original on August 23, 2018. Retrieved August 23, 2018.

99. ^ Palazzolo, Joe; Rothfeld, Michael (April 13, 2018). *"Trump Lawyer Michael Cohen Negotiated $1.6 Million Settlement for Top Republican Fundraiser"*. *The Wall Street Journal*. *Archived* from the original on April 13, 2018. Retrieved April 13, 2018.

100. ^ Ruiz, Rebecca R.; *Rutenberg, Jim* (April 13, 2018). *"R.N.C. Official Who Agreed to Pay Playboy Model $1.6 Million Resigns"*. *The New York Times*. *Archived* from the original on April 16, 2018. Retrieved April 16, 2018.

101. ^ Voreacos, David (April 16, 2018). *"Cohen Says He Gave Legal Advice to Three Clients in Past Year"*. *Bloomberg News*. *Archived*from the original on May 13, 2018. Retrieved May 23, 2018.

102. ^ Jump up to:_a_ _b_ _c_ Lee, MJ; _Sara, Sidner_; Scannell, Kara; Foran, Clare (April 13, 2018). _"Michael Cohen facilitated $1.6 million agreement on behalf of GOP fundraiser"_. _CNN_. _Archived_ from the original on April 13, 2018. Retrieved April 13, 2018.

103. ^ _Campos, Paul_ (May 8, 2018). _"Here's a Theory About That $1.6 Million Payout From a GOP Official to a Playboy Model"_. _New York_. _Archived_ from the original on August 12, 2018. Retrieved July 22,2018.

104. ^ _Prokop, Andrew_ (July 6, 2018). _"Shera Bechard lawsuit: Model who Trump donor paid hush money to sues - Vox"_. _Vox_. _Vox Media_. _Archived_ from the original on July 23, 2018. Retrieved July 22, 2018.

105. ^ _Dillon, Nancy_ (July 6, 2018). _"Ex-Playboy model sues Trump donor Elliott Broidy and_

Michael Avenatti over hush-money pact tied to secret pregnancy". *New York Daily News*. Archived from the original on July 7, 2018. Retrieved July 7, 2018.

106.    ^ Rothfeld, Michael; Palazzolo, Joe (July 6, 2018). "Ex-Playmate Files Suit Against GOP Donor Elliott Broidy Over Hush-Money Deal". *The Wall Street Journal*. Archived from the original on July 6, 2018.

107.    ^ Stris, Peter K.; Brannen, Elizabeth R.; Berkowitz, Dana; Stokes, John; Martin, Shaun P. (July 6, 2018). "Plaintiff's Memorandum of Points and Authorities in Support of Ex Parte Application to Conditionally Seal the Complaint for 45 Days" (PDF). Stris & Maher LLP via *The Wall Street Journal*. Archived from the original (PDF) on July 7, 2018.

108.    ^ Cohen, Michael (October 17, 2016). "State of Delaware Limited Liability Company Certificate of Formation" (PDF). *The Wall Street*

*Journal*. *Secretary of State of Delaware (Jeffrey W. Bullock)*. *Archived* (PDF) from the original on April 17, 2018. Retrieved May 9,2018.

109.  ^ Jump up to:*a* *b* *c* *d* *e* McIntire, Mike; Protess, Ben; *Rutenberg, Jim* (May 8, 2018). *"Firm Tied to Russian Oligarch Made Payments to Michael Cohen"*. *The New York Times*. *Archived* from the original on May 9, 2018. Retrieved May 9, 2018.

110.  ^ *Larson, Erik*; Martin, Andrew (May 8, 2018). *"Russian Oligarch Tied to Trump Lawyer in Stormy Bombshell"*. *Bloomberg L.P.* *Archived*from the original on May 8, 2018. Retrieved May 9, 2018.
Larson, Erik; Martin, Andrew (May 8, 2018). *"Russian Oligarch Tied to Trump Lawyer in Stormy Bombshell"* (MP3) (audio). *Bloomberg L.P.**Archived* from the original on

May 10, 2018. Retrieved March 2,2019.

111. ^ Lach, Eric (May 8, 2018). _"Why the Revelations About Michael Cohen's Business Dealings Could Be a Very Big Deal"_. _The New Yorker_. Archived from the original on May 9, 2018. Retrieved May 9,2018.

112. ^ Jump up to:[a] [b] Finnegan, Michael (May 9, 2018). _"Firm linked to Russian mogul paid $500,000 to Trump attorney Michael Cohen"_. _Los Angeles Times_. Archived from the original on May 9, 2018. Retrieved May 9,2018.

113. ^ May, Ruth (August 3, 2017). _"GOP campaigns took $7.35 million from oligarch linked to Russia"_. _The Dallas Morning News_. Archived from the original on May 18, 2018. Retrieved May 9, 2018.

114. ^ Avenatti, Michael. _"Executive Summary"_. Archived from the

original on June 12, 2018.
Retrieved May 9, 2018 – via Scribd.

115. ^ Johnson, Ted (May 9, 2018). "AT&T Says It Paid Michael Cohen's Firm for 'Insights' Into Trump Administration". Variety. Archivedfrom the original on May 9, 2018. Retrieved May 9, 2018.

116. ^ Shachtman, Noah; Briquelet, Kate (May 8, 2018). "Michael Cohen Took Cash From Oligarch-Connected Firm After Election". The Daily Beast. Archived from the original on May 8, 2018. Retrieved May 9,2018.

117. ^ Stelter, Brian; Gold, Hadas (May 11, 2018). "AT&T CEO says hiring Michael Cohen 'was a big mistake'". CNNMoney. Archived from the original on August 24, 2018. Retrieved August 23, 2018.

118. ^ Sagonowsky, Eric. "Novartis, Bayer CEOs get time with Trump as he meets with EU business leaders during Davos trip". FiercePharma. Archived from the

original on May 9, 2018. Retrieved May 9, 2018.

119. ^ Jump up to:*ª ᵇ* Blake, Aaron (May 10, 2018). *"Analysis | Michael Cohen epitomizes just how much the swamp has thrived under Trump"*. *The Washington Post*. ISSN 0190-8286. Archived from the original on May 10, 2018. Retrieved May 10, 2018.

120. ^ Rothfeld, Michael; Ballhaus, Rebecca; Palazzolo, Joe; Hong, Nicole (August 2, 2018). *"Top Trump Donor Agreed to Pay Michael Cohen $10 Million for Nuclear Project Push"*. *The Wall Street Journal*. Archived from the original on August 2, 2018.

121. ^ Winter, Tom; Edelman, Adam (April 16, 2018). *"Fox News host Sean Hannity revealed as Michael Cohen's mystery client"*. *NBC News*. Archived from the original on April 16, 2018. Retrieved April 16, 2018.

122.   ^ Strobel, Warren; Walcott, John (April 10, 2018). "FBI raids offices, home of Trump's personal lawyer: sources". *Reuters*. Archived from the original on April 10, 2018. Retrieved April 10, 2018.

123.   ^ Watkins, Eli. "FBI raids Trump lawyer Michael Cohen's office". *CNN*. Archived from the original on October 6, 2018. Retrieved May 3, 2018.

124.   ^ Jump up to:[a][b][c] Apuzzo, Matt (April 9, 2018). "F.B.I. Raids Office of Trump's Longtime Lawyer Michael Cohen". *The New York Times*. Archived from the original on April 9, 2018. Retrieved August 23, 2018.

125.   ^ Karl, Jonathan; Margolin, Josh (April 10, 2018). "Trump-appointed US attorney recused from Michael Cohen investigation". *ABC News*. Archived from the original on April 11, 2018. Retrieved April 11, 2018.

126. ^ Smith, Allan (April 10, 2018). _"The Justice Department had to go to extraordinary lengths to conduct a raid on top Trump lawyer Michael Cohen"_. _Business Insider_. _Archived_ from the original on May 2, 2018. Retrieved May 3, 2018.

127. ^ Orden, Erica; Ballhaus, Rebecca; Rothfeld, Michael (April 9, 2018). _"Agents Raid Office of Trump Lawyer Michael Cohen in Connection With Stormy Daniels Payments"_. _The Wall Street Journal_. _Archived_ from the original on April 11, 2018. Retrieved April 11, 2018.

128. ^ Lovelace, Ryan (April 9, 2018). _"After FBI Raid, Squire Says It Severed Ties to Trump Lawyer Michael Cohen"_. _The National Law Journal_. _Archived_ from the original on April 11, 2018. Retrieved April 11, 2018.

129. ^ _Haberman, Maggie; Apuzzo, Matt; Schmidt, Michael S._ (April 11,

2018). _"Raid on Trump's Lawyer Sought Records on 'Access Hollywood' Tape"._ _The New York Times._ _Archived_ from the original on April 11, 2018. Retrieved April 11, 2018.

130.    ^ _Borger, Gloria_; _Sidner, Sara_; Glover, Scott (April 13, 2018). _"Exclusive: FBI seized recordings between Trump's lawyer and Stormy Daniels' former lawyer"._ _CNN._ _Archived_ from the original on April 14, 2018. Retrieved April 14, 2018.

131.    ^ _Joy Reid_ (interviewer), _Michael Avenatti_ & _Lisa Bloom_ (interviewees) (April 14, 2018). _Avenatti and Bloom on A.M. Joy._ _A.M. Joy._ _MSNBC._ _Archived_ from the original on February 27, 2019. Retrieved December 9, 2018.

132.    ^ Rosenzweig, Paul (April 10, 2018). _"Michael Cohen, Attorney-Client Privilege and the Crime-Fraud Exception"._ _Lawfare._ _Archived_ from

the original on April 11, 2018. Retrieved April 11, 2018.

133. ^ Blake, Aaron (April 10, 2018). _"How Trump may have unwittingly invited the Michael Cohen raid"_. _The Washington Post_. _ISSN_ _0190-8286_. _Archived_ from the original on April 11, 2018. Retrieved April 11, 2018.

134. ^ _"Special Master in Cohen Case Finds Few Seized Materials Are Privileged"_. _Archived_ from the original on September 5, 2018. Retrieved September 5, 2018.

135. ^ Stockman, Rachel (April 9, 2018). _"Analysis: The FBI Raid Means Michael Cohen Should Be Really, Really Scared He's Next"_. _Law & Crime_. _Archived_ from the original on April 10, 2018. Retrieved April 10, 2018.

136. ^ Delk, Josh (April 10, 2018). _"FBI search warrant on Cohen covered taxi medallion ownership"_. _The Hill_. _Archived_ from

the original on April 11, 2018. Retrieved April 10, 2018.

137. ^ Graham, David A. (April 12, 2018). "What Exactly Was Michael Cohen Doing for Donald Trump?". *The Atlantic*. Archived from the original on April 13, 2018. Retrieved April 12, 2018.

138. ^ Stone, Peter; Gordon, Greg (April 13, 2018). "Sources: Mueller has evidence Cohen was in Prague in 2016, confirming part of dossier". *McClatchy DC Bureau*. Archived from the original on April 13, 2018. Retrieved April 16, 2018.

139. ^ Bump, Philip (April 14, 2018). "Michael Cohen's visiting Prague would be a huge development in the Russia investigation". *The Washington Post*. Archived from the original on April 15, 2018. Retrieved April 16, 2018.

140. ^ *"Special counsel has evidence Michael Cohen traveled to Prague: McClatchy"*. *Reuters*. April 14, 2018. *Archived* from the original on April 16, 2018. Retrieved April 16, 2018.

141. ^ Porter, Tom (April 14, 2018). *"Trump Attorney Lied About Prague Trip, Mueller Investigation Reveals, As New Evidence Comes To Light"*. *Newsweek*. *Archived* from the original on April 15, 2018. Retrieved April 16, 2018.

142. ^ *"Michael Cohen says he's "never" been to Prague. He told me a different story"*. *Mother Jones*. *Archived* from the original on December 30, 2018. Retrieved July 4, 2018.

143. ^ Winter, Tom; Ainsley, Julia (May 3, 2018). *"Feds monitored Trump lawyer Michael Cohen's phones"*. *Archived* from the original on May 3, 2018. Retrieved May 3, 2018.

144. ^ McLaughlin, Aidan. "Breaking: NBC News Issues Major Correction, Michael Cohen Was Not Wiretapped". *Mediaite*. Archived from the original on May 4, 2018. Retrieved May 3, 2018.

145. ^ Mangan, Dan; Breuninger, Kevin (July 26, 2018). "Trump Org. CFO mentioned in Michael Cohen tape called by grand jury to testify: WSJ". *CNBC*. Archived from the original on August 21, 2018. Retrieved August 22, 2018.

146. ^ "Michael Cohen reportedly under investigation for $20M in bank fraud". *New York Post*. August 19, 2018. Archived from the original on August 20, 2018. Retrieved August 20, 2018.

147. ^ Neumeister, Larry; Hays, Tom. "Ex-Trump lawyer Cohen pleads guilty in hush-money scheme, campaign finance violations". *Chicago Tribune*. Associated Press. Archived from the

original on August 21, 2018.
Retrieved August 21, 2018.

148.   ^ "Trump is latching on to a popular right-wing talking point about Michael Cohen that experts say is 'nonsense'". Business Insider. Archived from the original on August 26, 2018.
Retrieved August 25,2018.

149.   ^ Hong, Nicole; Ballhaus, Rebecca (August 21, 2018). "Michael Cohen Pleads Guilty, Says He Acted at Trump's Direction". The Wall Street Journal. Archived from the original on August 21, 2018.
Retrieved August 21, 2018.

150.   ^ Jump up to:ᵃ ᵇ "Ex-Trump lawyer admits campaign violation". BBC News. August 21, 2018. Archived from the original on August 21, 2018. Retrieved August 21, 2018.

151.   ^ Higgins, Tucker; Breuninger, Kevin (August 21, 2018). "Trump's former lawyer Michael Cohen pleads

guilty, admits to making illegal payments at direction of candidate to influence election". *CNBC*. Archived from the original on August 21, 2018. Retrieved August 21,2018.

152.    ^ *"Trump ex-lawyer 'happy' to aid Russia probe"*. *BBC News*. August 22, 2018. Archived from the original on August 22, 2018. Retrieved August 22, 2018.

153.    ^ Becker, Isaac. *"Cohen lawyer Lanny Davis suggests his client has knowledge implicating Trump in 'criminal conspiracy' to hack Democratic emails"*. *The Washington Post*. Archived from the original on August 22, 2018. Retrieved August 22, 2018.

154.    ^ Vazquez, Maegan (August 22, 2018). *"Cohen lawyer says he would testify to Congress about Trump without immunity"*. *CNN*. Archived from the original on August 22, 2018. Retrieved August 22, 2018.

155. ^ Dwyer, Colin; Lucas, Ryan. _"Michael Cohen's Lawyer Says His Client Would Never Accept Pardon From 'Corrupt' Trump"_. _Morning Edition_. _NPR_. _Archived_ from the original on August 22, 2018. Retrieved August 22, 2018.

156. ^ _"Putin news conference drove Michael Cohen away from Trump"_. _Sky News_. August 22, 2018. _Archived_ from the original on August 23, 2018. Retrieved August 22, 2018.

157. ^ Rashbaum, William K. (August 22, 2018). _"Cohen Wasn't Alone: Records Suggest Others in Trump Circle Had Role in Hush Money Arrangements"_. _The New York Times_. _Archived_ from the original on August 23, 2018. Retrieved August 22, 2018.

158. ^ Fox, Emily Jane (October 15, 2018). "He Is Trying to Make It Right": As the Midterms Approach, Michael Cohen Is Doubling Down on

His Civic Duty Archived November 28, 2018, at the Wayback Machine, *Vanity Fair*.

159. ^ *"Michael Cohen spoke to Mueller team for hours; asked about Russia, possible collusion"*. *ABC News*. September 20, 2018. Archived from the original on September 21, 2018. Retrieved September 20, 2018.

160. ^ Jump up to:*a* *b* *c* Cone, Allen; Adamczyk, Ed (December 13, 2018). Michael Cohen sentenced to 3 years in prison stemming from plea dealArchived December 15, 2018, at the Wayback Machine, United Press International.

161. ^ Hamilton, Colby (December 12, 2018). Cohen's 'Blind Loyalty' Leads to 3-Year Prison Term Archived December 15, 2018, at the Wayback Machine, *New York Law Journal*.

162. ^ Jump up to:*a* *b* *"Ex-Trump lawyer Cohen jailed for 36

months". *BBC News*. December 12, 2018. Archived from the original on December 12, 2018. Retrieved December 12, 2018.

163. ^ *"Michael Cohen, Trump's former lawyer, is sentenced to three years in prison for 'dirty deeds'"*. *USA Today*. December 12, 2018. Archived from the original on December 12, 2018. Retrieved December 12, 2018.

164. ^ Jump up to:<u>a</u> <u>b</u> <u>c</u> Barrett, Devlin; Zapotosky, Matt; Helderman, Rosalind S. *"Michael Cohen, Trump's former lawyer, pleads guilty to lying to Congress about Moscow project"*. *The Washington Post*. Archived from the original on November 29, 2018. Retrieved November 29, 2018.

165. ^ *"Trump ex-lawyer admits lying to Congress"*. *BBC News*. November 29, 2018. Archived from the original on November 30, 2018. Retrieved December 1, 2018.

166. ^ "Robert Mueller probe: Ex-Trump lawyer Michael Cohen pleads guilty to lying to Congress". *USA Today*. November 29, 2018. Archived from the original on November 30, 2018. Retrieved November 30, 2018.

167. ^ "Ex-lawyer says he told Trump about Kremlin contact: court filing". *Reuters*. December 1, 2018. Archived from the original on December 1, 2018. Retrieved December 1, 2018.

168. ^ Sullivan, Kate (January 18, 2019). "BuzzFeed: Sources say Trump directed Michael Cohen to lie to Congress about proposed Moscow project". *CNN*. Archived from the original on January 18, 2019. Retrieved January 18, 2018.

169. ^ Elfrink, Tim (January 18, 2019). "Democrats demand investigation after report that Trump ordered Michael Cohen to lie to Congress". *The Washington*

*Post*. *Archived* from the original on January 18, 2019. Retrieved January 18, 2019.

170.    ^ Polantz, Katelyn; Kelly, Caroline (January 19, 2019). *"Mueller's office disputes BuzzFeed report that Trump directed Michael Cohen to lie to Congress"*. *CNN*. *Archived* from the original on January 19, 2019. Retrieved January 19, 2019.

171.    ^ Orden, Erica; Tatum, Sophie (August 22, 2018). *"New York tax investigators subpoena Michael Cohen in Trump Foundation probe"*. *CNN*. *Archived* from the original on August 22, 2018. Retrieved August 23, 2018.

172.    ^ Isidore, Chris; Schuman, Melanie (June 14, 2018). *"New York attorney general sues Trump Foundation"*. *CNN*. *Archived* from the original on August 24, 2018. Retrieved August 23, 2018.

173.    ^ Haberman, Maggie; Fandos, Nicholas (January 10,

2019). _"Michael Cohen Agrees to Testify to Congress About Work for Trump"_. _The New York Times_. Archived from the original on January 10, 2019. Retrieved January 10, 2019.

174. ^ Larramendia, Eliana; Hill, James (January 16, 2019). _"Michael Cohen fears Trump rhetoric could put his family at risk: Sources"_. _ABC News_. Archived from the original on February 27, 2019. Retrieved January 25, 2019.

175. ^ Gualtieri, Allison Elyse. Who is Michael Cohen's father-in-law? Trump says he should be investigated Archived January 24, 2019, at the Wayback Machine, _Washington Examiner_, January 12, 2019. Retrieved January 24, 2019.

176. ^ Jump up to:ᵃ ᵇ Hettena, Seth. A Brief History of Michael Cohen's Criminal Ties From the Russian mob to money launderers, Trump's personal attorney has long

been a subject of interest to federal investigatorsArchived January 16, 2019, at the Wayback Machine, *Rolling Stone*, April 10, 2018. Retrieved January 24, 2019.

177. ^ Jump up to:[a] [b] *Prokop, Andrew (January 24, 2019). "Michael Cohen's claim that President Trump is threatening his family, explained". Vox. Archived from the original on January 25, 2019. Retrieved January 25, 2019.*

178. ^ *Ward, Stephanie Francis (January 15, 2019). "Legal experts weigh in on Trump's Cohen comments and whether they amount to witness intimidation". ABA Journal. Archived from the original on January 26, 2019. Retrieved January 25, 2019.*

179. ^ *Haberman, Maggie (January 23, 2019). "Michael Cohen Indefinitely Postpones Testimony to Congress, Citing Fears of Family's*

Safety". *The New York Times*. Archived from the original on January 24, 2019. Retrieved January 24, 2019.

180.    ^ *"Analysis | Michael Cohen says Trump and Giuliani threatened him. Does that amount to witness tampering?"*. *The Washington Post*. Archived from the original on January 24, 2019. Retrieved January 24, 2019.

181.    ^ Montoya-Galvez, Camilo (February 25, 2019). *"Cohen to face questions on Trump Tower deal, BuzzFeed report at closed-door hearing"*. CBS News. Archived from the original on March 6, 2019. Retrieved March 4, 2019.

182.    ^ Cillizza, Chris (February 27, 2019). *"A high-profile Trump ally in Congress just straight-up threatened Michael Cohen"*. CNN. Archived from the original on February 28, 2019. Retrieved February 28, 2019.

183.    ^ Stieb, Matt (February 27, 2019). *"GOP Congressman*

*Threatens Michael Cohen on Twitter, Then Apologizes". New York. Archived from the original on February 28, 2019. Retrieved February 28, 2019.*

184.    ^ *Fandos, Nicholas (February 27, 2019). "Florida Bar Will Investigate Matt Gaetz's Threat Against Cohen". The New York Times. Archived from the original on February 27, 2019. Retrieved February 28, 2019.*

185.    ^ *"'I am not protecting Mr. Trump anymore.' Michael Cohen ties the president to ongoing criminal probes". USA Today. February 27, 2019. Archived from the original on March 1, 2019. Retrieved March 4, 2019.*

186.    ^ *Ewing, Philip (February 27, 2019). "Michael Cohen Calls Trump A 'Racist' And A 'Con Man' In Scathing Testimony". NPR. Archived from the original on March 4, 2019. Retrieved March 4, 2019.*

187. ^ "Michael Cohen will return to Congress March 6, Felix Sater to testify March 14". CNN. February 28, 2019. Archived from the original on March 4, 2019. Retrieved March 4, 2019.

188. ^ Hettena, Seth (April 10, 2018). "A Brief History of Michael Cohen's Criminal Ties". Rolling Stone. Archived from the original on June 16, 2018. Retrieved August 23, 2018.

189. ^ Jump up to:ª ᵇ ᶜ Rashbaum, William K.; Hakim, Danny; Rosenthal, Brian M.; Flitter, Emily; Drucker, Jesse (May 5, 2018). "How Michael Cohen, Trump's Fixer, Built a Shadowy Business Empire". The New York Times. Archived from the original on May 5, 2018. Retrieved May 5, 2018.

190. ^ Megerian, Chris; Sharp, Sonja (December 12, 2018). "Michael Cohen, Trump's longtime lawyer, sentenced to three years in prison". Los Angeles

*Times*. *Archived* from the original on December 13, 2018. *Retrieved December 13, 2018.*

191.   ⌃ Kwong, Jessica. (December 3, 2018). "Who is Michael Cohen's wife? Laura Shusterman never charged though prosecutors had evidence implicating her, according to report." Newsweek website ArchivedJanuary 16, 2019, at the Wayback Machine *Newsweek*. Retrieved December 16, 2018.

192.   ⌃ Hettena, Seth (May 2018). *Trump / Russia: A Definitive History*. *Melville House*. *p. 80. ISBN 978-1612197395*. *Archived* from the original on January 31, 2019. *Retrieved December 18, 2018.*

193.   ⌃ Cadenas, Kerensa (December 2, 2018). *"Alec Baldwin Returns to S.N.L. as Trump with Ben Stiller as Michael Cohen"*. *Vanity Fair*. *Archived* from the original on

*February 27, 2019.*
*Retrieved December 13, 2018.*

## External links

- [Michael Cohen](#) on [IMDb](#)
- [American University alumni](#)

Rick Gates Biography-Witch # 4
Political Consultant (c. 1972–)

- 
- 
- 
- 
- 

Rick Gates is an American political consultant and associate of veteran campaign operative Paul Manafort's. In 2018, he pleaded guilty to fraud for falsifying financial documents and concealing millions of dollars in earnings from their overseas work.

**Who Is Rick Gates?**

Rick Gates first found his footing in the world of political consulting as an intern for Washington insider Paul Manafort's firm in the mid-1990s. The following decade he rejoined Manafort in Ukraine, where they allied themselves with powerful businessmen and political figures and allegedly concealed much of the income they made while doing so. They then joined Donald Trump's presidential campaign in 2016, though news reports of their overseas history hinted at the troubles ahead. Gates and Manafort were indicted by special counsel Robert Mueller on conspiracy and money laundering charges in October 2017, prompting Gates to agree to a plea deal and testify against his old boss the following year.

Richard Gates arrives at the Prettyman Federal Courthouse for a bail hearing November 6, 2017 in Washington, D.C.
(Photo: Mark Wilson_Getty Images)
**Paul Manafort Trial Witness**

On August 6, 2018, six days after the start of Paul Manafort's trial on 18 felony counts of tax and bank fraud charges in Alexandria, Virgina, his protégé, Rick Gates, took the stand as the prosecution's star witness.

The two had been ensnared in special counsel Robert Mueller's wide-ranging investigation into Russian attempts to influence the 2016 U.S. presidential race, which uncovered their illicit financial activities on foreign shores.

Gates testified as to how, under the instructions of Manafort, he concealed millions of dollars received from their work in Ukraine for former President Viktor Yanukovych and powerful oligarchs over a period spanning 2006 to 2015. He said he had set up 15 bank accounts in the names of shell companies in Cyprus, Saint Vincent and the Grenadines and the Seychelles, through which they avoided paying taxes on some $16.47 million in earnings. After their cash flow dried up, Gates said he altered financial documents to help Manafort qualify for loans stateside so he could pay off his mortgages and maintain a lavish lifestyle.

Gates was then subjected to withering cross-examination, with the defense describing him as the mastermind behind the fraudulent activities and Manafort too busy to notice. They pressed him about his lengthy list of misdeeds, which included embezzling hundreds of thousands from his boss and hiding $3 million of his own income, and even attempted to paint him as a serial adulterer who lied to his wife and investigators about his numerous affairs. When asked why the jury should trust his account of events, Gates replied, "I made a decision — I'm here to tell the truth," adding that he took responsibility for his actions and was "trying to change."

## Working for Manafort

Gates first came into Manafort's orbit in the mid-1990s as a research intern at Black, Manafort, Stone, Kelly, a Washington consulting firm that counted foreign dictators like the Phillippines' Ferdinand Marcos and entities like the Trump Organization among its clients. While Manafort left the firm shortly afterward, the hardworking Gates made a strong impression on its remaining members, including well-connected lobbyist Rick Davis.

In 2006 Gates reunited with his old mentors at their new company, Davis Manafort. Based in the Ukranian capital of Kiev, the men used their expertise to rebrand the political prospects of Prime Minister Viktor Yanukovych, helping him earn election to the country's presidency in 2010. They also forged connections with oligarchs like aluminum magnate Oleg Deripaska, who became a primary investor in the Davis Manafort private equity fund Pericles. When Davis left the company to manage John McCain's 2008 presidential campaign, Gates assumed many of his duties and strengthened his relationship with Manafort.

This period was not without its difficulties, as the two men were named in a 2011 racketeering lawsuit filed in the U.S. over their work for Yanukovych, and later were questioned by the FBI as part of a joint American-Ukrainian forfeiture investigation. Of greater concern was Yanukovych's departure from office in 2014, which robbed the company of its most lucrative client and left Manafort in deep debt by the start of 2016.

**Trump Campaign Aide and Supporter**

In the spring of 2016, when Manafort joined the upstart presidential campaign of Donald Trump as chief strategist, he brought Gates into the fold as his trusted second. Gates helped his boss track delegates for the Republican nomination, along the way forging relationships with key campaign members like digital director Brad Parscale and Trump's first chief of staff, Reince Priebus.

Manafort's ascension to campaign manager in June placed Gates in the position of deputy campaign manager, though the arrangement was short-lived: In August, with the media reporting on the duo's work in the Ukraine, Manafort was dismissed from the campaign. Gates survived, though he was transferred to the role of liaison to the Republican National Committee.

Gates eventually struck up a friendship with wealthy investor and Trump confidant Tom Barrack, who tapped the younger operative to assist him on the Presidential Inaugural Committee. From there, Gates joined Parscale and other former campaign associates to found the pro-Trump nonprofit America First Policies.

In March 2017, with Manafort and Gates back in the news over reports of their professional dealings, Gates was let go from America First. He subsequently became a consultant for Barrack's company, Colony NorthStar, and reportedly maintained access to White House personnel for months afterward.

## Gates's Indictments and Plea Deal

On October 30, 2017, special counsel Robert Mueller indicted Manafort and Gates on 12 charges apiece on counts that included conspiracy to launder money, conspiracy against the U.S. and failure to report foreign financial accounts and transactions. Both men pleaded not guilty, with Gates released on a $5 million bond and confined to house arrest.

After Mueller unsealed a new indictment of 32 counts against the two in February 2018, Gates changed his tune and pleaded guilty to financial fraud and lying to federal investigators. In exchange for his cooperation, prosecutors said they would recommend a reduced prison sentence ranging from four years, nine months to six years.

## Background and Schools

Little is publicly known about the early life of Richard W. Gates III. Reportedly born on April 27, 1972, he is the son of a career Army officer, lieutenant colonel Richard W. Gates Jr., and spent much of his childhood abroad before the family settled in Prince George County, Virginia.

Gates graduated with a B.A. in Government from the College of William & Mary in 1994, and later earned his

Master's in Public Policy from George Washington University.

## Other Companies

Following his time at Black, Manafort, Stone, Kelly, Gates worked at the gaming companies GTech and Scientific Games Corporation. He also continued his political consulting work with Business Strategies and Insight, LLC and co-founded Capital Strategies, LLC.

Gates was on the board of directors for ID Watchdog Inc., an identity-theft protection company, from 2011 to '16. He also served as chairman of the advisory board of his father's management consultant business, Gates Group International.

## Personal

Gates lives in the Near West End area of Richmond, Virginia, with his wife, Sarah Brooke Gates, and four children. Neighbors say he has been active in the community as a youth soccer coach.

## Citation Information

Article Title

Rick Gates Biography

Author

Biography.com Editors

Website Name

The Biography.com website

URL

https://www.biography.com/people/rick-gates

Access Date

Publisher

A&E Television Networks

Last Updated

August 14, 2018

Original Published Date

August 14, 2018

- 
- 
-

# George Papadopoulas-Witch # 5

By Alex Johnson

George Papadopoulos, the first person to plead guilty in special counsel Robert Mueller's investigation into Donald Trump's presidential campaign, is a specialist in Mediterranean oil and gas policy who sought to become a key intermediary between Russia and the United States.

And, by almost all accounts, he failed.

Papadopoulos, 30, who volunteered as a foreign policy adviser to the Trump campaign, secretly pleaded guilty on Oct. 5 to a single count of making false statements to federal investigators — a charge that carries a maximum sentence of five years in prison.

George Papadopoulos Pleads Guilty to Making False Statements to FBI

But prosecutors agreed to recommend that Papadopoulos be sentenced to no more than six months in return for his continued cooperation with Mueller's investigation into allegations of collusion between Russia and the Trump campaign.

The guilty plea was a surprise development that was revealed as Mueller's office indicted former Trump campaign manager Paul Manafort and his associate Rick

Gates on charges of conspiracy against the United States, money laundering, being an unregistered foreign agent and seven counts of failing to file reports of foreign bank and financial accounts.

According to federal prosecutors, Papadopoulos lied to the FBI about both the timing and the significance of extensive conversations with people whom he believed to be close to the Russian government during the 2016 campaign. He believed one of those people was the niece of Russian President Vladimir Putin, even though she wasn't, prosecutors said in a statement of criminal information filed in U.S. District Court in Washington.

George Papadopoulos, third from left, meets with then-presidential candidate Donald Trump at a "National Security Meeting" in Washington, in a photo posted to Instagram on March 31, 2016.**@reaDonaldTrump / Instagram**

White House Press Secretary Sarah Huckabee Sanders said Monday that Papadopoulos, who previously had been an adviser to the failed campaign of Ben Carson, now the secretary of housing and urban development, had an "extremely limited" role with the Trump campaign.

Corey Lewandowski, who preceded Manafort as Trump campaign manager, on Tuesday called Papadopoulos a "low level volunteer" who was "not involved with day-to-day operations of the campaign."

████████████████████████████████

Prosecutors painted a picture of an eager young political operative who appeared to be currying favor with his superiors in the Trump campaign by repeatedly trying to set up a meeting between Trump and Putin or other senior Russian leaders. He sought himself to meet with top Russian officials, and he plied his bosses with promises that the Russians had "thousands of emails" full of "dirt" on Democratic presidential nominee Hillary Clinton.

Those meetings never occurred, and those emails never materialized, at least not through Papadopoulos' efforts, prosecutors said.

At one point, they said, a campaign official made it clear in an internal message that "DT" — presumably Trump — "is not doing these trips." That message should be conveyed by "someone low level in the campaign," wrote the unnamed campaign official — who suggested that ignoring Papadopoulos was a reasonable option, according to prosecutors.

According to multiple biographies of Papadopoulos on **his LinkedIn page** and various think tank websites, Papadopoulos is a political science graduate of DePaul University in Chicago with a master's degree from University College London. His master's dissertation examined the impact of regulation on government policies in the Middle East.

George Papadopoulos in an undated photograph.

Papadopoulos' own writings say that one of his first jobs was as a research associate at the Hudson Institute, a conservative think tank, where he specialized in the energy policies of Greece, Cyprus, Egypt, Israel and Lebanon, and examined Eastern Mediterranean and Caspian hydrocarbon reserves. The Hudson Institute on Monday described Papadopoulos as an intern who left the organization in 2014.

Papadopoulos then worked for Energy Stream, a London energy consultancy, for four months, before joining the Carson campaign, which he left in February 2016 as Carson was preparing to drop out of the Republican race.

From there, he joined the London Center of International Law Practice as director of the organization's Center for International Energy and Natural Resources Law & Security, **according to a staff directory** preserved on the Internet Archive. After about three months in that job, he left in March 2016 to sign on with Trump, who described him in **an interview with The Washington Post** at the time as "an oil and energy consultant."

It's unclear when, how or why Papadopoulos turned his focus to U.S. relations with Russia, but almost immediately, he was telling his campaign bosses that he was in contact with the woman he thought was Putin's niece and that he might be able to arrange a meeting between Trump and Putin, prosecutors said.

That account was backed up in August, in part, by Ivan Timofeev, director of programs of the Russian International Affairs Council, a Moscow-based think tank founded in 2010 by the Russian Foreign Affairs Ministry and the Russian news agency Interfax.

**In an Aug. 21 interview** with the Russian news site Gazeta, Timofeev said Papadopoulos approached him sometime in spring 2016 seeking to arrange "a visit to Russia either for Trump himself or for a member of his team 'to discuss Russia-U.S. relations.'" He said Papadopoulos represented himself as a member of the Trump campaign.

Timofeev described Papadopoulos as "an enthusiast with little experience."

"Our conversations made it clear that George was not well acquainted with the Russian foreign political landscape," Timofeev said. "You obviously can't just go and set up a meeting with the president, for instance. Things just aren't done that way."

He said he recommended some public reports and "analytical materials" for Papadopoulos to read to get up to speed.

Papadopoulos' LinkedIn page appears to lend credence to characterizations that he was a relative neophyte who was trying to wedge his way into the U.S.-Russia discussion.

In a reference that was later removed — but which is preserved on the Internet Archive — Papadopoulos listed at the top of his list of awards and honors that he was a U.S. representative at the Model United Nations. That's a mock U.N. session where high school and college students practice being U.N. delegates.

LinkedIn page of Trump foreign policy adviser Papadopoulos lists Model UN as credential.
**https://www.linkedin.com/in/gpapadopoulos7 …**

And on the still-live version of his LinkedIn biography, Papadopoulos claims to have been a speaker at the Republican National Convention in Cleveland in July 2016.

There are no records of that in convention schedules, news accounts or C-SPAN's complete recordings of Papadopoulos' having spoken at the convention. But a **news report in the Cleveland Jewish News** does recount Papadopoulos' having been one of six members of a panel discussion that the American Jewish Committee hosted on July 20 at The City Club of Cleveland.

The Cleveland Jewish News report includes a photograph showing Papadopoulos seated at a table with the other panelists in a small room in front of an American Jewish Committee sign.

Alex Johnson
Alex Johnson is a senior writer for NBC News covering general news, with an emphasis on explanatory journalism, data analysis, technology and religion. He is based in Los Angeles.

## Roger Stone-Witch # 6

Roger Jason Stone Jr. (born August 27, 1952) is an American **political consultant**,[2] author, **lobbyist** and **strategist** known for his use of **opposition research**, usually for candidates of the **Republican Party**.[3] Since the 1970s, Stone has worked on the campaigns of Republican politicians including **Richard Nixon, Ronald Reagan, Jack Kemp, Bob Dole, and Donald Trump.**

In addition to frequently serving as a campaign advisor, Stone was previously a political lobbyist. In 1980, he co-founded a Washington, D.C.–based lobbying firm with **Paul Manafort and Charles R. Black Jr.**[4][5][6] **The firm recruited Peter G. Kelly and was renamed Black,**

**Manafort, Stone and Kelly in 1984.**[7]:124 **During the 1980s, BMSK** became a top lobbying firm by leveraging its White House connections to attract high-paying clients including U.S. corporations, trade associations, and foreign governments. By 1990, it was one of the leading **lobbyists for American companies** and foreign organizations.[7]:125

Stone has been variously described as a "**dirty trickster,**"[8] a "**renowned infighter,**" a "**seasoned** practitioner of hard-edged politics," a "mendacious windbag," a "veteran Republican strategist,"[9][10][11][12][13][14][15] and a political **fixer**.[16] Over the course of the **2016 Trump presidential campaign**, Stone promoted a number of falsehoods and conspiracy theories.[17][18][19][20][21][22][23][24] He has described his political **modus operandi** as "Attack, attack, attack – never defend" and "Admit nothing, deny everything, launch counterattack."[25] Stone first suggested Trump run for President in early 1998 while Stone was Trump's casino business lobbyist in Washington.[26] The **Netflix** documentary film **Get Me Roger Stone** focuses on Stone's past and his role in the presidential campaign of Donald Trump.[27]

Stone officially left the Trump campaign on August 8, 2015; however, as part of the ongoing investigation into **Russian interference in the 2016 United States election**, two associates of Stone have said he collaborated with **WikiLeaks** founder **Julian Assange** during the 2016 presidential campaign to discredit **Hillary Clinton.** Both men have repeatedly denied this.[28][29][30] On January 25, 2019, Stone was arrested at his **Fort Lauderdale, Florida, home in connection with Robert Mueller's Special Counsel investigation** and charged in an indictment with **witness tampering,** obstructing an official proceeding, and five counts of making false statements.[31][32] Stone pleaded not guilty and denied wrongdoing in press interviews.[33]

# Contents

## Early life and political work

Stone was born on August 27, 1952,[13] in Norwalk, Connecticut,[34] to Gloria Rose (Corbo) and Roger J. Stone.[35] He grew up in Lewisboro, New York, in a family of Hungarian and Italian descent. His mother was a small-town reporter, his father a well driller[36] and business owner. He has described his family as middle-class, blue-collar Catholics.[34]

Stone said that as an elementary school student in 1960, he broke into politics to further John F. Kennedy's presidential campaign: "I remember going through the cafeteria line and telling every kid that Nixon was in favor of school on Saturdays ... It was my first political trick."[36]

When he was a junior and vice president of student government at his high school in northern Westchester County, New York, he manipulated the ouster of the president and succeeded him. Stone recalled how he ran for election as president for his senior year:

I built alliances and put all my serious challengers on my ticket. Then I recruited the most unpopular guy in the school to run against me. You think that's mean? No, it's smart.[37]

Given a copy of Barry Goldwater's The Conscience of a Conservative, Stone became a convert to conservatism as a child and a volunteer in Goldwater's 1964 campaign. In 2007, Stone indicated he was a staunch conservative but with libertarian leanings.[36]

As a student at George Washington University in 1972, Stone invited Jeb Magruder to speak at a Young Republicans Club meeting, then asked Magruder for a job with Richard Nixon's Committee to Re-elect the President.[38] Magruder agreed and Stone then left college to work for the committee.[39]

Career

1970s: Nixon campaign, Watergate and Reagan 1976

Stone's political career began in earnest on the 1972 Nixon campaign, with activities such as contributing money to a possible rival of Nixon in the name of the Young Socialist Alliance – then slipping the receipt to the Manchester Union-Leader. He also hired a spy in the Hubert Humphrey campaign who became Humphrey's driver. According to Stone, during the day he was officially a scheduler in the Nixon campaign, but "By night, I'm trafficking in the black arts. Nixon's people were obsessed with intelligence."[3] Stone maintains he never did anything illegal during Watergate.[39] The Richard Nixon Foundation later clarified that Stone had been a 20-year-old junior scheduler on the campaign, and that to characterize Stone as one of Nixon's aides or advisers was a "gross misstatement".[40]

After Nixon won the 1972 presidential election, Stone worked for the administration in the Office of Economic Opportunity. After Nixon resigned, Stone went to work for Bob Dole, but was later fired after columnist Jack Anderson publicly identified Stone as a Nixon 'dirty trickster'.[41]

In 1975, Stone helped found the National Conservative Political Action Committee, a New Right organization that helped to pioneer independent expenditure political advertising.[42]

In 1976, he worked in Ronald Reagan's campaign for President. In 1977, at age 24, Stone won the presidency of the Young Republicans in a campaign managed by his friend Paul Manafort; they had compiled a dossier for each of the 800 delegates that gathered, which they called "whip books".[43]

1980s: Reagan 1980, lobbying, and Bush 1988

Stone with President Ronald Reagan and then-Vice PresidentGeorge H. W. Bush in 1982

Roger Stone and his then-wife Ann Stone with President Ronald Reagan and First Lady Nancy Reagan in 1984

Stone greeting President Ronald Reagan in 1985

Stone went on to serve as chief strategist for Thomas Kean's campaign for governor of New Jersey in 1981 and for his re-election campaign in 1985.[13]

Stone, the "keeper of the Nixon flame",[44] was an adviser to the former President in his post-presidential years, serving as "Nixon's man in Washington".[45] Stone was a protégé of former Connecticut Governor John Davis Lodge, who introduced the young Stone to then former Vice President Nixon in 1967.[46] After Stone was indicted in 2019, the Nixon Foundation released a statement distancing Stone's ties to Nixon.[47][48][49]John Sears recruited Stone to work in Ronald Reagan's 1980 presidential campaign, coordinating the Northeast. Stone said that Roy Cohn helped him arrange for John B. Anderson to get the nomination of the Liberal Party of New York, a move that would help split the opposition to Reagan in the state. Stone said Cohn gave him a suitcase that Stone avoided opening and that, as instructed by Cohn, he dropped off at the office of a lawyer influential in Liberal Party circles. Reagan carried the state with 46% of the vote. Speaking after the statute of limitations for bribery had expired, Stone later said, "I paid his law firm. Legal fees. I don't know what he did for the money, but whatever it was, the Liberal party reached its right conclusion out of a matter of principle."[3]

In 1980, after their key roles in the Reagan campaign, Stone and Manafort decided to go into business together, with partner Charlie Black, creating a political consulting and lobbying firm to cash in on their relationships within the new administration. Black, Manafort & Stone (BMS), became one of Washington D.C.'s first mega-lobbying firms[50][51]and was described as instrumental to the success of Ronald Reagan's 1984 campaign. Republican political strategist Lee Atwater joined the firm in 1985, after serving in the #2 position on Reagan-Bush 1984.

Because of BMS's willingness to represent brutal third-world dictators like Mobutu Sese Seko in the Republic of the Congo and Ferdinand Marcos in the Philippines, the firm was branded "The Torturers' Lobby". BMS also represented a host of high-powered corporate clients, including Rupert Murdoch's News Corp, The Tobacco Institute and, starting in the early 1980s, Donald Trump.[52][53][54]

In 1987–88, Stone served as senior adviser to Jack Kemp's presidential campaign, which was managed by consulting partner Charlie Black.[55] In that same election, his other partners worked for George H. W. Bush (Lee Atwater as campaign manager, and Paul Manafort as director of operations in the fall campaign).[56]

In April 1992, Time alleged that Stone was involved with the controversial Willie Horton advertisements to aid George H. W. Bush's 1988 presidential campaign, which were targeted against Democratic opponent Michael Dukakis.[57] Stone has said that he urged Lee Atwater not to include Horton in the ad.[13] Stone denied making or distributing the advertisement, and said it was Atwater's doing.[13]

In the 1990s, Stone and Manafort sold their business. Although their careers went in different directions, their relationship remained close.[citation needed]

Stone married his first wife Anne Elizabeth Wesche in 1974. Using the name Ann E.W. Stone, she founded the group Republicans for Choice in 1989. They divorced in 1990.[58]

### 1990s: early work with Donald Trump, Dole 1996

In 1995, Stone was the president of Republican Senator Arlen Specter's campaign for the 1996 Republican presidential nomination.[59] Specter withdrew early in the campaign season with less than 2% support.

Stone was for many years a lobbyist for Donald Trump on behalf of his casino business[26] and also was involved in opposing expanded casino gambling in New York State, a position that brought him into conflict with Governor George Pataki.[60]

Stone resigned from a post as a consultant to the 1996 presidential campaign for Senator Bob Dole after *The National Enquirer* reported that Stone had placed ads and pictures in racy swingers' publications and a website, seeking sexual partners for himself and Nydia Bertran Stone, his second wife, married in Las Vegas in 1992. Stone initially denied the report.[36][37] On the *Good Morning America* program he falsely stated, "An exhaustive investigation now indicates that a domestic employee, who I discharged for substance abuse on the second time that we learned that he had a drug problem, is the perpetrator who had access to my home, access to my computer, access to my password, access to my postage meter, access to my post-office box key."[36] In a 2008 interview with *The New Yorker* Stone admitted that the ads were authentic.[13]

**2000s: Florida recount, Killian memos, conflict with Eliot Spitzer**

In 2000, Stone served as campaign manager of Donald Trump's aborted campaign for President in the Reform Party primary.[39] Investigative journalist Wayne Barrett accused Stone of persuading Trump to publicly consider a run for the Reform nomination to sideline Pat

Buchanan and sabotage the Reform Party in an attempt to lower their vote total to benefit George W. Bush.[61]

Later that year, according to Stone and the film *Recount*, Stone was recruited by James Baker to assist with public relations during the Florida recount. His role in the Brooks Brothers riot, the demonstration by Republican operatives against the recount, remains controversial.[39]

In 2002, Stone was associated with the campaign of businessman Thomas Golisano for governor of New York State.[60]

During the 2004 presidential campaign, Democrat Al Sharpton responded to accusations that Stone was working on his campaign, stating, "I've been talking to Roger Stone for a long time. That doesn't mean that he's calling the shots for me. Don't forget that Bill Clinton was doing more than talking to Dick Morris."[62] Critics suggested that Stone was only working with Sharpton as a way to undermine the Democratic Party's chances of winning the election. Sharpton denies that Stone had any influence over his campaign.[63]

In that election a blogger accused Stone of responsibility for the Kerry–Specter campaign materials which were circulated in Pennsylvania.[64] Such signs were considered controversial because they were seen as an effort to get Democrats who supported Kerry to vote for then Republican Senator Arlen Specter in heavily Democratic Philadelphia.

During the 2004 general election, Stone was accused by then-DNC Chairman Terry McAuliffe of forging the Killian memos that led CBS News to report that President Bush had not fulfilled his service obligations while enlisted in the Texas Air National Guard. McAuliffe cited a report in the *New York Post* in his accusations. For his part, Stone denied having forged the documents.[39][65]

In 2007, Stone, a top adviser at the time to Joseph Bruno (the Majority Leader of the New York State Senate), was forced to resign by Bruno after allegations that Stone had threatened Bernard Spitzer, the then-83-year-old father of Democratic gubernatorial candidate Eliot Spitzer.[10][66] On August 6, 2007, an expletive-laced message was left on the elder Spitzer's answering machine threatening to prosecute the elderly man if he did not implicate his son in wrongdoing. Bernard Spitzer hired a private detective agency that traced the call to the phone of Roger Stone's wife. Roger Stone denied leaving the message, despite the fact that his voice was recognized, claiming he was at a movie that was later shown not to have been screened that night. Stone was accused on an episode of *Hardball with Chris Matthews* on August 22, 2007, of being the voice on an expletive-laden voicemail threatening Bernard Spitzer, father of Eliot, with subpoenas.[67][68] Donald Trump is quoted as saying of the incident, "They caught Roger red-handed, lying. What he did was ridiculous and stupid."[69]

Stone consistently denied the reports. Thereafter, however, he resigned from his position as a consultant to the New York

State Senate Republican Campaign Committee at Bruno's request.[66]

In January 2008, Stone founded Citizens United Not Timid, an anti-Hillary Clinton 527 group with an intentionally obscene acronym.[70]

Stone is featured in *Boogie Man: The Lee Atwater Story*, documentary on Lee Atwater made in 2008. He also was featured in *Client 9: The Rise and Fall of Eliot Spitzer*, the 2010 documentary of the Eliot Spitzer prostitution scandal.

Former Trump aide Sam Nunberg considers Stone his mentor during this time, and "surrogate father".[71]

## 2010s: Libertarian Party involvement, Donald Trump campaign and media commentary

In February 2010, Stone became campaign manager for Kristin Davis, a madam linked with the Eliot Spitzer prostitution scandal, in her bid for the Libertarian Party nomination for governor of New York in the 2010 election. Stone said that the campaign "is not a hoax, a prank or a publicity stunt. I want to get her a half-million votes."[72] However, he later was spotted at a campaign rally for Republican gubernatorial candidate Carl Paladino,[73] of whom Stone has spoken favorably.[74] Stone admittedly had been providing support and advice to both campaigns on the grounds that the two campaigns had different goals: Davis was seeking to gain permanent ballot access for her party, and Paladino was in the race to win (and was Stone's preferred candidate). As such,

Stone did not believe he had a conflict of interest in supporting both candidates.[75] While working for the Davis campaign, Warren Redlich, the Libertarian nominee for Governor, alleged that Stone collaborated with a group entitled "People for a Safer New York" to send a flyer labeling Redlich a "sexual predator" and "sick, twisted pervert" based on a blog post Redlich had made in 2008.[76] Redlich later sued Stone in a New York court for defamation over the flyers, and sought $20,000,000 in damages. However, the jury in the case returned a verdict in favor of Stone in December 2017, finding that Redlich failed to prove Stone was involved with the flyers.[77]

Stone volunteered as an unpaid advisor to comedian Steve Berke ("a libertarian member of his so-called After Party") in his 2011 campaign for mayor of Miami Beach, Florida in 2012.[78] (Berke lost the race to incumbent mayor Matti Herrera Bower.[79])

In February 2012, Stone said that he had changed his party affiliation from the Republican Party to the Libertarian Party. Stone predicted a "Libertarian moment" in 2016 and the end of the Republican party.[80]

In June 2012, Stone said that he was running a super PAC in support of former New Mexico governor and Libertarian presidential candidate Gary Johnson, whom he had met at a Reason magazine Christmas party two years earlier.[81] Stone told the Huffington Post that Johnson had a real role to play, although "I have no allusions [sic] of him winning."[81]

Stone meeting a fan in 2014

Stone considered running as a **Libertarian** candidate for governor of Florida in 2014, but in May 2013 said in a statement that he would not run, and that he wanted to devote himself to campaigning in support of a **2014 constitutional amendment on the Florida ballot to legalize medical marijuana**.[82]

Stone served as an advisor to the **2016 presidential campaign** of Donald Trump.[83] Stone left the campaign on August 8, 2015, amid controversy, with Stone claiming he quit and Trump claiming that Stone was fired.[84] Despite this, Stone still supported Trump.[85][86] A few days later, Stone wrote an **op-ed** called "The man who just resigned from Donald Trump's campaign explains how Trump can still win" for *Business Insider*.[87]

Despite calling Stone a "stone-cold loser" in a 2008 interview[39] and accusing him of seeking too much publicity in a statement shortly after Stone left the campaign,[84] Donald Trump praised him during an appearance in December 2015 on **Alex Jones**' radio show that was orchestrated by Stone. "Roger's a good guy," Trump said. "He's been so loyal and so wonderful."[88] Stone remained an informal advisor to and media surrogate for Trump throughout the campaign.[89][90]

During the course of the 2016 campaign, Stone was banned from appearing on CNN and MSNBC after making a series of offensive Twitter posts disparaging television personalities.[91] Stone specifically referred to a CNN commentator as an "entitled diva bitch" and imagined her "killing herself", and called another CNN personality a "stupid negro" and a "fat negro".[92] Erik Wemple, media writer for *The Washington Post*, described Stone's tweets as "nasty" and "bigoted".[92] In February 2016, CNN said that it would no longer invite Stone to appear on its network, and MSNBC followed suit, confirming in April 2016 that Stone had also been banned from that network.[93] In a June 2016 appearance on *On Point*, Stone told Tom Ashbrook: "I would have to admit that calling Roland Martin a 'fat negro' was a two-martini tweet, and I regret that. As for my criticism of Ana Navarro not being qualified ... I don't understand why she's there, given her lack of qualifications."[91]

In March 2016, an article in the tabloid magazine *National Enquirer* stated that Ted Cruz, Trump's Republican primary rival, had extramarital affairs with five women. The article quoted Stone as saying, "These stories have been swirling about Cruz for some time. I believe where there is smoke there is fire."[94] Cruz denied the allegations (calling it "garbage" and a "tabloid smear") and accused the Trump campaign, and Stone specifically, of planting the story as part of an orchestrated smear campaign against him.[94] Cruz stated, "It is a story that quoted one source on the record, Roger Stone, Donald Trump's chief political adviser. And I would note that Mr. Stone is a man who has 50 years of dirty tricks behind him. He's a man for whom a term was coined for copulating with a rodent."[94][95] In April 2016, Cruz again criticized Stone, saying on Sean Hannity's radio show of Stone: "He is pulling the strings on Donald Trump. He planned the Trump campaign, and he is Trump's henchman and dirty trickster. And this pattern, Donald keeps associating himself with people who encourage violence."[96] Stone responded by comparing Cruz to Richard Nixon and accusing him of being a liar.[97]

In April 2016, Stone formed a pro-Trump activist group, Stop the Steal, and threatened "Days of Rage" if Republican party leaders tried to deny the nomination to Trump at the Republican National Convention in Cleveland.[98][99] The *Washington Post* reported that Stone "is organizing [Trump] supporters as a force of intimidation", noting that Stone "has ... threatened to publicly disclose the hotel room numbers of delegates who work against Trump".[99] Republican National Committee Chairman Reince Priebus said that Stone's threat to publicize the hotel room numbers of delegates was "just totally over the line".[100]

After Trump had been criticized at the Democratic National Convention for his comments on Muslims by Khizr Khan, a Pakistani American whose son received a posthumous Bronze Star Medal and Purple Heart in Operation

Iraqi Freedom in 2004, Stone made headlines defending Trump's criticism by accusing Khan of sympathizing with the enemy.[101]

In 2017, Stone was the subject of a Netflix documentary film, titled *Get Me Roger Stone*, which focuses on his past and on his role in the 2016 presidential campaign of Donald Trump.[27] Stone first suggested Trump run for President in early 1998 while Stone was Trump's casino business lobbyist in Washington.[26]

During the campaign, Stone frequently promoted conspiracy theories, including the false claim that Clinton aide Huma Abedin was connected to the Muslim Brotherhood.[102][17][18][19][20][21][22][23] In December 2018, as part of a defamation settlement, Stone agreed to retract a false claim he had made during the campaign: that Guo Wengui had donated to Hillary Clinton.[103]

In early 2018, ahead of an appearance at the annual Republican Dorchester Conference in Salem, Oregon, Stone sought out the Proud Boys, a right-wing group known for street brawling, to act as his "security" for the event; photos posted online showed Stone drinking with several Proud Boys.[104]

**Alleged relations with Wikileaks and Russian hackers before the 2016 United States elections**

*Further information: Russian interference in the 2016 United States elections and Special Counsel investigation (2017–present)*

Roger Stone indictment for one count of obstruction of an official proceeding, five counts of false statements, and one count of witness tampering

Stone making the **V sign** after his arrest and indictment, on January 25, 2019

During the 2016 campaign, Stone was accused by Hillary Clinton campaign chairman **John Podesta** of having prior knowledge of the publishing by **WikiLeaks** of **Podesta's private emails obtained by a hacker**.[105] Stone tweeted before the leak, "It will soon [*sic*] the Podesta's time in the barrel". Five days before the leak, Stone tweeted, "Wednesday Hillary Clinton is done. #Wikileaks."[106] Stone has denied having any advance knowledge of the Podesta email hack or any connection to Russian intelligence, stating that his earlier tweet was referring to reports of the **Podesta Group**'s own ties to Russia.[107][108] In his opening statement before the **United States House Permanent Select Committee on Intelligence** on September 26, 2017, Stone reiterated this claim: "Note that my tweet of August 21, 2016, makes no mention, whatsoever, of Mr. Podesta's email, but does accurately predict that the Podesta brothers' business activities in Russia ... would come under public scrutiny."[109]

Stone has repeatedly acknowledged that he had established a back-channel with WikiLeaks founder **Julian Assange** to obtain information on **Hillary Clinton**[110][105] and has pointed to this intermediary as the source for his advance knowledge about the release of Podesta's e-mails by WikiLeaks.[111] Stone ultimately named **Randy Credico**, who had interviewed both Assange and Stone for a radio show, as his intermediary with Assange.[112] A January 2019 indictment claimed Stone communicated with additional contacts knowledgeable about WikiLeaks plans.[113][114]

In February 2017, *The New York Times* reported that as part of its ongoing investigation into the Trump campaign, the FBI was looking into any contacts Stone may have had with Russian operatives.[115] The following month, *The Washington Times* reported that Stone had direct-messaged alleged DNC hacker **Guccifer 2.0** on Twitter. Stone acknowledged contacts with the mysterious persona and made public excerpts of the messages. Stone said the messages were just innocent praise of the hacking.[116] U.S. intelligence agencies believe Guccifer 2.0 to be a persona created by Russian intelligence to obscure its role in the DNC hack.[117] The Guccifer 2.0 persona was ultimately linked with an IP address associated with the Russian intelligence agency, GRU, in Moscow when a user with a Moscow IP address logged into one of the Guccifer social media accounts without using a VPN.[118]

In March 2017, the Senate Intelligence Committee asked Stone to preserve all documents related to any Russian contacts.[119] The Committee Vice Chair, Senator Mark Warner (D-VA), called on Stone to testify before the committee, saying he "hit the trifecta" of shady dealings with Russia. Stone denied any wrongdoing in an interview on *Real Time with Bill Maher* on March 31, 2017, and said he was willing to testify before the committee.[106]

On September 26, 2017, Stone testified before the House Intelligence Committee behind closed doors. He also provided a statement to the Committee and the press. *The Washington Post* annotated Stone's statement by noting his affiliations with *Infowars*, Breitbart, and Barack Obama citizenship conspiracy theories promulgator, Jerome Corsi. Stone also made personal attacks on Democratic committee members Adam Schiff, Eric Swalwell and Dennis Heck.[120]

On October 28, 2017, following a news report by CNN that indictments would be announced within a few days, Stone's Twitter account was suspended by Twitter for what it called "targeted abuse" of various CNN personnel in a series of derogatory, threatening and obscenity-filled tweets.[121]

On March 13, 2018, two sources close to Stone, former Trump aide Sam Nunberg and a person speaking on condition of anonymity, acknowledged to *The Washington Post* that Stone had established contact with WikiLeaks owner Julian Assange and that the two had a telephone conversation discussing emails related to the Clinton campaign which had been leaked to WikiLeaks.[28] According to Nunberg, who claimed he spoke to the paper after being asked to do so by Special Counsel Robert Mueller,[28] Stone joked to him that he had taken a trip to London to personally meet with Assange, but declined to do so, had only wanted to have telephone conversations to remain undetected and did not have advance notice of the leaked emails.[28] The other source, who spoke on anonymity, stated that the conversation occurred before it was publicly known that hackers had obtained the emails of Podesta and of the Democratic National Committee, documents that WikiLeaks released in July and October 2016.[28] Stone afterwards denied that he had contacted Assange or had known in advance about the leaked emails.[122]

In May 2018, Stone's social media consultant, Jason Sullivan, was issued grand jury subpoenas from the Mueller investigation.[123][124]

On July 3, 2018, U.S. District Court Judge Ellen Huvelle dismissed a lawsuit brought by political activist group Protect Democracy, alleging that Donald Trump's campaign and Stone conspired with Russia and WikiLeaks to publish hacked Democratic National Committee emails during the 2016 presidential election race. The judge found that the suit was brought in the wrong jurisdiction.[125][126] The next week, Stone was identified by two government officials as the anonymous person mentioned in the indictment released by Deputy Attorney General Rod Rosenstein that charged twelve Russian military intelligence officials with conspiring to interfere in the 2016 elections, as somebody the Russian hackers operating the online persona Guccifer 2.0 communicated with, and who the indictment alleged was in regular contact with senior members of the presidential campaign.[127]

On January 25, 2019, in a pre-dawn raid by 29 FBI agents acting on both an arrest warrant and a search warrant[128] at his Fort Lauderdale, Florida home, Stone was arrested on seven criminal charges of an indictment in the Mueller investigation: one count of obstruction of an official proceeding, five counts of false statements, and one count of witness tampering.[129][130][131] The same day, a federal magistrate judge released Stone on a USD$250,000 signature bond and declared that he was not a flight risk.[132][133] Stone said he would fight the charges, which he called politically motivated, and would refuse to "bear false witness" against Trump.[134] He called Robert Mueller a "rogue prosecutor".[135] In the charging document, prosecutors alleged that after the first WikiLeaks release of hacked DNC emails in July 2016, a senior Trump campaign official was directed to contact Stone about any additional releases and determine what other damaging information WikiLeaks had regarding the Clinton campaign. Stone thereafter told the

Trump campaign about potential future releases of damaging material by WikiLeaks, the indictment alleged. The indictment also alleged that Stone had discussed WikiLeaks releases with multiple senior Trump campaign officials.[136][137]

On February 18, 2019, Stone posted on Instagram a photo of the federal judge overseeing his case, Amy Berman Jackson, with what resembled rifle scope crosshairs next to her head.[138] Later that day, Stone filed an apology with the court. Jackson then imposed a full gag order on Stone, citing her belief that Stone would "pose a danger" to others without the order.[139]

### Books and other writings

Since 2010, Stone has been an occasional contributor to the conservative website *The Daily Caller*, serving as a "male fashion editor".[140][141] Stone also writes for his own fashion blog, *Stone on Style*.[141]

Stone has written five books, all published by Skyhorse Publishing of New York City.[142] His books have been described as "hatchet jobs" by the *Miami Herald*[143] and *Tampa Bay Times*.[144]

*The Man Who Killed Kennedy: The Case Against LBJ* (with Mike Colapietro contributing) (Skyhorse Publishing, 2013): Stone contends that Lyndon B. Johnson was behind a conspiracy to kill John F. Kennedy and was complicit in at least six other murders.[145] In a review for *The Washington Times*, Hugh Aynesworth wrote: "The title pretty much explains the book's theory. If a reader doesn't let facts get in the way, it could be an interesting adventure."[146] Aynesworth, who covered the assassination for the *Dallas Morning News*, said that the book "is totally full of all kinds of crap".[143]

*Nixon's Secrets: The Rise, Fall and Untold Truth about the President, Watergate, and the Pardon* (Skyhorse Publishing, 2014): Stone discusses Richard Nixon and his career. About two-thirds of the book "is a conventional biography that is by no means a whitewash of Nixon. Stone writes that the President took campaign money from the mob, had a long-running affair with a Hong Kong woman who may have been a Chinese spy, and even once unwittingly smuggled three pounds of marijuana into the United States when carrying the suitcase of jazz great Louis Armstrong." The remaining one-third of the book is an unconventional account of the Watergate scandal.[143] Stone portrays Nixon as a "confused victim" and claims that John Dean orchestrated the break-in (which he depicts as ordinary politics of the time[147]) to cover up involvement in a prostitution ring. This account is rejected by experts, such as Watergate researchers Anthony Summers and Max Holland. Holland said of Stone: "He's out of his ever-lovin' mind."[143]Dean said in 2014 that Stone's book and his defense of Nixon are "typical of the alternative universe out there" and "pure bullshit".[148]

*The Clintons' War on Women* (with Robert Morrow of Austin, Texas) (Skyhorse Publishing, 2015): This book, according to *Politico*, is a "sensational" work that contains "explosive, but highly dubious, revelations about both <u>Bill Clinton</u> and <u>Hillary Clinton</u>", with a focus on <u>Bill Clinton sexual misconduct allegations</u>, and a claim that <u>Webster Hubbell</u> is the biological father of <u>Chelsea Clinton</u>. This book was promoted by Trump, who posted a Twitter message containing the book's Amazon.com page.[149] <u>David Corn</u>, writing in *Mother Jones*, writes that the book is "apparently designed to smear the Clintons – by depicting Bill as a serial rapist, Hillary as an enabler, and both members of the power couple as a diabolical duo bent on destroying anyone who stands in their way" and said that the book was part of a wider "extreme anti-Clinton project" by Stone.[142]

*Jeb! and the Bush Crime Family* (with Saint John Hunt) (Skyhorse Publishing, 2016): The book focuses on <u>Jeb Bush</u> and the <u>Bush family</u>.[144]

*The Making of the President 2016: How Donald Trump Orchestrated a Revolution* (Skyhorse Publishing, 2017): Susan J. McWilliams, Professor of Politics at Pomona College, wrote in her review of the book that "[a]side from some minor revelations about how long Trump planned what would later appear to be spontaneous decisions—he trademarked the slogan "Make America Great Again" in 2013—there's very little Trump, doing very little orchestrating, in these pages" and that "[t]here are many provocative political musings here, but they get lost in Stone's avaricious appetite for self-promotion and grudge-holding."[150]

*Stone's Rules: How to Win at Politics, Business, and Style* (Skyhorse Publishing, 2018)

*The Myth of Russian Collusion: The Inside Story of How Donald Trump REALLY Won* (Skyhorse Publishing, 2019) (paperback edition of Stone's 2016 book "The Making of the President 2016" with an added "Introduction 2019")[151]

## Personal style and habits

Stone's personal style has been described as flamboyant.[152][153] In a 2007 *Weekly Standard* profile written by Matt Labash, Stone was described as a "lord of mischief" and the "boastful black prince of Republican sleaze."[3][154] Labash wrote that Stone "often sets his pronouncements off with the utterance 'Stone's Rules,' signifying to listeners that one of his shot-glass commandments is coming down, a pithy dictate uttered with the unbending certitude one usually associates with the Book of Deuteronomy." Examples of Stone's Rules include "Politics with me isn't theater. It's performance art, sometimes for its own sake."[3]

Stone does not wear socks – a fact that Nancy Reagan brought to her husband's attention during his 1980 presidential campaign.[155] Labash described him as "a dandy by disposition who boasts of having not bought off-the-rack since he was 17," who has "taught reporters how to achieve perfect double-dimples underneath their tie knots."[154] Washington journalist Victor Gold has noted Stone's reputation as one of the "smartest dressers" in Washington.[156] Stone's longtime tailor is Alan Flusser. Stone dislikes single-vent jackets (describing them as the sign of a "heathen"); says he owns 100 silver-colored neckties; and has 100 suits in storage.[3] Fashion stories have been written about him in *GQ* and *Penthouse*.[3] Stone has written of his dislike for jeans and ascots and has praised seersucker three-piece suits, as well as Madras jackets in the summertime and velvet blazers in the winter.[141][145]

In 1999, Stone credited his facial appearance to "decades of following a regimen of Chinese herbs, breathing therapies, tai chi and acupuncture."[37] Stone wears a diamond pinkie ring in the shape of a horseshoe and in 2007 he had Richard Nixon's face tattooed on his back.[3] He has said: "I like English tailoring, I like Italian shoes. I like French wine. I like vodka martinis with an olive, please. I like to keep physically fit."[157] Stone's office in Florida has been described as a "Hall of Nixonia" with framed pictures, posters, and letters associated with Nixon.[3]

## References-Recommended Further Reading

^ Theis, Paul Anthony; Henshaw, Edmund Lee (January 1, 1991). *Who's Who in American Politics*. Bowker. ISBN 9780835230124 – via Google Books.

^ Warner, Margaret (February 29, 1996). *"Money and the Presidency"*. NewsHour with Jim Lehrer. PBS.

^ Jump up to:<u>a</u> <u>b</u> <u>c</u> <u>d</u> <u>e</u> <u>f</u> <u>g</u> <u>h</u> <u>i</u> **Labash, Matt** (November 5, 2007). *"Roger Stone, Political Animal, 'Above all, attack, attack, attack — never defend.'"*. The Weekly Standard.

^ Edsall, Thomas B. (May 14, 2012). *"The Lobbyist in the Gray Flannel Suit"*. The Opinion Page. The New York Times Blog. Retrieved June 16, 2017.

^ *"A Political Power Broker"*. The New York Times. June 21, 1989. Retrieved June 16, 2017.

^ *"Registration with the Foreign Agents Registration Act (FARA)"*(PDF). Department of Justice. August 1982. Retrieved June 16, 2017.

^ Jump up to:<u>a</u> <u>b</u> Choate, Pat (1990). Agents of Influence. Simon and Schuster. p. 307. ISBN 978-0671743390.

^ Haberman, Maggie (March 21, 2017). *"Roger Stone, the 'Trickster' on Trump's Side, Is Under F.B.I. Scrutiny"*. The New York Times. Retrieved December 4, 2018.

^ Michael Gerson (November 29, 2018). *"Trump's inner circle has always been a cesspool"*. The Washington Post.

^ Jump up to:<u>a</u> <u>b</u> Danny Haki (August 23, 2007). *"Politics Seen in Nasty Call to Spitzer's Father"*. The New York Times.

^ **Toner, Robin** (March 19, 1990). *"The Trouble With Politics: Running vs. Governing: 'Wars' Wound Candidates and the Process"*. The New York Times.

^ Haberman, Maggie (March 21, 2017). *"Roger Stone, the 'Trickster' on Trump's Side, Is Under FBI Scurtiny"*. The New York Times. Retrieved May 17, 2017.

^ **Jump up to:**[a] [b] [c] [d] [e] [f] Toobin, Jeffrey (June 2, 2008). *"The Dirty Trickster"*. The New Yorker. Retrieved May 17, 2017.

^ Schreckinger, Ben (August 6, 2015). *"Trump's debate 'dirty trickster'"*. Politico. Retrieved May 17, 2017.

^ Murphy, Jarret (October 13, 2004). *"If You Ain't Got That Swing, Any Voters Still Up for Grabs? The Campaigns Seem to Disagree"*. CBS News.

^ *"The FBI's ridiculous riot gear and pre-dawn raid on Roger Stone was excessive and unnecessary"*. Washington Examiner. January 25, 2019.

^ **Jump up to:**[a] [b] Rogin, Josh (August 12, 2016). *"Trump allies, WikiLeaks and Russia are pushing a nonsensical conspiracy theory about the DNC hacks"*. The Washington Post. ISSN 0190-8286.

^ **Jump up to:**[a] [b] Milbank, Dana (November 1, 2016). *"Latest from the Trump conspiracy factory: Bill Clinton's black son"*. The Washington Post. ISSN 0190-8286.

^ **Jump up to:**[a] [b] Elise Viebeck (December 21, 2016). *"Schooled on Benghazi and Pizzagate, Trump team is heavy on conspiracy theorists"*. PowerPost. The Washington Post.

^ Jump up to:<sup>a b</sup> Roig-Franzia, Manuel (November 17, 2016). *"How Alex Jones, conspiracy theorist extraordinaire, got Donald Trump's ear"*. *The Washington Post*. ISSN 0190-8286.

^ Jump up to:<sup>a b</sup> Chozick, Amy (May 23, 2016). *"As Trump and Clinton Clash, 2 Operatives Duke It Out in Their Shadows"*. *The New York Times*. ISSN 0362-4331.

^ Jump up to:<sup>a b</sup> Robertson, Campbell (October 17, 2016). *"In Donald Trump, Conspiracy Fans Find a Campaign to Believe In"*. *The New York Times*. ISSN 0362-4331. Retrieved February 26, 2017.

^ Jump up to:<sup>a b</sup> Parker, Ashley; Eder, Steve (July 3, 2016). *"Inside the Six Weeks Donald Trump Was a Nonstop 'Birther'"*. *The New York Times*. ISSN 0362-4331.

^ Elfrink, Tim (May 26, 2017). *"Roger Stone Keeps Pushing Seth Rich Conspiracy Theories Despite Family Pleas"*. *Miami New Times*.

^ *"The Dirty Trickster"*. *The New Yorker*. Retrieved December 4, 2018.

^ Jump up to:<sup>a b c</sup> Duffy, Michael; Cooper, Matthew (September 20, 1999). *"Take my party, please"*. *CNN*.

^ Jump up to:<sup>a b</sup> Mohr, Ian (March 29, 2017). *"Roger Stone Netflix doc to premiere at Tribeca Film Fest"*. *New York Post*.

^ **Jump up to:**_a b c d e_ Hamburger, Tom; Dawsey, Josh; Leonnig, Carol D.; Harris, Shane (March 13, 2018). _"Roger Stone claimed contact with WikiLeaks founder Julian Assange in 2016, according to two associates"_ – via www.washingtonpost.com.

^ _"Emails about WikiLeaks publisher Julian Assange being 'mischaracterized': Roger Stone"_. ABC News. December 2, 2018. Retrieved January 26, 2019.

^ _"Roger Stone's indictment offers more proof of no contacts between him and Julian Assange – WikiLeaks"_. RT International. Retrieved January 26, 2019.

^ Kocieniewski, David. _"Trump Associate Stone Charged With Obstruction in Mueller Probe"_. www.bloomberg.com. Retrieved January 25, 2019.

^ _"Roger Stone Arrested on Obstruction Charges in Mueller Investigation"_. Time. Retrieved January 25, 2019.

^ CNN, Katelyn Polantz. _"Roger Stone enters not guilty plea"_. CNN.

^ **Jump up to:**_a b_ Edsall, Thomas B. (April 7, 1985). "Partners in Political PR Firm Typify Republican New Breed". Washington Post.

^ _"Roger J. Stone's Obituary on The Hour"_.

^ **Jump up to:**_a b c d e_ Segal, David (August 25, 2007). _"Mover, Shaker, And Cranky Caller? A GOP Consultant Who Doesn't_

*Mince Words Has Some Explaining to Do"*. *Washington Post*. p. C1.

^ **Jump up to:**<u>*a*</u> <u>*b*</u> <u>*c*</u> Hoffman, Jan (18 November 1999). *"The Ego Behind the Ego in a Trump Gamble"*. *The New York Times*.

^ *Paybarah, Azi (September 7, 2007). "Roger Stone's Nixon Thing". **The New York Observer**. Archived from the original on June 24, 2008. Retrieved July 8, 2008.*

^ **Jump up to:**<u>*a*</u> <u>*b*</u> <u>*c*</u> <u>*d*</u> <u>*e*</u> *f* *"The Dirty Trickster"*. *The New Yorker*.

^ *Kelly, Caroline (January 25, 2019). "Nixon Foundation distances itself from Roger Stone after Mueller indictment". CNN Politics. Retrieved January 27, 2019.*

^ *Mansfield, Stephanie (June 16, 1986). "The Rise and Gall of Roger Stone". The Washington Post.*

^ *Edsall, Thomas B. (April 7, 1985). "Partners in Political PR Firm Typify Republican New Breed". The Washington Post.*

^ *Foer, Franklin (March 2018). "Paul Manafort, American Hustler". theatlantic.com. Retrieved November 24, 2018.*

^ *Dowd, Maureen (December 21, 1995). "Liberties; Nix 'Nixon' – Tricky Pix". The New York Times.*

^ *Pareene (March 24, 2008). "Roger Stone Knew Guv's Terrible Secret, According to Roger Stone". Gawker.com. Archived from the original on August 28, 2009.*

^ "Rothstein Rosenfeldt Adler bios". 2006. Archived from the original on November 20, 2008. Retrieved September 13, 2009.; see **Scott W. Rothstein**

^ "Nixon Foundation objects to calling Roger Stone an 'aide' to disgraced ex-president". NBC News.

^ Foundation, Nixon (January 25, 2019). "This morning's widely-circulated characterization of Roger Stone as a Nixon campaign aide or adviser is a gross misstatement. Mr. Stone was 16 years old during the Nixon presidential campaign of 1968 and 20 years old during the reelection campaign of 1972. 1/2".

^ Foundation, Nixon (January 25, 2019). "Mr. Stone, during his time as a student at George Washington University, was a junior scheduler on the Nixon reelection committee. Mr. Stone was not a campaign aide or adviser. Nowhere in the Presidential Daily Diaries from 1972 to 1974 does the name "Roger Stone" appear. 2/2".

^ Thomas, Evan (March 3, 1986). "The Slickest Shop in Town". Time.

^ Toner, Robin (July 31, 1990). "Washington at Work; The New Spokesman for the Republicans: a Tough Player in a Rough Arena". The New York Times.

^ "Paul Manafort's Wild and Lucrative Philippine Adventure". Politico. Retrieved August 15, 2016.

^ _"Black, Manafort, Stone and Kelly, Public Affairs Company document for U.S. Department of Justice"_ (PDF). U.S. Foreign Agents Registration Act website (FARA.gov). Retrieved August 15, 2016.

^ _"Mobutu in Search of an Image Boost"_. Washington Post. Retrieved August 15, 2016.

^ The Almanac of 1988 Presidential Politics. Campaign Hotline/ American Political Network. 1989. p. 14. _ISBN_ _978-0-9621971-0-9_.

^ The Almanac of 1988 Presidential Politics. Campaign Hotline/ American Political Network. 1989. p. 5. _ISBN_ _978-0-9621971-0-9_.

^ Michael Kerner (April 20, 1992). _"The Political Interest It's Not Going To Be Pretty"_. Time Magazine.

^ Sherrill, Martha (April 4, 1992). _"The GOP's abortion-rights upstart"_. The Washington Post. Retrieved January 25, 2019.

^ Holmes, Steven A. (November 10, 1995). _"96 Aspirants Filling Breach Left By Powell"_. The New York Times.

^ Jump up to:_a_ _b_ Tomasky, Michael (June 17, 2002). _"The Right Stuff"_. _New York Metro_. Archived from _the original_ on December 9, 2004. Retrieved May 3, 2005.

^ _"In Netflix's Get Me Roger Stone, the notorious GOP operative plays both narrator and villain"_. vox.com. Retrieved November 24, 2018.

^ Ireland, Doug (February 19, 2004). "A Prayer for Rev. Al". LA Weekly.

^ Barrett, Wayne; Suh, Jennifer (February 3, 2004). "Sharpton's Cynical Campaign Choice". The Village Voice.

^ Bunch, Will (October 15, 2004). "Arlen's spectre: Roger Stone". Campaign Extra!. Philadelphia Daily News. [permanent dead link]

^ "Chairman McAuliffe, Please Shut Up".

^ Jump up to:ᵃ ᵇ Hakim, Danny; Confessore, Nicholas (August 23, 2007). "Political Consultant Resigns After Allegations of Threatening Spitzer's Father". The New York Times. p. B1.

^ Barnicle, Mike (August 23, 2007). "August 22nd transcript". Hardball with Chris Matthews. MSNBC.

^ assumed to be Roger Stone (August 2007). Bernard Spitzer's voicemail (MP3) (voicemail). The New York Times. And there's not a goddamn thing your phony, psycho, piece-of-shit son can do about it.

^ "The Dirty Trickster". The New Yorker.

^ Labash, Matt (January 28, 2008). "Making Political Trouble: Roger Stone shows how its done—again". The Weekly Standard.

^ Aaron Blake (March 7, 2018). _"The Fix Analysis; Roger Stone's conspicuously worded denials of wrongdoing in the Russia probe"_. **The Washington Post**. Retrieved March 8, 2018. This led to plenty of speculation that Nunberg sensed trouble for his mentor, Stone. (with link)

^ _"Kristin Davis, alleged Eliot Spitzer madam, to run for New York governor with GOP Roger Stone's help"_. **New York Daily News**. February 7, 2010.

^ Vielkind, Jimmy (April 6, 2010). Hi, Roger! Archived April 12, 2010, at the **Wayback Machine**. Capitol Confidential (Albany Times Union). Retrieved April 6, 2010.

^ Stone, Roger (March 24, 2010). "New York GOP Rumble". _The Stone Zone_. Retrieved April 6, 2010.

^ Hakim, Danny. "Opposing Campaigns, with One Unlikely Link: Roger Stone Plays Role in Two Opposing Campaigns". _The New York Times_. Retrieved August 12, 2010.

^ Vielkind, Jimmy (October 29, 2010). "Stone: I pushed for Redlich mailer". Albany Times-Union. Retrieved November 1, 2010.

^ _"Roger Stone wins lawsuit and is cleared of defamation charges"_. December 16, 2017.

^ Lizette Alvarez, "Comedian Is Serious, Mostly, as Candidate", _New York Times_ (October 29, 2011).

^ Douglas Hanks (September 18, 2013). *"Entertainer Steve Berke has aspirations for Miami Beach City Hall and MTV"*. *Miami Herald*.

^ "GOP trickster Roger Stone defects to Libertarian party", *Washington Post* (February 16, 2012).

^ Jump up to:*a b* Sam Stein, "Roger Stone, Nixon Operative and Famed Dirty Trickster, Building Gary Johnson Super PAC", *Huffington Post* (June 5, 2012).

^ Caputo, Marc (May 27, 2013). *"Roger Stone: Why I won't run for Florida governor"*. *Tampa Bay Times*. Archived from *the original* on September 26, 2013.

^ Schreckinger, Ben (August 6, 2015). "Donald Trump's debate dirty trickster". *Politico*.

^ Jump up to:*a b* Robert Costa (August 8, 2015). *"Trump ends relationship with longtime political adviser Roger Stone"*. *Washington Post*.

^ Nelson, Louis (August 11, 2015). *"Ex-adviser Roger Stone: I still believe in Trump"*. *Politico*. Retrieved May 21, 2017.

^ Diaz, Daniella (August 12, 2015). *"Jesse Ventura hopes Trump considers him for VP"*. *CNN*. Retrieved May 21, 2017.

^ Stone, Roger (August 11, 2015). *"The man who just resigned from Donald Trump's campaign explains how Trump can still win"*. *Business Insider*.

^ *The Alex Jones Channel (December 2, 2015). "Alex Jones & Donald Trump Bombshell Full Interview" – via YouTube.*

^ Philip Rucker & Robert Costa, "While the GOP worries about convention chaos, Trump pushes for 'showbiz' feel", *The Washington Post* (April 17, 2016).

^ Jenna Johnson, "Again: Nothing is off limits for Donald Trump, including spouses", *Washington Post* (March 23, 2016).

^ Jump up to:*a b* "Former Trump Advisor Roger Stone: 'Trump's Going To Be The Next President'", *On Point with Tom Ashbrook*, WBUR (June 6, 2016).

^ Jump up to:*a b* Erik Wemple, "CNN bans Trump supporter Roger Stone after nasty, bigoted tweets", *Washington Post* (February 23, 2016) (citing and linking to Eric Hananoki, "'Diva Bitch,' 'Stupid Negro': CNN Rewards Trump Supporter With Airtime Despite Anti-CNN Diatribes", Media Matters for America (April 5, 2016).

^ Eric Hananoki, "MSNBC Removes Trump Ally Roger Stone From Its Airing Of With All Due Respect", Media Matters for America (April 5, 2016).

^ Jump up to:*a b c* Nolan D. McCaskill, "Cruz accuses Trump of planting National Enquirer story alleging affairs", *Politico* (March 25, 2016).

^ Dan Nowicki, "Roger Stone, blasted by Ted Cruz, working for Kelli Ward?", *Arizona Republic* (March 28, 2016).

^ Tim Hains, "Ted Cruz: Roger Stone Incites Violence Like A Mobster, He Is 'Pulling The Strings On Donald Trump'", *Real Clear Politics*(April 12, 2016).

^ Tim Hains, "Roger Stone: 'Tricky' Ted Cruz 'Continues To Lie About Me,' Reminds Me of Richard Nixon", *Real Clear Politics* (April 12, 2016).

^ Jim DeFede, "Roger Stone: Inside the World of a Political Hitman", CBS Miami (April 17, 2016).

^ Jump up to:*a b* "While the GOP worries about convention chaos, Trump pushes for 'showbiz' feel", *Washington Post* (April 17, 2016).

^ Callum Borchers, "Could Donald Trump surrogate Roger Stone be charged with 'menacing' GOP convention delegates", *Washington Post* (April 8, 2016).

^ *Katherine Krueger (August 1, 2016). "Roger Stone, Trump Allies Smear Muslim War Hero as Al-Qaeda Double Agent". Talking Points Memo.*

^ *Victor, Daniel; Stack, Liam (November 14, 2016). "Stephen Bannon and Breitbart News, in Their Words". The New York Times. ISSN 0362-4331. A June 2016 article by Dan Riehl chronicled the belief of Mr. Stone, a Trump adviser, that Ms. Abedin, an aide to Hillary Clinton, was connected to a terrorist conspiracy.*

^ "Ex-Trump adviser Roger Stone admits to spreading lies online in lawsuit settlement". NBC News. Retrieved December 18, 2018.

^ Elise Herron, Right-Wing Provocateur Roger Stone Asked Proud Boys For Protection at Dorchester Conference Last Weekend, *Willamette Week* (March 7, 2018).

^ Jump up to:*a* *b* "Trump Ally Roger Stone Admits 'Back-Channel' Tie to WikiLeaks".

^ Jump up to:*a* *b* Stern, Marlow (April 1, 2017). "Bill Maher Grills Shady Trump Crony Roger Stone on Trump-Russia Ties". The Daily Beast.

^ Farley, Robert (March 28, 2017). "Misrepresenting Stone's Prescience". FactCheck.org. Retrieved October 18, 2017.

^ "Stone 'happy to cooperate' with FBI on WikiLeaks, Russian hacking probes".

^ Bertrand, Natasha (September 26, 2017). "Top Trump confidant points to dubious report to justify conversation with Russian cyber spy". Business Insider. Retrieved October 18, 2017.

^ Fang, Marina (March 5, 2017). "Former Trump Adviser Roger Stone Admits Collusion with WikiLeaks, Then Deletes It". Huffington Post – via Huff Post.

^ "Top Trump confidant points to dubious report to justify conversation with Russian cyber spy".

^ Raju, Manu; Herb, Jeremy (November 29, 2017). _"New York radio personality was Roger Stone's WikiLeaks contact"_. CNN. Retrieved November 30, 2017.

^ _"U.S. v. Roger Jason Stone Jr: The full indictment"_.

^ _"Indicting Roger Stone, Mueller Shows Link Between Trump Campaign and WikiLeaks"_.

^ Mazzetti, Michael S. Schmidt, Mark; Apuzzo, Matt (February 14, 2017). _"Trump Campaign Aides Had Repeated Contacts With Russian Intelligence"_ – via NYTimes.com.

^ Korade, Gloria Borger and Matt. _"Trump associate plays down Twitter contact with Guccifer 2.0"_. CNN.

^ _"Conversations with a hacker: What Guccifer 2.0 told me"_. BBC News. January 14, 2017.

^ Gallagher, Sean (March 23, 2018). _"DNC "lone hacker" Guccifer 2.0 pegged as Russian spy after opsec fail"_. Ars Technica.

^ Haberman, Maggie (March 18, 2017). _"Senators Ask Trump Adviser to Preserve Any Russia-Related Documents"_ – via NYTimes.com.

^ Roger Stone's defiant congressional testimony on Trump and Russia, annotated, _Washington Post_, Callum Borchers, September 26, 2017. Retrieved January 4, 2017.

^ Miller, Ryan (October 29, 2017). _"Roger Stone suspended from Twitter"_. USA Today. Retrieved October 29, 2017.

^ CNN, Maegan Vazquez,. _"Stone denies report that he had contact with Assange in 2016"_.

^ Mark Hosenball (May 16, 2018). _"Mueller issues grand jury subpoenas to Trump adviser's social media consultant"_. Reuters. Retrieved May 17, 2018.

^ Shannon Pettypiece, Billy House, and Kevin Cirilli (May 16, 2018). _"Mueller Turns His Focus to Longtime Trump Adviser Roger Stone"_. Bloomberg. Retrieved May 17, 2018.

^ _"Judge tosses suit alleging Trump campaign conspired with Russia in DNC hack"_. politico.com. Retrieved November 24, 2018.

^ _"Judge dismisses suit alleging Trump campaign conspired with Russia to hack DNC"_. washingtonexaminer.com. July 4, 2018. Retrieved November 24, 2018.

^ Mark Mazzetti and Katie Benner (July 13, 2018). _"12 Russian Agents Indicted in Mueller Investigation"_. The New York Times. Retrieved July 14, 2018.

^ _"Video shows FBI's predawn raid on Trump associate Roger Stone's house"_. www.cbsnews.com.

^ Harris, Andrew M.; Kocieniewski, David; Voreacos, David (January 25, 2019). _"Trump Associate Roger Stone Arrested in_

*Florida as Part of Special Counsel Probe"*. **Bloomberg. Retrieved January 25, 2019.**

^ *"Roger Stone Arrested on Obstruction Charges in Mueller Investigation"*. **Time. Retrieved January 25, 2019.**

^ *"Read the full indictment against Roger Stone, an informal Trump adviser"*. **USA Today. Retrieved January 25, 2019.**

^ **January 25, Raychel Lean; PM, 2019 at 02:15.** *"'I Will Defeat This': Roger Stone Released on $250,000 Bail in Broward Federal Court"*. **Daily Business Review.**

^ **Thomsen, Jacqueline (January 25, 2019).** *"Federal judge orders Stone released on $250K bond"*. **TheHill. Retrieved January 25,2019.**

^ *"Roger Stone Pledges to Fight Mueller Charges, Will Appear on 'Tucker Carlson Tonight'"*. **Fox News Insider. Retrieved 2019-01-25.**

^ *"Stone calls Mueller a 'rogue prosecutor' and America the 'new Soviet Union'"*. **The Washington Times. January 25, 2019.**

^ *"'Get Me Roger Stone': What to Make of the 'Dirty Trickster's' Indictment"*. **Lawfare. January 25, 2019.**

^ **CNN, Katelyn Polantz, Sara Murray and David Shortell.** *"Mueller indicts Roger Stone, says he was coordinating with Trump officials about WikiLeaks' stolen emails"*. **CNN.**

^ *Campbell, Andy (February 18, 2019). "Roger Stone Attacks Judge Presiding Over His Case In Bizarre Instagram Post". Huffington Post. Retrieved 21 February 2019.*

^ *"Judge imposes gag order on Trump confidant Stone". Associated Press. February 21, 2019. Retrieved 21 February 2019.*

^ Archive of Stone's columns at *The Daily Caller*.

^ Jump up to:*a b c* Sridhar Pappu, Roger Stone Rides Donald Trump's Well-Tailored Coattails, *The New York Times* (August 26, 2015).

^ Jump up to:*a b* David Corn, "Trump's No. 1 Booster Goes Real Dirty to Attack the Clintons: With his new book and video project, can Roger Stone get any lower?", *Mother Jones* (September 18, 2015)

^ Jump up to:*a b c d* Glenn Garvin, "Hatchet job: Roger Stone's edgy takes on history and politics", *Miami Herald* (October 14, 2014).

^ Jump up to:*a b* Smith, Adam C. (January 6, 2016). *"Roger Stone's book on 'Bush crime family' coming soon". Tampa Bay Times. Archived from the original on May 6, 2016.*

^ Jump up to:*a b* David Freedlander, Roger Stone's New Book 'Solves' JFK Assassination: Johnson Did It!, *Daily Beast* (May 14, 2013).

^ *Aynesworth, Hugh (February 25, 2014). "Nook Review 'The Man Who Killed Kennedy'". The Washington Times.* Washington, D.C. Retrieved November 6, 2014.

^ Nikki Schwab, "Did Richard Nixon Have a Mistress?", *U.S. News & World Report* (October 22, 2014).

^ Joe Strupp, "Former Nixon Counsel John Dean: Right-Wing Media Impeachment Calls, Watergate Comparisons 'Absolutely Silliness'", Media Matters of America (August 19, 2014).

^ Nick Hass, "Trump embraces sensational anti-Clinton book by former aide Roger Stone", *Politico* (October 14, 2015).

^ *McWilliams, Susan. "The Making of the President 2016: How Donald Trump Orchestrated a Revolution". New York Journal of Books. Retrieved March 2, 2019.*

^ *Hsu, Spencer S. (March 1, 2019). "Judge orders Roger Stone to explain imminent release of book that may violate gag order". The Washington Post. Retrieved March 2, 2019.*

^ Slackman, Michael, The Consultant: Sharpton's Bid Aided by an Unlikely Source, *The New York Times* (January 25, 2004).

^ Greg Cwik, Donald Trump and Top Adviser Roger Stone Split as Campaign Turmoil Intensifies, *New York* (August 8, 2015) ("Stone, a legendary political operator known for his colorful tactics and flamboyant persona ...").

^ Jump up to:<u>ᵃ ᵇ</u> Andrew Prokop, <u>A top Donald Trump adviser either just quit or was just fired</u> (August 8, 2015).

^ Taylor, Stuart, and Binder, David, <u>Washington Talk: Briefing; Sockless Strategist</u>, *The New York Times* (August 11, 1988) ("'I told him, "I'm not wearing socks until the Soviets are out of Afghanistan,"' Mr. Stone recalled. 'I had to say something, and that answer seemed acceptable to Governor Reagan.'").

^ Gold, Victor, "Hail to the tie", *San Antonio Express-News*, February 17, 1994/.

^ Metz, Andrew, "Golisano's Not-So-Secret Weapon / Adviser lobs political bombs", *Newsday,* September 23, 2002, accessed via Newsbank.com subscription archive April 28, 2008

Donald John Trump—Witch # 7

Donald John Trump (born June 14, 1946) is the <u>45th</u> and current <u>president of the United States</u>. Before entering politics, he was a businessman and television personality.

Trump was born and raised in the <u>New York City</u> borough of <u>Queens</u> and received an economics degree from the <u>Wharton School</u>. He was appointed president of his family's real estate business in 1971, renamed it <u>The Trump Organization</u>, and expanded it from <u>Queens</u> and <u>Brooklyn</u> into <u>Manhattan</u>. The company built or renovated skyscrapers, hotels, casinos, and golf courses. Trump later started various side ventures, including licensing his name for real estate and consumer products. He managed the company until **his 2017 inauguration**. He co-authored **several books**, including *The Art of the Deal*. He owned the **Miss Universe** and **Miss USA** beauty pageants from 1996 to 2015, and he produced and hosted *The Apprentice*, a **reality television** show, from 2003 to 2015. *Forbes* estimates his net worth to be $3.1 billion.

Trump entered the **2016 presidential race** as a **Republican** and defeated sixteen opponents in the **primaries**. His campaign received extensive **free media** coverage. Commentators described **his political positions** as **populist**, **protectionist**, and **nationalist**. Trump **has made many false or misleading statements** during his campaign and presidency. The statements have been documented by **fact-checkers**, and the media have widely described the phenomenon as unprecedented in American politics. Trump was elected president in a surprise victory over Democratic nominee **Hillary Clinton**. He became **the oldest** and **wealthiest** person ever to assume the presidency, the first without **prior military or government service**, and **the fifth** to have won the election while losing the popular vote.[b] His election and policies have sparked **numerous protests**. Many of his **comments and actions** have been perceived as racially charged or racist.

During **his presidency**, Trump **ordered a travel ban** on citizens from several Muslim-majority countries, citing security concerns; after **legal challenges**, the Supreme Court upheld the policy's third revision. He enacted a tax cut package for individuals and businesses, which also rescinded the individual health insurance mandate and allowed oil drilling in the Arctic Refuge. He partially repealed the Dodd-Frank Act that had imposed stricter constraints on banks in the aftermath of the 2008 financial crisis. He has pursued his America First agenda in foreign policy, withdrawing the U.S. from the Trans-Pacific Partnership trade negotiations, the Paris Agreement on climate change, and the Iran nuclear deal. He recognized Jerusalem as the capital of Israel, imposed import tariffs on various goods, triggering a trade war with China, and negotiated with North Korea seeking denuclearization. He successfully nominated two justices to the Supreme Court: Neil Gorsuch and Brett Kavanaugh.

After Trump dismissed FBI Director James Comey, the Justice Department appointed Robert Mueller as special counsel to proceed with investigating links between the Trump campaign and the Russian government regarding its election interference, and any matters arising from the probe. The ongoing investigation has led to guilty pleas by several Trump associates to criminal charges including lying to investigators, campaign finance violations, and tax fraud. Trump has repeatedly denied accusations of collusion and obstruction of justice, calling the investigation a politically motivated "witch hunt". In 2019, several House committees launched or expanded investigations of Trump's presidency, business, and personal life.

# Contents

## Family and personal life

## Early life and education

Donald John Trump was born on June 14, 1946, at the Jamaica Hospital in the <u>Queens</u> borough of <u>New York City</u>.[1][2] His parents were <u>Frederick Christ Trump</u>, a real estate developer, and <u>Mary Anne MacLeod</u>.[3] Trump grew up in the <u>Jamaica Estates</u> neighborhood of Queens, and attended the <u>Kew-Forest School</u> from kindergarten through seventh grade.[4][5] At age 13, he was enrolled in the <u>New York Military Academy</u>,[6][7] a private boarding school, after his parents discovered that he had made frequent trips into <u>Manhattan</u> without their permission.[8][9] In 1964, Trump enrolled at <u>Fordham University</u>.[6][10] After two years, he transferred to the <u>Wharton School</u> of the <u>University of Pennsylvania</u>.[10][11] While at Wharton, he worked at the family business, Elizabeth Trump & Son.[12] He graduated in May 1968 with a <u>B.S.</u> in economics.[10][13][14]

Senior yearbook photo of Trump in 1964 wearing the uniform of his private boarding school, New York Military Academy

While in college from 1964 to 1968, Trump obtained four student deferments from serving in the military.[15][16] In 1966, he was deemed fit for service based upon a medical examination and in July 1968, after graduating from college, was briefly classified as eligible to serve by a local draft board. In October 1968, he was given a medical deferment which he later attributed to spurs in both heels, and classified as 1-Y: "Unqualified for duty except in the case of a national emergency."[17] In the December 1969 draft lottery, Trump's birthday, June 14, received a high number which would have given him a low probability to be called to military service even without the 1-Y.[17][18][19] In 1972, he was reclassified as 4-F, disqualifying him from service.[18][20]

The New York Times reported in 1973, and again in 1976, that Trump had graduated first in his class at Wharton. However, a 1984 Times profile of Trump noted he had never made honor roll. In 1988, New York magazine reported Trump conceding, "Okay, maybe not 'first,' as myth has it, but he had 'the highest grades possible.'"[21]Michael Cohen, Trump's former attorney, testified to the House Oversight Committee in February 2019 that Trump "directed me to threaten his high school, his colleges and the College Board to never release his grades or SAT scores."[22] Days after Trump stated in 2011, "I heard [Barack Obama] was a terrible student, terrible. How does a bad student go to Columbia and then to Harvard?...Let him show his records,"[23] the headmaster of Trump's alma mater, New York Military Academy, was instructed by his manager to secure Trump's academic records so they could not be released, reportedly at the direction of "prominent, wealthy alumni of the school who were Mr. Trump's friends"[24]

## Ancestry and parents

*Further information: Trump family*

Trump's ancestors originated from the German village of Kallstadt in the Palatinate on his father's side, and from the Outer Hebrides in Scotland on his mother's side. All of his grandparents and his mother were born in Europe.[25]

Trump's paternal grandfather, Frederick Trump, first immigrated to the United States in 1885 at the age of 16 and became a citizen in 1892.[26] He amassed a fortune operating boomtown restaurants and boarding houses in the Seattle area and the Klondike region of Canada during its gold rush.[26] On a visit to Kallstadt, he met Elisabeth Christ and married her in 1902. The couple permanently settled in New York in 1905.[27] Frederick died from influenza during the 1918 pandemic.[28]

Trump's father Fred was born in 1905 in the Bronx. Fred started working with his mother in real estate when he was 15, shortly after his father's death. Their company, "E. Trump & Son",[c] founded in 1923,[33] was primarily active in the New York boroughs of Queens and Brooklyn. Fred eventually built and sold thousands of houses, barracks, and apartments.[28][34] In spite of his **German ancestry**, "Fred Trump sought to pass himself off as **Swedish** amid **anti-German sentiment** sparked by World War II."[35] Donald Trump "reaffirmed the myth" in *The Art of the Deal*.[35][36][37]

Trump's mother Mary Anne MacLeod was born in **Tong, Lewis**, Scotland. At age 18 in 1930, she immigrated to New York, where she worked as a maid.[38] Fred and Mary were married in 1936 and raised their family in Queens.[38][39]

**Wives, siblings, and descendants**

*Main article: Family of Donald Trump*

Trump grew up with three elder siblings—**Maryanne**, Fred Jr., and Elizabeth—as well as a younger brother named Robert. Maryanne is an inactive **Federal Appeals Court**judge on the **Third Circuit**.[40]

Trump has five children by three marriages, as well as nine grandchildren.[41][42] In 1977, Trump married **Czech** model **Ivana Zelníčková** at the **Marble Collegiate Church** in Manhattan, in a ceremony performed by the Reverend **Norman Vincent Peale**.[43][44] They had three children: **Donald Jr.** (born 1977), **Ivanka** (born 1981), and **Eric** (born 1984). Ivana became a naturalized United States citizen in 1988.[45] The couple divorced in 1992, following Trump's affair with actress **Marla Maples**.[46] In October 1993, Maples gave birth to Trump's daughter, who was named **Tiffany** in honor of high-end retailer **Tiffany & Company**.[47] Maples and Trump were married two months later in December 1993.[48] They divorced in 1999,[49] and Tiffany was raised by Marla in **California**.[50]

**Trump is sworn in** as president on January 20, 2017. From left to right: Trump, his wife **Melania**, and his children **Donald Jr.**, **Barron**, **Ivanka**, **Eric**, and **Tiffany**.

Having first met in 1998,[51] Trump married his third wife, **Slovenian** model **Melania Knauss**, at **Bethesda-by-the-Sea** Episcopal Church in **Palm Beach, Florida**, in 2005.[52] In 2006, she gained United States citizenship[53] and gave birth to a son, **Barron**.[54][55] Melania became **First Lady** when Trump took office as president in January 2017.[56]

Upon his inauguration, Trump delegated the management of his real estate business to his two adult sons, Eric and Don Jr.[57] His daughter Ivanka resigned from the Trump Organization and moved to Washington, D.C., with her husband **Jared Kushner**. She serves as an assistant to the president,[58] and he is a **Senior Advisor** in the White House.[59]

## Religion

Trump is a **Presbyterian**.[60][61][62] His ancestors were **Lutheran** on his paternal grandfather's side in Germany[63] and **Presbyterian** on his mother's side in

Scotland.[64] His parents married in a Manhattan Presbyterian church in 1936.[65] As a child, he attended the First Presbyterian Church in Jamaica, Queens, where he had his confirmation.[44] In the 1970s, his parents joined the Marble Collegiate Church in Manhattan,[66] part of the Reformed Church.[67] The pastor at Marble, Norman Vincent Peale, ministered to Trump's family and mentored him until Peale's death in 1993.[68][66] In August 2015 Trump told reporters, "I am Presbyterian Protestant. I go to Marble Collegiate Church," adding that he attends many different churches because he travels a lot.[69] The Marble Collegiate Church then issued a statement noting that Trump and his family have a "longstanding history" with the church, but that he "is not an active member".[67]

Trump said he was "not sure" whether he ever asked God for forgiveness, stating "If I do something wrong, I just try and make it right. I don't bring God into that picture." He said he tries to take Holy Communion as often as possible because it makes him "feel cleansed".[60] While campaigning, Trump referred to *The Art of the Deal* as his second favorite book after the Bible, saying, "Nothing beats the Bible."[70] *The New York Times* reported that evangelical Christians nationwide thought "that his heart was in the right place, that his intentions for the country were pure."[71]

Trump has associations with a number of Christian spiritual leaders, including Florida pastor Paula White, who has been called his "closest spiritual confidant."[72] In 2015, he released a list of religious advisers, including James Dobson, Jerry

Falwell Jr., Ralph Reed, Michele Bachmann, Robert Jeffress, and others.[73][74]

## Health

*Main article: Health of Donald Trump*

Trump does not drink alcohol, a reaction to his older brother Fred Trump Jr.'s alcoholism and early death.[75][76] He has stated that he has never smoked cigarettes or consumed drugs, including marijuana.[77] In December 2015, Trump's personal physician, Harold Bornstein, released a superlative-laden letter of health which stated that Trump's "physical strength and stamina are extraordinary."[78][79] Bornstein later said that Trump himself had dictated the contents.[80] A follow-up medical report showed Trump's blood pressure, liver and thyroid functions to be in normal ranges, and that he takes a statin.[81][82] In January 2018, Trump was examined by White House physician Ronny Jackson, who stated that he was in excellent health and that his cardiac assessment revealed no medical issues,[83] although his weight and cholesterol level were higher than recommended.[84] Several outside cardiologists commented that Trump's weight, lifestyle, and LDL cholesterol level ought to have raised serious concerns about his cardiac health.[85] In February 2019, Trump underwent another physical examination; White House physician Sean Conley said Trump was in "very good health overall", although Trump had gained weight and was now clinically obese.[86]

## Wealth

*Main article: Wealth of Donald Trump*

Trump was listed on the initial *Forbes List* of wealthy individuals in 1982 as having a share of his family's estimated $200 million net worth. His financial losses in the 1980s caused him to be dropped from the list between 1990 and 1995, and reportedly obliged him to borrow from his siblings' trusts in 1993.[87] In its 2019 billionaires ranking, *Forbes* estimated Trump's net worth at $3.1 billion[a] (715th in the world, 259th in the U.S.)[90] making him one of the richest politicians in American history and the first billionaire American president.[90] During the three years since Trump announced his presidential run in 2015, Forbes estimated his net worth declined 31% and his ranking fell 138 spots.[91] When he filed mandatory financial disclosure forms with the Federal Elections Commission (FEC) in July 2015, Trump claimed a net worth of about $10 billion;[92] however FEC figures cannot corroborate this estimate because they only show each of his largest buildings as being worth over $50 million, yielding total assets worth more than $1.4 billion and debt over $265 million.[93] Trump reported hundreds of millions of dollars of yearly income from 2014 to 2018.[92][94][95] Trump stated in a 2007 deposition, "My net worth fluctuates, and it goes up and down with markets and with attitudes and with feelings, even my own feelings."[96]

Journalist Jonathan Greenberg reported in April 2018 that Trump, using a pseudonym "John Barron," called him in 1984 to falsely assert he then owned "in excess of 90 percent" of the Trump family's business in an effort to secure a higher ranking on the Forbes 400 list of wealthy Americans.[97]

Trump has often said that he began his career with "a small loan of one million dollars" from his father, and that he had to pay it back with interest.[98] In October 2018, *The New York Times* reported that Trump "was a millionaire by age 8", borrowed at least $60 million from his father, and largely failed to reimburse him, and had received $413 million (adjusted for inflation) from his father's business empire over his lifetime.[99][100]According to the report, Trump and his family committed tax fraud, which a lawyer for Trump denied; the tax department of New York says it is "vigorously pursuing all appropriate avenues of investigation" into it.[101][102] Analyses by *The Economist* and *The Washington Post* have concluded that Trump's investments have under-performed the stock market.[103][104] Forbes estimated in October 2018 that the value of Trump's personal brand licensing business had declined by 88% since 2015, to $3 million.[105]

**Business career**

*Main article: Business career of Donald Trump*

*Further information: Business projects of Donald Trump in Russia*

## Real estate

The distinctive façade of **Trump Tower**, the headquarters of The Trump Organization, in **Midtown Manhattan**

In 1968, Trump began his career at his father Fred's real estate development company, E. Trump & Son, which, among other interests, owned middle-class rental housing in New York City's outer boroughs.[106][107] Trump worked for his father to revitalize the Swifton Village apartment complex in Cincinnati, Ohio, which the elder Trump had bought in 1964.[108][109]The management of the property was sued for racial discrimination in 1969; the suit "was quietly settled at Fred Trump's direction."[109] The Trumps sold the property in 1972, with vacancy on the rise.[109]

When his father became chairman of the board in 1971, Trump was promoted to president of the company and renamed it The Trump Organization.[110][111] In 1973, he and his father **drew wider attention** when the **Justice Department** contended in a lawsuit that their company systematically discriminated against African Americans who wished to rent apartments. The Department alleged that the Trump Organization had screened out people based on race and not low income as the Trumps had stated. Under an agreement reached in 1975, the Trumps made no admission of wrongdoing and made the Urban League an intermediary for qualified minority applicants.[112][113] Trump's attorney at the time was Roy Cohn, who valued both positive and negative publicity, and responded to attacks with forceful counterattacks; Trump later emulated Cohn's style.[114]

## Manhattan developments

In 1978, Trump launched his Manhattan real estate business by purchasing a 50 percent stake in the derelict Commodore Hotel, located next to Grand Central Terminal. The purchase was funded largely by a $70 million construction loan that was guaranteed jointly by Fred Trump and the Hyatt hotel chain.[115][116] When the remodeling was finished, the hotel reopened in 1980 as the Grand Hyatt Hotel.[117]

The same year, Trump obtained the rights to develop Trump Tower, a 58-story, 664-foot-high (202 m) skyscraper in Midtown Manhattan.[118][119] To make way for the new building, a crew of undocumented Polish workers demolished the historic Bonwit Teller store, including art deco features that had initially been marked for preservation.[120] The building was completed in 1983 and houses both the primary penthouse condominium residence of Trump and the headquarters of The Trump Organization.[121][122] Architectural critic Paul Goldberger said in 1983 that he was surprised to find the tower's atrium was "the most pleasant interior public space to be completed in New York in some years".[123][124]

<u>Central Park</u>'s <u>Wollman Rink</u> after the Trump renovation

Repairs on the <u>Wollman Rink</u> in <u>Central Park</u>, built in 1955, were started in 1980 by a <u>general contractor</u> unconnected to Trump, with an expected 2 ½-year construction schedule, but were not completed by 1986. Trump took over the project, completed it in three months for $1.95 million, which was $775,000 less than the initial budget, and then operated the rink for one year with some profits going to charity in exchange for the rink's <u>concession</u> rights.[125][126][127] According to journalist <u>Joyce Purnick</u>, Trump's "Wollman success was also the stuff of a carefully crafted, self-promotional legend."[128]

In 1988, Trump acquired the <u>Plaza Hotel</u> in Manhattan for $407 million and appointed his wife Ivana to manage its operation.[129] Trump invested $50 million to restore the building, which he called "the Mona Lisa".[130] According to hotel expert Thomas McConnell, the Trumps boosted it from a three-star to a four-star ranking. They sold it in 1995, by which time Ivana was no longer involved in the hotel's day-to-day operations.[131]

In 1994, Trump's company refurbished the Gulf and Western Building on **Columbus Circle** with design and structural enhancements turning it into a 44-story luxury residential and hotel property[132][133] known as **Trump International Hotel and Tower**.[134]

In 1996, Trump acquired the Bank of Manhattan Trust Building, which was a vacant seventy-one story skyscraper on Wall Street. After an extensive renovation, the high-rise was renamed the Trump Building at **40 Wall Street**.[135] In 1997, he began construction on **Riverside South**, which he dubbed **Trump Place**, a multi-building development along the **Hudson River**. He and the other investors in the project ultimately sold their interest for $1.8 billion in 2005 in what was then the biggest residential sale in the history of New York City.[136] From 1994 to 2002, Trump owned a 50 percent share of the **Empire State Building**. He intended to rename it "Trump Empire State Building Tower Apartments" if he had been able to boost his share.[137][138] In 2001, Trump completed **Trump World Tower**.[139] In 2002, Trump acquired the former Hotel Delmonico, which was renovated and reopened in 2004 as the **Trump Park Avenue**; the building consisted of 35 stories of luxury condominiums.[140]

**Palm Beach estate**

*Main article: Mar-a-Lago*

Mar-a-Lago in 2009

In 1985, Trump acquired the Mar-a-Lago estate in Palm Beach, Florida, for $10 million, $7 million for the real estate and $3 million for the furnishings.[141][142] His initial offer of $28 million had been rejected, and he was able to obtain the property for the lower price after a real-estate market "slump".[143] The home was built in the 1920s by heiress and socialite Marjorie Merriweather Post.[144] After her death, her heirs unsuccessfully tried to donate the property to the government before putting it up for sale.[144][145] In addition to using a wing of the estate as a home, Trump turned Mar-a-Lago into a private club. In order to join, prospective members had to pay an initiation fee[146] and annual dues.[147]The initiation fee was $100,000 until 2016; it was doubled to $200,000 in January 2017.[148][149]

**Atlantic City casinos**

After New Jersey legalized casino gambling in 1977, Trump traveled to Atlantic City to explore new business opportunities. Seven years later, he opened Harrah's at Trump Plaza hotel and casino; the project was built by Trump with financing from the Holiday Corporation, who also managed its operation.[150] It was renamed "Trump Plaza" soon after it opened.[151] The casino's poor financial results exacerbated disagreements between Trump and Holiday Corporation, which led to Trump paying $70 million in May 1986 to buy out their interest in the property.[152][153] Trump also acquired a partially completed building in Atlantic City from the Hilton Corporation for $320 million; when completed in 1985, that hotel and casino became Trump Castle, and Trump's wife Ivana managed the property until 1988.[154][155]

Entrance of the Trump Taj Mahal in Atlantic City

Trump acquired his third casino in Atlantic City, the Taj Mahal, in 1988 while it was under construction, through a complex transaction with Merv Griffin and Resorts International.[156] It was completed at a cost of $1.1 billion and opened in April 1990.[157][158] The project was financed with $675 million in junk bonds[159] and was a major gamble by Trump.[160] The project underwent debt restructuring the following year,[161] leaving Trump with 50 percent ownership.[162] Facing "enormous debt", he gave up control of his money-losing airline, Trump Shuttle, and sold his 282-foot (86 m) megayacht, the *Trump Princess*, which had been indefinitely docked in Atlantic City while leased to his casinos for use by wealthy gamblers.[163][164][165]

In 1995, Trump founded **Trump Hotels & Casino Resorts** (THCR), which assumed ownership of Trump Plaza, Trump Castle, and the **Trump Casino** in **Gary, Indiana**.[166] THCR purchased Taj Mahal in 1996 and underwent bankruptcy restructuring in 2004 and 2009, leaving Trump with 10 percent ownership in the Trump Taj Mahal and other Trump casino properties.[167] Trump remained chairman of THCR until 2009.[168]

## Golf courses

*Main article: Donald Trump and golf*

**Turnberry Hotel** and golf course in **Ayrshire**, Scotland

As of December 2016, the Trump Organization owns or operates 18 golf course and golf resorts in the United States and abroad.[169] According to Trump's FEC personal financial disclosure, his 2015 golf and resort revenue amounted to $382 million,[170][94] while his three European golf courses did not show a profit.[171]

Trump began acquiring and constructing golf courses in 1999; his first property was the **Trump International Golf Club, West Palm Beach** in **Florida**.[172] By 2007, he owned four courses around the U.S.[172] Following the **financial crisis of 2007–2008**, he began purchasing existing golf courses and re-designing them.[173] His use of these courses during his presidency was controversial. Despite frequently criticizing his predecessor **Barack Obama** for his numerous golf outings, Trump golfed 11 times during his first eight weeks in office.[174] According to **CNN**, Trump visited Trump-owned golf courses 91 times in 2017, although the White House does not disclose whether or not the president actually played on each of those visits.[175]

## Branding and licensing

*See also: **List of things named after Donald Trump***

Trump International Hotel and Tower in Chicago

The Trump Organization expanded its business into branding and management by licensing the Trump name for a large number of building projects that are owned and operated by other people and companies. In the late 2000s and early 2010s, The Trump Organization expanded its footprint beyond New York with the branding and management of various developers' hotel towers around the world. These included projects in Chicago, Las Vegas, Washington D.C., Panama City, Toronto, and Vancouver. There are also Trump-branded buildings in Dubai, Honolulu, Istanbul, Manila, Mumbai, and Indonesia.[176]

The Trump name has also been licensed for various consumer products and services, including foodstuffs, apparel, adult learning courses, and home furnishings. In 2011, *Forbes*'financial experts estimated the value of the Trump brand at $200 million. Trump disputed this valuation, saying his brand was worth about $3 billion.[177] According to an analysis by *The Washington Post*, there are more than 50 licensing or management deals involving Trump's name, which have generated at least $59 million in yearly revenue for his companies.[178]*The Post* reported in April 2018 that — of the 19 consumer goods companies Trump said in 2015 were licensing his name — only two continue to do so, in Panama and Turkey.[179]

**Lawsuits and bankruptcies**

*Main article: Legal affairs of Donald Trump*

As of April 2018, Trump and his businesses had been involved in more than 4,000 state and federal legal actions, according to a running tally by *USA Today*.[180] As of 2016, he or one of his companies had been the plaintiff in 1,900 cases and the defendant in 1,450. With Trump or his company as plaintiff, more than half the cases have been against gamblers at his casinos who had failed to pay off their debts. With Trump or his company as a defendant, the most common type of case involved personal injury cases at his hotels. In cases where there was a clear resolution, Trump's side won 451 times and lost 38.[181][182]

Trump has never filed for personal bankruptcy, although in 1990 he came within one missed bank loan payment of doing so, agreeing to a deal that temporarily ceded management control of his company to his banks and put him on a spending allowance.[183] Trump claimed to have initiated this deal with his banks as he saw the downturn in the real estate market, but bankers involved in the matter stated they initiated the negotiations before Trump had realized there was a problem.[184] His hotel and casino businesses have been declared bankrupt six times between 1991 and 2009 in order to re-negotiate debt with banks and owners of stock and bonds.[185][186] Because the businesses used Chapter 11 bankruptcy, they were allowed to operate while negotiations proceeded. Trump was quoted by *Newsweek* in 2011 saying, "I do play with the bankruptcy laws – they're very good for me" as a tool for trimming debt.[187][188] The six bankruptcies were the result of over-leveraged hotel and casino businesses in Atlantic City and New York: Trump Taj Mahal (1991), Trump Plaza Hotel and Casino (1992), Plaza Hotel (1992), Trump Castle Hotel and Casino (1992), Trump Hotels and Casino Resorts (2004), and Trump Entertainment Resorts (2009).[189][190]

During the 1980s, more than 70 banks had lent Trump $4 billion,[184] but in the aftermath of his corporate bankruptcies of the early 1990s, most major banks declined to lend to him, with a notable exception of Deutsche Bank.[191]

## Side ventures

After Trump took over the family real estate firm in 1971 and renamed it The Trump Organization, he expanded its real estate operations and ventured into other business activities. The company eventually became the umbrella organization for several hundred individual business ventures and partnerships.[192]

## Sports

In September 1983, Trump purchased the New Jersey Generals—an American football team that played in the United States Football League (USFL). After the 1985 season, the league folded largely due to Trump's strategy of moving games to a fall schedule where they competed with the NFL for audience, and trying to force a merger with the NFL by bringing an antitrust lawsuit against the organization.[193][194]

Trump operated golf courses in several countries.[193] He hosted several boxing matches at the Trump Plaza in Atlantic City, including Mike Tyson's 1988 heavyweight championship fight against Michael Spinks.[195]He also acted as a financial advisor to Mike Tyson.[196] In 1989 and 1990, Trump lent his name to the Tour de Trump cycling stage race, which was an attempt to create an American equivalent of European races such as the Tour de France or the Giro d'Italia.[197]

**Trump Shuttle**

*Main article: Trump Shuttle*

In 1988, Trump bought the Air-Shuttle, including 21 planes and landing rights at three airports in New York City, Boston, and the Washington, D.C., area, from Eastern Airlines which had filed for Chapter 11 bankruptcy. He financed the purchase price of $380 million through 22 banks. The airline operated as the Trump Shuttle from 1989 to 1992, offering charter services in addition to scheduled shuttle flights. It lost money from the start, and its control reverted to the banks in mid-1990. It was sold to USAir Group in 1992.[198][199][200][201]

During the first Gulf War the U.S. government contracted with Trump Shuttle to carry Armed Forces personnel between locations in the U.S., which may have led to the erroneous claim by a former Marine at a Trump campaign rally that Trump had dispatched his personal jet to transport a group of Marines from North Carolina to Florida. The falsehood was publicized on *Hannity* and confirmed by the Trump campaign.[200][202]

## Miss Universe

Trump's star on the Hollywood Walk of Fame, installed in 2007

From 1996 to 2015, Trump owned part or all of the Miss Universe pageants.[203][204] The pageants include Miss USA and Miss Teen USA. His management of this business involved his family members—daughter Ivanka once hosted Miss Teen USA.[205] He became dissatisfied with how CBS scheduled the pageants, and took both Miss Universe and Miss USA to NBC in 2002.[206][207] In 2007, Trump received a star on the Hollywood Walk of Fame for his work as producer of Miss Universe.[208]

Following Trump's controversial statements about illegal Mexican immigrants during his 2015 presidential campaign kickoff speech, NBC ended its business relationship with him, stating that it would no longer air the Miss Universe or Miss USA pageants on its networks.[209] In September 2015, Trump bought NBC's share of the Miss Universe Organization and then sold the entire company to the WME/IMG talent agency.[210]

## Trump University

*Main article: Trump University*

Trump University was a for-profit education company that was founded by Trump and his associates, Michael Sexton and Jonathan Spitalny. The company ran a real estate training program and charged between $1,500 and $35,000 per course.[211][212][213] In 2005, New York State authorities notified the operation that its use of the word "university" was misleading and violated state law. After a second such notification in 2010, the name of the company was changed to the "Trump Entrepreneurial Institute".[214] Trump was also found personally liable for failing to obtain a business license for the operation.[215]

Ronald Schnackenberg, a sales manager for Trump University, said in a testimony that he was reprimanded for not trying harder to sell a $35,000 real estate class to a couple who could not afford it.[216]Schnackenberg said that he believed "Trump University was a fraudulent scheme" which "preyed upon the elderly and uneducated to separate them from their money."[216]

In 2013, New York State filed a $40 million civil suit against Trump University; the suit alleged that the company made false statements and defrauded consumers.[214][217] In addition, two class-action civil lawsuits were filed in federal court relating to Trump University; they named Trump personally as well as his companies.[218] During the **presidential campaign**, Trump criticized presiding Judge **Gonzalo P. Curiel**, alleging bias in his rulings because of his Mexican heritage.[219][220] Shortly after Trump won the presidency, the parties agreed to a settlement of all three pending cases, whereby Trump paid a total of $25 million and denied any wrongdoing.[221][222]

## Foundation

*Main article: Donald J. Trump Foundation*

The Donald J. Trump Foundation is a U.S.-based private foundation[223] that was established in 1988 for the initial purpose of giving away proceeds from the book *Trump: The Art of the Deal*.[224][225] The foundation's funds have mostly come from donors other than Trump,[226] who has not given personally to the charity since 2008.[226]

The foundation's tax returns show that it has given to health care and sports-related charities, as well as conservative groups.[227] In 2009, for example, the foundation gave $926,750 to about 40 groups, with the biggest donations going to the **Arnold Palmer Medical Center Foundation** ($100,000), the **New York–Presbyterian Hospital** ($125,000), the **Police Athletic League** ($156,000), and the **Clinton Foundation** ($100,000).[228][229] From 2004 to 2014, the top donors to the foundation were Vince and Linda McMahon of WWE, who donated $5 million to the foundation after Trump appeared at WrestleMania in 2007.[226]

In 2016, *The Washington Post* reported that the charity had committed several potential legal and ethical violations, including alleged self-dealing and possible tax evasion.[230] Also in 2016, the New York State Attorney General's office notified the Trump Foundation that the foundation appeared to be in violation of New York laws regarding charities, ordering it to immediately cease its fundraising activities in New York.[231][232][233] A Trump spokesman called the Attorney General's investigation a "partisan hit job".[231] In response to mounting complaints, Trump's team announced in late December 2016 that the Trump Foundation would be dissolved to remove "even the appearance of any conflict with [his] role as President."[234] According to an IRS filing in November 2017, the foundation intended to shut down and distribute its assets (about $970,000) to other charities. However, the New York Attorney General's office had to complete their ongoing investigation before the foundation could legally shut down,[235] and in June 2018 they filed a civil suit against the foundation for $2.8 million in restitution and additional penalties.[236] The suit names Trump himself as well as his adult children Donald Jr., Eric, and Ivanka.[237]

## Conflicts of interest

Before being inaugurated as president, Trump moved his businesses into a revocable trust run by his eldest sons and a business associate.[238][239] According to ethics experts, as long as Trump continues to profit from his businesses, the measures taken by Trump do not help to avoid conflicts of interest.[240] Because Trump would have knowledge of how his administration's policies would affect his businesses, ethics experts recommend that Trump sell off his businesses.[239] While Trump has said that his organization would eschew "new foreign deals", the Trump Organization has since pursued expansions of its operations in Dubai, Scotland, and the Dominican Republic.[240] Multiple lawsuits have been filed alleging that Trump is violating the emoluments clause of the United States Constitution, which forbids presidents from taking money from foreign governments, due to his business interests; they argue that these interests allow foreign governments to influence him.[240][241] Previous presidents in the modern era have either divested their holdings or put them in blind trusts,[238] and he is the first president to be sued over the emoluments clause.[241] A suit, *D.C. and Maryland v. Trump*, brought in June 2017 by the attorneys general of Maryland and the District of Columbia, cleared three judicial hurdles to proceed to the discovery phase during 2018,[242][243][244] with prosecutors issuing 38 subpoenas to Trump's businesses and cabinet departments in December before the Fourth Circuit Court of Appeals issued a stay days later at the behest of the Justice Department, pending hearings in March 2019.[245][246][247]

## Media career

### Books

*Main article: Bibliography of Donald Trump*

Trump has published numerous books. His first published book in 1987 was *Trump: The Art of the Deal*, in which Trump is credited as co-author with Tony Schwartz, who has stated that he did all the writing for the book.[248][249][250] It reached the top of the *New York Times* Best Seller list, stayed there for 13 weeks, and altogether held a position on the list for 48 weeks.[249] According to *The New Yorker*, "The book expanded Trump's renown far beyond New York City, promoting an image of himself as a successful dealmaker and tycoon."[249] Trump's published writings shifted post-2000 from stylized memoirs to financial tips and political opinion.[251]

## Film and television

### Wrestling

In 1988 and 1989, Trump hosted WrestleMania IV and V at the Trump Plaza in Atlantic City.[252][253] Trump headlined WrestleMania 23 in 2007 and a Monday Night Raw in 2009;[253] the catchphrase "You're fired" he used on *The Apprentice* was also used by WWE owner Vince McMahon.[253] In 2013, he was inducted into the WWE Hall of Fame during *WrestleMania* 29.[254]

### The Apprentice

In 2003, Trump became the executive producer and host of the NBC reality show *The Apprentice*, in which contestants competed for a one-year management job with the Trump Organization; applicants were successively eliminated from the game with the catchphrase "You're fired".[255][248][256] He went on to be co-host of *The Celebrity Apprentice*, in which celebrities compete to win money for their charities.[255][256][257]

In February 2015, Trump stated that he was "not ready" to sign on for another season of the show because of the possibility of a presidential run.[258] Despite this, NBC announced they were going ahead with production of a 15th season.[259] In June, after widespread negative reaction stemming from Trump's campaign announcement speech, NBC released a statement saying, "Due to the recent derogatory statements by Donald Trump regarding immigrants, NBCUniversal is ending its business relationship with Mr. Trump."[260]

**Acting**

*Main article: Donald Trump filmography*

Trump has made cameo appearances in 12 films and 14 television series,[261] including as the father of one of the characters in *The Little Rascals*.[262][263] He performed a song with Megan Mullally at the 57th Primetime Emmy Awards in 2005.[264][265]

Trump receives a pension as a member of the Screen Actors Guild.[266] His financial disclosure forms mentioned an annual pension of $110,000 in 2016 and $85,000 in 2017.[266][267][268]

## Radio and television commentary

Starting in the 1990s, Trump was a guest about 24 times on the nationally syndicated *Howard Stern Show* on talk radio.[269] Trump also had his own short-form talk radio program called *Trumped!* (one to two minutes on weekdays) from 2004 to 2008.[270][271][272] In 2011, Trump was given a weekly unpaid guest commentator spot on *Fox & Friends* that continued until he started his presidential candidacy in 2015.[273][274][275][276]

## Public profile

## Approval ratings

Presidential approval polls taken during the first ten months of Trump's term have shown him to be the least popular U.S. president in the history of modern opinion polls.[277][278][279] A Pew Research Center global poll conducted in July 2017, found "a median of just 22 percent has confidence in Trump to do the right thing when it comes to international affairs". This compares to a median of 64 percent rate of confidence for his predecessor Barack Obama. Trump received a higher rating in only two countries: Russia and Israel.[280] An August 2017 POLITICO/Morning consult poll found on some measures "that majorities of voters have low opinions of his character and competence".[281] By December 2018, Trump's approval ratings, averaged over many polls, stood at roughly 42%, two points below Obama's 44% at the same time in his presidency, and one point above Ronald

Reagan.[282] Trump's two-year average Gallup approval rating was the lowest of any president since World War II.[283]

Trump is the only elected president who did not place first on Gallup's poll of Americans' most admired men in his first year in office, coming in second behind Obama.[284][285] The Gallup poll near the end of Trump's second year in office named him the second most admired man in America – behind Obama – for the fourth consecutive year.[286][285]

## False statements

*Main article: Veracity of statements by Donald Trump*

As president, Trump has frequently made false statements in public speeches and remarks.[287][288][289] The statements have been documented by fact-checkers, and the media have widely described the phenomenon as unprecedented in American politics.[290][291][292][293][294] His falsehoods have also become a distinctive part of his political identity.[292]

Trump uttered "at least one false or misleading claim per day on 91 of his first 99 days" in office according to *The New York Times*,[287] and 1,318 total in his first 263 days in office according to the "Fact Checker" political analysis column of *The Washington Post*.[295] By Trump's 773rd day in office, the *Post*'s tally stood at 9,014 false or misleading claims.[296] For the seven weeks leading up to the midterm elections, it rose to an average of 30 per day[297] from 4.9 during his first 100 days in office.[298] The *Post* found that Trump averaged 15 false statements per day during 2018.[299]

## Racial views

*Main article: <u>Racial views of Donald Trump</u>*

Trump has a history of making racially controversial remarks and taking actions that are perceived as racially motivated.[300] In 1975, he settled a 1973 Department of Justice lawsuit that alleged housing discrimination against black renters.[107][301][302] He was accused of racism for insisting that a group of black and Latino teenagers were guilty of raping a white woman in the 1989 <u>Central Park jogger attack</u>, even after they were exonerated by DNA evidence in 2002. He continued to maintain this position as late as 2016.[303]

Starting in 2011, Trump was a major proponent of <u>"birther" conspiracy theories</u> alleging that Barack Obama was born in Kenya, and questioned his eligibility to serve as president.[304][305] Trump later took credit for pushing the White House to release the "long-form" birth certificate from <u>Hawaii</u>,[306][307][308] and he stated during his presidential campaign that his stance had made him "very popular".[309] In September 2016, he publicly acknowledged that Obama was born in the United States, and falsely asserted that the rumors had been started by <u>Hillary Clinton</u> and her <u>2008 presidential campaign</u>.[310]

Trump makes a statement (begins at 7:20 into the video) on the Unite the Right rally in Charlottesville published by the White House.

According to an analysis in *Political Science Quarterly*, Trump made "explicitly racist appeals to whites" during his 2016 presidential campaign.[311] Trump launched his campaign with a speech in which he stated: "When Mexico sends its people, they're not sending their best. ... They're bringing drugs, they're bringing crime, they're rapists, and some, I assume, are good people."[312][313][314][315] Later, his attacks on a Mexican-American judge were criticized as racist.[316] His comments following a 2017 far-right rally in Charlottesville, Virginia, were seen as implying a moral equivalence between the white supremacist marchers and those who protested them.[317] In a January 2018 Oval Officemeeting to discuss immigration legislation with Congressional leaders, Trump reportedly referred to El Salvador, Haiti, Honduras, and African countries as "shitholes".[318] His remarks were condemned as racist worldwide, as well as by many members of Congress.[319][320][321] Trump has denied accusations of racism multiple times, saying he is the "least racist person".[322][323]

Trump's racially insensitive statements and actions[301] have been condemned by many observers in the U.S. and around the world,[324][325] but accepted by his supporters either as a rejection of political correctness[326][327] or because they harbor similar racial sentiments.[328][329] Several studies and surveys have stated that racist attitudes and racial resentment have fueled Trump's political ascendance, and have become more significant than economic factors in determining party allegiance of voters.[329][330] In a June 2018 Quinnipiac University poll, 49 percent of respondents believed that Trump is racist while 47 percent believed he is not. Additionally, 55 percent said he "has emboldened people who hold racist beliefs to express those beliefs publicly."[331][332]

**Relationship with the press**

President Trump talking to the press, March 2017

*Further information: Presidency of Donald Trump § Relationship with the media*

Throughout his career, Trump has sought media attention. His interactions with the press turned into what some sources called a "love-hate" relationship.[333][334][335] Trump began promoting himself in the press in the 1970s.[336]

Throughout his 2016 presidential campaign and his presidency, Trump has repeatedly accused the press of intentionally misinterpreting his words and of being biased, calling them "fake news media" and "the enemy of the people".[337][338] In the campaign, Trump benefited from a record amount of free media coverage, elevating his standing in the Republican primaries.[339] After winning the election, Trump told journalist **Lesley Stahl** that he intentionally demeaned and discredited the media "so when you write negative stories about me no one will believe you".[340] Into his presidency, much of the press coverage of Trump and his administration was negative.[341][342] Trump has privately and publicly mused about taking away critical reporters' White House press credentials (despite, during his campaign, promising not to do so once he became president).[343]

A study found that between October 7 and November 14, 2016, while one in four Americans visited a **fake news website**, "Trump supporters visited the most fake news websites, which were overwhelmingly pro-Trump" and "almost 6 in 10 visits to fake news websites came from the 10 percent of people with the most conservative online information diets".[344][345] **Brendan Nyhan**, one of the authors of the study, stated in an interview on NBC News: "People got vastly more misinformation from Donald Trump than they did from fake news websites".[346]

**Popular culture**

*Main articles: Donald Trump in popular culture and Donald Trump in music*

Trump has been the subject of comedians, flash cartoon artists, and online caricature artists. He has been parodied regularly on *Saturday Night Live* by **Phil Hartman**, **Darrell**

Hammond, and **Alec Baldwin**, and in *South Park* as **Mr. Garrison**. *The Simpsons* episode "**Bart to the Future**", written during his **2000 campaign for the Reform party**, anticipated a future Trump presidency. A dedicated parody series called *The President Show* debuted in April 2017 on **Comedy Central**, while another one called *Our Cartoon President* debuted on **Showtime** in February 2018.[347]

Trump's wealth and lifestyle had been a fixture of **hip hop** lyrics since the 1980s, as he was named in hundreds of songs, most often in a positive tone.[348][349] Mentions of Trump turned negative and pejorative after he ran for office in 2015.[348][350][351]

**Social media**

*Main article: **Donald Trump on social media***

Trump's presence on social media has attracted attention worldwide since he joined **Twitter** in March 2009. He communicated heavily on Twitter during the 2016 election campaign, and has continued to use this channel during his presidency. The attention on Trump's Twitter activity has significantly increased since he was sworn in as president. He uses Twitter as a direct means of communication with the public, sidelining the press.[352] Many of the assertions he tweeted have been proven false.[353][354][355]

**Recognition**

*Further information: List of honors and awards received by Donald Trump*

In 2015, **Robert Gordon University** revoked the honorary Doctor of Business Administration (DBA) it had granted Trump in 2010, stating that "Mr. Trump has made a number of statements that are wholly incompatible with the ethos and values of the university."[356] In December 2016, *Time* named Trump as its "**Person of the Year**".[357] In an interview on *The Today Show*, he said he was honored by the "award", but he took issue with the magazine for referring to him as the "President of the Divided States of America."[358][359] In the same month, he was named *Financial Times* **Person of the Year**[360] and was ranked the **second most powerful person in the world** after **Vladimir Putin**, by *Forbes*.[361]

## Political career

## Political activities up to 2015

Trump's political party affiliation has changed numerous times over the years. He registered as a Republican in Manhattan in 1987,[362] switched to the Reform Party in 1999, the Democratic Party in 2001, and back to the Republican Party in 2009.[362] He made donations to both the Democratic and the Republican party, party committees, and candidates until 2010 when he stopped donating to Democrats and increased his donations to Republicans considerably.[363]

In 1987 Trump spent $94,801 (equivalent to $209,068 in 2018) to place full-page advertisements in three major newspapers, proclaiming that "America should stop paying to defend countries that can afford to defend themselves."[364] The advertisements also advocated for "reducing the budget deficit, working for peace in Central America, and speeding up nuclear disarmament negotiations with the Soviet Union."[365] After rumors of a presidential run, Trump was invited by then U.S. Senator John Kerry (Democrat from Massachusetts), House Speaker Jim Wright of Texas, and Arkansas congressman Beryl Anthony Jr., to host a fundraising dinner for Democratic Congressional candidates and to switch parties. Anthony told *The New York Times* that "the message Trump has been preaching is a Democratic message." Asked whether the rumors were true, Trump denied being a candidate, but said, "I believe that if I did run for President, I'd win."[365] According to a Gallup poll in December 1988, Trump was the tenth most admired man in America.[366][367]

**2000 presidential campaign**

*Main article: Donald Trump 2000 presidential campaign*

In 1999, Trump filed an exploratory committee to seek the nomination of the Reform Party for the 2000 presidential election.[368][369] A July 1999 poll matching him against likely Republican nominee George W. Bushand likely Democratic nominee Al Gore showed Trump with seven percent support.[370] Trump eventually dropped out of the race, but still went on to win the Reform Party primaries in California and Michigan.[369][371]After his run, Trump left the party due to the involvement of David Duke, Pat Buchanan, and Lenora

Fulani.[368] Trump also considered running for president in 2004.[372] In 2005, Trump said that he voted for George W. Bush.[373] In 2008, he endorsed Republican **John McCain** for president.[374]

Trump speaking at the **Conservative Political Action Conference** in February 2011

## 2012 presidential speculation

Trump publicly speculated about running for president in **the 2012 election**, and made his first speaking appearance at the **Conservative Political Action Conference** (CPAC) in February 2011. The speech is credited for helping kick-start his political career within the Republican Party.[375] On May 16, 2011, Trump announced he would not run for president in the 2012 election.[376] In February 2012, Trump endorsed **Mitt Romney** for president.[377]

Trump's presidential ambitions were generally not taken seriously at the time.[378] Trump's moves were interpreted by some media as possible promotional tools for his reality show *The Apprentice*.[376][379][380] Before the 2016 election, *The New York Times* speculated that Trump "accelerated his ferocious efforts to gain stature within the political world" after Obama lampooned him at the <u>White House Correspondents' Association</u> Dinner in April 2011.[381]

## 2013–2015

In 2013, Trump was a featured CPAC speaker.[382] In a sparsely-attended speech, he railed against illegal immigration while seeming to encourage immigration from Europe, bemoaned Obama's "unprecedented media protection", advised against harming Medicare, Medicaid, and Social Security, and suggested that the government "take" Iraq's oil and use the proceeds to pay a million dollars each to families of dead soldiers.[383][384] He spent over $1 million that year to research a possible 2016 candidacy.[385]

In October 2013, New York Republicans circulated a memo suggesting Trump should run for governor of the state in 2014 against <u>Andrew Cuomo</u>. Trump responded that while New York had problems and its taxes were too high, he was not interested in the governorship.[386] A February 2014 Quinnipiac poll had shown Trump losing to the more popular Cuomo by 37 points in a hypothetical election.[387] In February 2015, Trump told NBC that he was not prepared to sign on for another season of *The Apprentice*, as he mulled his political future.[388]

## 2016 presidential campaign

## Republican primaries

*Main article: <u>2016 Republican Party presidential primaries</u>*

Trump campaigning in <u>Laconia, New Hampshire</u>, July 2015

On June 16, 2015, Trump announced his candidacy for President of the United States at Trump Tower in Manhattan. In the speech, Trump discussed <u>illegal immigration</u>, <u>offshoring</u> of American jobs, the <u>U.S. national debt</u>, and <u>Islamic terrorism</u>, which all remained large priorities during the campaign. He also announced his campaign slogan: "<u>Make America Great Again</u>".[313][312] Trump said his wealth would make him immune to pressure from campaign donors.[389] He declared that he was funding his own campaign,[390] but according to *The Atlantic*, "Trump's claims of self-funding have always been dubious at best and actively misleading at worst."[391]

In the primaries, Trump was one of seventeen candidates vying for the 2016 Republican nomination; this was the largest presidential field in American history.[392] Trump's campaign was initially not taken seriously by political analysts, but he quickly rose to the top of opinion polls.[393]

On <u>Super Tuesday</u>, Trump won the plurality of the vote, and he remained the front-runner throughout the remainder of the primaries. By March 2016, Trump was poised to win the

Republican nomination.[394] After a landslide win in Indiana on May 3, 2016—which prompted the remaining candidates Cruz and John Kasich to suspend their presidential campaigns— RNC Chairman Reince Priebus declared Trump the presumptive Republican nominee.[395]

**General election campaign**

*Main article: Donald Trump 2016 presidential campaign*

After becoming the presumptive Republican nominee, Trump shifted his focus to the general election. Trump began campaigning against Hillary Clinton, who became the presumptive Democratic nominee on June 6, 2016.

Clinton had established a significant lead over Trump in national polls throughout most of 2016. In early July, Clinton's lead narrowed in national polling averages following the FBI's re-opening of its investigation into her ongoing email controversy.[396][397][398]

Candidate Trump and running mate Mike Pence at the Republican National Convention, July 2016

On July 15, 2016, Trump announced his selection of Indiana Governor Mike Pence as his running mate.[399] Four days later on July 19, Trump and Pence were officially nominated by the Republican Party at the Republican National Convention.[400] The list of convention speakers and attendees included former presidential nominee Bob Dole, but the other prior nominees did not attend.[401][402]

Two days later, Trump officially accepted the nomination in a 76-minute speech. The historically long speech received mixed reviews, with net negative viewer reactions according to CNN and Gallup polls.[403][404][405]

On September 26, 2016, Trump and Clinton faced off in their first presidential debate, which was held at Hofstra University in Hempstead, New York, and moderated by NBC News anchor Lester Holt.[406] The TV broadcast was the most watched presidential debate in United States history.[407] The second presidential debate was held at Washington University in Saint Louis, Missouri. The beginning of that debate was dominated by references to a recently leaked tape of Trump making sexually explicit comments, which Trump countered by referring to alleged sexual misconduct on the part of Bill Clinton. Prior to the debate, Trump had invited four women who had accused Clinton of impropriety to a press conference. The final presidential debate was held on October 19 at the University of Nevada, Las Vegas. Trump's refusal to say whether he would accept the result of the election, regardless of the outcome, drew particular attention, with some saying it undermined democracy.[408][409]

## Political positions

*Main article: **Political positions of Donald Trump***

Trump's campaign platform emphasized renegotiating <u>U.S.–China relations</u> and free trade agreements such as <u>NAFTA</u> and the <u>Trans-Pacific Partnership</u>, strongly enforcing immigration laws, and building <u>a new wall</u>along the U.S.–Mexico border. His other campaign positions included pursuing <u>energy independence</u> while opposing climate change regulations such as the <u>Clean Power Plan</u> and the <u>Paris Agreement</u>, modernizing and expediting <u>services for veterans</u>, repealing and replacing the <u>Affordable Care Act</u>, abolishing <u>Common Core</u> education standards, <u>investing in infrastructure</u>, simplifying the <u>tax code</u> while reducing taxes for all economic classes, and imposing <u>tariffs</u> on imports by companies that offshore jobs. During the campaign, he also advocated a largely <u>non-interventionist</u> approach to foreign policy while increasing military spending, extreme vetting or banning immigrants from Muslim-majority countries[410] to pre-empt domestic Islamic terrorism, and aggressive military action against the <u>Islamic State of Iraq and the Levant</u>. During the campaign Trump repeatedly called <u>NATO</u> "obsolete".[411]

His political positions have been described as <u>populist</u>,[412][413][414] and some of his views cross party lines. For example, his economic campaign plan calls for large reductions in income taxes and deregulation,[415]consistent with Republican Party policies, along with significant infrastructure investment,[416] usually considered a Democratic

Party policy.[417][418] According to political writer Jack Shafer, Trump may be a "fairly conventional American populist when it comes to his policy views", but he attracts free media attention, sometimes by making outrageous comments.[419][420]

Trump has supported or leaned toward varying political positions over time.[421][422][423] *Politico* has described his positions as "eclectic, improvisational and often contradictory",[423] while NBC News counted "141 distinct shifts on 23 major issues" during his campaign.[424]

## Campaign rhetoric

In his campaign, Trump said that he disdained political correctness; he also stated that the media had intentionally misinterpreted his words, and he made other claims of adverse media bias.[337][425][426] In part due to his fame, and due to his willingness to say things other candidates would not, and because a candidate who is gaining ground automatically provides a compelling news story, Trump received an unprecedented amount of free media coverage during his run for the presidency, which elevated his standing in the Republican primaries.[339]

Fact-checking organizations have denounced Trump for making a record number of false statements compared to other candidates.[427][428][429] At least four major publications—*Politico*, *The Washington Post*, *The New York Times*, and the *Los Angeles Times*—have pointed out lies or falsehoods in his campaign statements, with the *Los Angeles Times* saying that "Never in modern presidential politics has a major candidate made false statements as routinely as Trump has".[430] NPR said that Trump's campaign statements were often opaque or suggestive.[431]

Trump's penchant for hyperbole is believed to have roots in the New York real estate scene, where Trump established his wealth and where puffery abounds.[432] Trump adopted his ghostwriter's phrase "truthful hyperbole" to describe his public speaking style.[432][293]

## Support from white supremacists

According to Michael Barkun, the Trump campaign was remarkable for bringing fringe ideas, beliefs, and organizations into the mainstream.[433] During his presidential campaign, Trump was accused of pandering to white supremacists.[434][435][436] He retweeted open racists,[437][438] and repeatedly refused to condemn David Duke, the Ku Klux Klan or white supremacists, in an interview on CNN's *State of the Union*, saying that he would first need to "do research" because he knew nothing about Duke or white supremacists.[439][440] Duke himself was an enthusiastic supporter of Trump throughout the 2016 primary and election, and has stated that he and like-minded people voted for Trump because of his promises to "take our country back".[441][442]

After repeated questioning by reporters, Trump said that he disavowed David Duke and the KKK.[443][444][445] Trump said on MSNBC's *Morning Joe*: "I disavowed him. I disavowed the KKK. Do you want me to do it again for the 12th time? I disavowed him in the past, I disavow him now."[445]

The alt-right movement coalesced around Trump's candidacy,[446] due in part to its opposition to multiculturalism and immigration.[447][448][449] Members of the alt-right enthusiastically supported Trump's campaign.[450]In August 2016, he appointed Steve Bannon—the executive chairman of Breitbart News—as his campaign CEO; Bannon described Breitbart News as "the platform for the alt-right."[451] In an interview days after the election, Trump condemned supporters who celebrated his victory with Nazi salutes.[444][452]

## Financial disclosures

As a presidential candidate, Trump disclosed details of his companies, assets, and revenue sources to the extent required by the FEC. His 2015 report listed assets above $1.4 billion and outstanding debts of at least $265 million.[93][453] The 2016 form showed little change.[94]

Trump did not release his tax returns during his presidential campaign or afterward,[454][455] contrary to usual practice by every candidate since Gerald Ford in 1976 and to his promise in 2014 to do so if he ran for office.[456][457][458] Trump's refusal led to speculation that he was hiding something.[459] He said that his tax returns were being audited, and his lawyers had advised him against releasing them.[460][461] Trump has told the press that his tax rate was none of their business, and that he tries to pay "as little tax as possible".[462][463][464]

In October 2016, portions of Trump's state filings for 1995 were leaked to a reporter from *The New York Times*. They show that Trump declared a loss of $916 million that year, which could have let him avoid taxes for up to 18 years. During the second presidential debate, Trump acknowledged using the deduction, but declined to provide details such as the specific years it was applied.[465] He said that he did use the tax code to avoid paying taxes.[466][467][468]

On March 14, 2017, the first two pages of Trump's 2005 federal income tax returns were leaked to Rachel Maddow and shown on MSNBC. The document states that Trump had a gross adjusted income of $150 million and paid $38 million in federal taxes. The White House confirmed the authenticity of these documents and stated: "Despite this substantial income figure and tax paid, it is totally illegal to steal and publish tax returns."[469][470]

## Sexual misconduct allegations

*Main articles: Donald Trump Access Hollywood tape and Donald Trump sexual misconduct allegations*

A total of 19 women have accused Trump of sexual misconduct as of December 2017.[471] Trump has denied all of the accusations, which he has called "false smears", and alleged a conspiracy against him.[472][473][474]

Two days before the second presidential debate, a 2005 recording surfaced in which Trump was heard bragging about forcibly kissing and groping women.[475][476][477] The hot mic recording was captured on a studio bus in which Trump and Billy Bush were preparing to film an episode of *Access Hollywood*. In the tape, Trump said: "I just start kissing them ... I don't even wait. And when you're a star, they let you do it, you can do anything ... grab 'em by the pussy."[478] During the recording, Trump also spoke of his efforts to seduce a married woman, saying he "moved on her very heavily".[478]

Trump's language on the tape was described by the media as "vulgar", "sexist", and descriptive of sexual assault. The incident prompted him to make his first public apology during the campaign,[479][480] and caused outrage across the political spectrum,[481][482] with many Republicans withdrawing their endorsements of his candidacy and some urging him to quit the race.[483] Subsequently, at least 15 women[484] came forward with new accusations of sexual misconduct, including unwanted kissing and groping, resulting in widespread media coverage.[485][486] In his two public statements in response to the controversy, Trump alleged that former president Bill Clinton had "abused women" and that Hillary had bullied her husband's victims.[487]

**Election to the presidency**

Main article: *2016 United States presidential election*

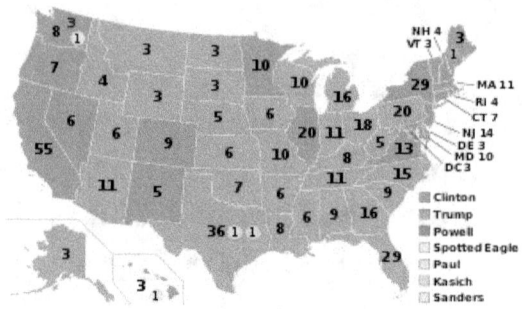

2016 electoral vote results

On November 8, 2016, Trump received 306 pledged underline electoral votes versus 232 for Clinton. The official counts were 304 and 227 respectively, after defections on both sides.[488] Trump received a smaller share of the popular vote than Clinton, which made him the fifth person to be elected president while losing the popular vote.[489][d] Clinton was ahead nationwide by 2.1 percentage points, with 65,853,514 votes (48.18%) to 62,984,828 votes (46.09%); neither candidate reached a majority.[492]

Trump's victory was considered a stunning political upset by most observers, as polls had consistently showed Hillary Clinton with a nationwide—though diminishing—lead, as well as a favorable advantage in most of the competitive states. Trump's support had been modestly underestimated throughout his campaign,[493] and many observers blamed errors in polls, partially attributed to pollsters overestimating Clinton's support among well-educated and nonwhite voters, while underestimating Trump's support among white working-class voters.[494] The polls were relatively accurate,[495] but media outlets and pundits alike showed overconfidence in a Clinton victory despite a large number of undecided voters and a favorable concentration of Trump's core constituencies in competitive states.[496]

Trump won 30 states, including Michigan, Pennsylvania, and Wisconsin, which had been considered a blue wall of Democratic strongholds since the 1990s. Clinton won 20 states and the District of Columbia. Trump's victory marked the return of a Republican White House combined with control of both chambers of Congress.

Trump is the wealthiest president in U.S. history, even after adjusting for inflation.[497] He is also the first president without prior government or military service.[498][499][500] Of the 43[e] previous presidents, 38 had held prior elective office, two had not held elective office but had served in the Cabinet, and three had never held public office but had been commanding generals.[500]

**Protests**

*Main article: Protests against Donald Trump*

Women's March in Washington on January 21, 2017, a day after the inauguration

Some rallies during the primary season were accompanied by protests or violence, including attacks on Trump supporters and vice versa both inside and outside the venues.[502][503][504] Trump's election victory sparked protests across the United States, in opposition to his policies and his inflammatory statements. Trump initially said on Twitter that these were "professional protesters, incited by the media", and were "unfair", but he later tweeted, "Love the fact that the small groups of protesters last night have passion for our great country."[505][506]

In the weeks following Trump's inauguration, massive anti-Trump demonstrations took place, such as the Women Marches, which gathered 2,600,000 people worldwide,[507]including 500,000 in Washington alone.[508] Moreover, marches against his travel ban began across the country on January 29, 2017, just nine days after his inauguration.[509]

**Presidency**

*Main article: Presidency of Donald Trump*

*For a chronological guide to this subject, see Timeline of the Donald Trump presidency.*

**Early actions**

*See also: Presidential transition of Donald Trump and First 100 days of Donald Trump's presidency*

Trump was inaugurated as the 45th president of the United States on January 20, 2017. During his first week in office, he signed six executive orders: interim procedures in anticipation of repealing the Patient Protection and Affordable Care Act (Obamacare), withdrawal from the Trans-Pacific Partnership negotiations, reinstatement of the Mexico City Policy, unlocking the Keystone XL and Dakota Access Pipelineconstruction projects, reinforcing border security, and beginning the planning and design process to construct a wall along the U.S. border with Mexico.[510]

On January 31, Trump nominated U.S. Appeals Court judge Neil Gorsuch to fill the seat on the Supreme Court previous held by Justice Antonin Scalia until his death in 2016.[511]

**Domestic policy**

**Economy and trade**

*Main articles: Economic policy of Donald Trump and Trump tariffs*

In December 2017, Trump signed the Tax Cuts and Jobs Act of 2017, which cut the corporate tax rate to 21 percent, lowered personal tax brackets, increased child tax credit, doubled the estate tax threshold to $11.2 million, and limited the state and local tax deduction to $10,000.[512] The reduction in individual tax rates ends in 2025. While people would generally get a tax cut, those with higher incomes would see the most benefit.[513][514] Households in the lower or middle class would also see a small tax increase after the tax cuts expire. The bill is estimated to increase deficits by $1.5 trillion over 10 years.[515][516]

Trump speaking to automobile workers in Michigan, March 2017

Trump adopted his current views on trade issues in the 1980s.[517] Trump has been described as a **protectionist**[518][519][520] because he criticized **NAFTA**,[521][522] cancelled negotiations towards the **Trans-Pacific Partnership** (TPP),[523] imposed tariffs on steel and aluminum,[524][525] and proposed to significantly raise tariffs on Chinese and Mexican exports to the United States.[526][527] He has also been critical of the **World Trade Organization**, threatening to leave unless his proposed tariffs are accepted.[528][529]

In March 2018, Trump signed an order imposing import tariffs of 25 percent on steel and 10 percent on aluminum, with exemptions for Canada, Mexico, and possibly other countries.[530] In response, the EU imposed retaliatory tariffs targeting $3.4 billion in U.S. exports.[531][532]

In July, the United States and China imposed tariffs on $34 billion of each other's goods,[533][534] expanded to $50 billion in August.[535]

In September the U.S. introduced a 10% tariff on $200 billion worth of Chinese goods, poised to increase to 25% by the end of the year, and threatened further tariffs on an additional $267 billion if China retaliates.[536] China countered the move with a 10% tariff on $60 billion of U.S. imports,[537] which, combined with the previous round of tariffs, covers almost all $110 billion of U.S. imports to China.[536] According to some analysts, the escalating trade war with China[538] could impact $2 trillion in global trade.[539][540]

## Energy and climate

*Main article: Environmental policy under the Trump administration*

While campaigning, Trump's energy policy advocated domestic support for both fossil and renewable energy sources in order to curb reliance on Middle-Eastern oil and possibly turn the U.S. into a net energy exporter.[541] However, following his election his "America First Energy Plan" did not mention renewable energy and instead focused on fossil fuels.[542] Environmentalists expressed concerns after he announced plans to make large budget cuts to programs that research renewable energy and to roll back Obama-era policies directed at curbing climate change and limiting environmental pollution.[543]

Trump rejects the scientific consensus on climate change[544][545] and his first Environmental Protection Agency chief, Scott Pruitt, does not believe that carbon emissions are the main cause of global warming. While acknowledging the climate is warming, Pruitt claimed this warming is not necessarily harmful and could be beneficial.[546] Based on numerous studies, climate experts disagree with his position.[547] On June 1, 2017, Trump announced the withdrawal of the United States from the Paris Agreement, making the U.S. the only nation in the world to not ratify the agreement.[548][549][550]

**Government size and deregulation**

Trump's early policies have favored rollback and dismantling of government regulations. He signed a Congressional Review Act disapproval resolution, the first in 16 years and second overall.[551] During his first six weeks in office, he delayed, suspended or reversed ninety federal regulations.[552][553]

On January 23, 2017, Trump ordered a temporary government-wide hiring freeze, except for those working in certain areas.[554][555] Unlike some past freezes, it barred agencies from adding contractors to make up for employees leaving.[556] The Comptroller General of the Government Accountability Office told a House committee that hiring freezes have not proven to be effective in reducing costs.[556] The hiring freeze was lifted in April 2017.[557]

A week later Trump signed Executive Order 13771, which directed administrative agencies to repeal two existing regulations for every new regulation they issue.[558][559] Agency defenders expressed opposition to Trump's criticisms, saying that the bureaucracy exists to protect people against well-organized, well-funded interest groups.[560]

## Health care

In 1999, Trump told *Larry King Live*: "I believe in universal healthcare."[561] Trump's 2000 book, *The America We Deserve*, argued strongly for a single-payer healthcare system based on the Canadian model,[562] and he has voiced admiration for the Scottish National Health Service.[561][563][564]

During his campaign, Trump repeatedly vowed to repeal and replace Patient Protection and Affordable Care Act (ACA or "Obamacare").[565][566] Shortly after taking office, he urged Congress to repeal and replace it. In May of that year, the House of Representatives voted to repeal it.[567] Over the course of several months' effort, however, the Senate was unable to pass any version of a repeal bill.[568] Trump has expressed a desire to "let Obamacare fail", and the Trump administration has cut the ACA enrollment period in half and drastically reduced funding for advertising and other ways to encourage enrollment.[569][570][571] The tax reform Trump signed into law at the end of his first year in office effectively repealed the individual health insurance mandate that was a major element of the Obamacare health insurance system; this repeal is scheduled to be implemented in 2019.[572][573][574]

## Social issues

*Main article: Social policy of Donald Trump*

Trump favored modifying the 2016 Republican platform opposing abortion, to allow for exceptions in cases of rape, incest, and circumstances endangering the health of the mother.[575] He has said that he is committed to appointing pro-life justices.[576] He says he personally supports "traditional marriage"[577] but considers the nationwide legality of same-sex marriage a "settled" issue.[576] Despite the statement by Trump and the White House saying they would keep in place a 2014 executive order from the Obama administration which created federal workplace protections for LGBT people,[578] in March 2017, the Trump administration rolled back key components of the Obama administration's workplace protections for LGBT people.[579]

Trump supports a broad interpretation of the Second Amendment and says he is opposed to gun control in general,[580][581] although his views have shifted over time.[582] Trump opposes legalizing recreational marijuana but supports legalizing medical marijuana.[583] He favors capital punishment,[584][585] as well as the use of waterboarding and "a hell of a lot worse" methods.[586][587]

## Immigration

*Main article: Immigration policy of Donald Trump*

Trump conferring with Vice President Mike Pence and Secretary of Homeland Security John F. Kelly, January 25, 2017

Trump's proposed immigration policies were a topic of bitter and contentious debate during the campaign. He promised to build a more substantial wall on the Mexico–United States border to keep out illegal immigrants and vowed that Mexico would pay for it.[588] He pledged to massively deport illegal immigrants residing in the United States,[589] and criticized birthright citizenship for creating "anchor babies".[590] He said that deportation would focus on criminals, visa overstays, and security threats.[591]

**Travel ban**

*Further information: Executive Order 13769 and Executive Order 13780*

Following the November 2015 Paris attacks, Trump made a controversial proposal to ban Muslim foreigners from entering the United States until stronger vetting systems could be implemented.[592][593][594] He later reframed the proposed ban to apply to countries with a "proven history of terrorism".[595][596][597]

On January 27, 2017, Trump signed Executive Order 13769, which suspended admission of refugees for 120 days and denied entry to citizens of Iraq, Iran, Libya, Somalia, Sudan, Syria, and Yemen for 90 days, citing security concerns. The order was imposed without warning and took effect immediately.[598] Confusion and protests caused chaos at airports.[599][600] The administration then clarified that visitors with a green card were exempt from the ban.[601][602]

On January 30, Sally Yates, the acting Attorney General, directed Justice Department lawyers not to defend the executive order, which she deemed unenforceable and unconstitutional;[603] Trump immediately dismissed her.[604][605] Multiple legal challenges were filed against the order, and on February 5 a federal judge in Seattle blocked its implementation.[606][607] On March 6, Trump issued a revised order, which excluded Iraq, gave specific exemptions for permanent residents, and removed priorities for Christian minorities.[608][598] Again federal judges in three states blocked its implementation.[609] On June 26, 2017, the Supreme Court ruled that the ban could be enforced on visitors who lack a "credible claim of a *bona fide* relationship with a person or entity in the United States."[610]

The temporary order was replaced by Presidential Proclamation 9645 on September 24, 2017, which permanently restricts travel from the originally targeted countries except Iraq and Sudan, and further bans travelers from North Korea and Chad, and certain Venezuelan officials.[611] After lower courts partially blocked the new restrictions with injunctions, the Supreme Court allowed the September version to go into full effect on December 4.[612] In January 2018, the Supreme Court announced that it would hear a challenge to the travel ban.[613] The Court heard oral arguments on April 25,[614][613] and ultimately upheld the travel ban in a June ruling.[615]

## DACA

While running for president, Trump said that he intended to repeal the **Deferred Action for Childhood Arrivals** (DACA) on "day one" of his presidency. The program, introduced in 2012, allowed people who had either entered or remained in the United States illegally as minors to receive a renewable two-year period of deferred action from deportation and be eligible for a work permit.[616]

In September 2017, Attorney General **Jeff Sessions** announced that the DACA program would be repealed after six months.[617] Trump argued that "top legal experts" believed that DACA was unconstitutional, and called on Congress to use the six-month delay to pass legislation solving the "Dreamers" issue permanently.[618] As of March 2018, when the delay expired, no legislation had been agreed on DACA.[619] Several states immediately challenged the DACA rescission in court.[620] Two injunctions in January and

February 2018 allowed renewals of applications and stopped the rolling back of DACA, and in April 2018 a federal judge ordered the acceptance of new applications; this would go into effect in 90 days.[621]

## Family separation at border

*Main article: Trump administration family separation policy*

In April 2018, Trump enacted a "zero tolerance" immigration policy that took adults irregularly entering the U.S. into custody for criminal prosecution and forcibly separated children from parents, eliminating the policy of previous administrations that made exceptions for families with children.[622][623] By mid-June, more than 2,300 children had been placed in shelters, including "tender age" shelters for babies and toddlers,[624]culminating in demands from Democrats, Republicans, Trump allies, and religious groups that the policy be rescinded.[625] Trump falsely asserted that his administration was merely following the law.[626][627][628] On June 20, Trump signed an executive order to end family separations at the U.S. border.[629] On June 26 a federal judge in San Diego issued a preliminary injunction requiring the Trump administration to stop detaining immigrants parents separately from their minor children, and to reunite family groups that had been separated at the border.[630]

## 2018–2019 federal government shutdown

*Main article: United States federal government shutdown of 2018–2019*

On December 22, 2018, the federal government was partially shut down after Trump declared that any funding extension must include $5.6 billion in federal funds for a <u>U.S.–Mexico border wall</u> to partly fulfill his campaign promise.[631] The shutdown was caused by a lapse in funding for nine federal departments, affecting about one-fourth of federal government activities.[632] Trump said he would not accept any bill that does not include funding for the wall, and Democrats, who control the House, said they would not support any bill that does. Senate Republicans have said they will not advance any legislation that Trump would not sign.[633] In earlier negotiations with Democratic leaders, Trump commented that he would be "proud to shut down the government for border security".[634][635][636]

On January 25, 2019, Congress passed and Trump signed a 3-week appropriation bill to fund the government while negotiations on border security funding take place.[637] This ended the 31-day shutdown, the longest such shutdown in U.S. history.[638] On February 14 both houses of Congress passed, and on February 15 Trump signed, a bill to fund the government until September 30, the balance of the fiscal year. At the same time he signed a declaration that there is a national emergency at the country's southern border, ordering that funds from drug interdiction programs and military construction projects be used to build barriers along the border.[639] On March 5, 2019, it was admitted by a senior republican member of Senate that Trump's declaration of emergency would be rejected by the Senate.[640]

## Foreign policy

*Main articles:* *Foreign policy of the Donald Trump administration* *and* *Foreign policy of Donald Trump*

President Trump together with other leaders at the **43rd G7 summit** in Italy

Trump, King **Salman of Saudi Arabia**, and Egyptian president **Abdel Fattah el-Sisi** at the **2017 Riyadh summit** in Saudi Arabia

Trump has been described as a **non-interventionist**[641][642] and as an **American nationalist**.[643] He has repeatedly stated that he supports an "**America First**" foreign policy.[644]He supports increasing United States military defense spending,[643] but favors decreasing United States spending on **NATO** and in the Pacific region.[645] He says America should look inward, stop "nation building", and re-orient its resources toward domestic needs.[642] Trump has praised **China**'s president **Xi Jinping**,[646] **Philippines** president **Rodrigo Duterte**,[647] **Egyptian** president **Abdel Fattah el-Sisi**,[648] **Turkey**'s president **Recep Tayyip Erdoğan**,[649] King **Salman of Saudi Arabia**,[650] Italy's prime minister **Giuseppe Conte**[651] and Brazil's president **Jair**

Bolsonaro.[652] Trump also praised __Poland__ under the EU-skeptic, anti-immigrant __Law and Justice__ party (PiS) as a defender of Western civilization.[653][654]

**ISIS and foreign wars**

In order to confront the __Islamic State of Iraq and Syria__ (ISIS), in 2015 Trump called for seizing the oil in ISIS-occupied areas, using U.S. air power and ground troops.[655] In 2016, Trump advocated sending 20,000 to 30,000 U.S. troops to the region, a position he later retracted.[656][657]

In April 2017, Trump ordered a __missile strike__ against a Syrian airfield in retaliation for the __Khan Shaykhun chemical attack__.[658] According to investigative journalist __Bob Woodward__, Trump had ordered his Defense Secretary James Mattis to assassinate __Syrian president__ __Bashar al-Assad__ after the chemical attack, but Mattis declined; Trump denied doing so.[659] In April 2018, he announced __missile strikes__ against Assad's regime, following a suspected chemical attack near __Damascus__.[660]

In December 2018, Trump declared "we have won against ISIS," and ordered the withdrawal of all troops from Syria, contradicting Department of Defense assessments.[661][662][663] Mattis resigned the next day over disagreements in foreign policy, calling this decision an abandonment of __Kurd__ allies that had played a key role in fighting ISIS.[664] One week after his announcement, Trump asserted he would not approve any extension of the American deployment in Syria.[665] On January 6, 2019, national security advisor John Bolton announced America would remain in Syria until ISIS is eradicated and Turkey guaranteed it would not strike America's Kurdish allies.[666]

Trump actively supported the Saudi Arabian-led intervention in Yemen against the Houthis and signed a $110 billion agreement to sell arms to Saudi Arabia.[667][668][669] Trump also praised his relationship with Saudi Arabia's powerful Crown Prince Mohammad bin Salman.[667]

U.S. troop numbers in Afghanistan increased from 8,500 to 14,000, as of January 2017.[670] reversing Trump's pre-election position critical of further involvement in Afghanistan.[671] U.S. officials said then that they aimed to "force the Taliban to negotiate a political settlement"; in January 2018, however, Trump spoke against talks with the Taliban.[672]

Iran

Main articles: Iran–United States relations § 2017–present: Trump administration, and United States withdrawal from the Joint Comprehensive Plan of Action

Trump has described the regime in Iran as "the rogue regime".[673] He has repeatedly criticized the Joint Comprehensive Plan of Action (JCPOA or "Iran nuclear deal") that was negotiated with the United States, Iran, and five other world powers in 2015, calling it "terrible" and saying that the Obama administration negotiated the agreement "from desperation."[674][675] At one point Trump said that despite opposing the content of the deal, he would attempt to enforce it rather than abrogate it.[676]

Protest against Trump's <u>recognition of Jerusalem as capital of Israel</u>, Tehran, December 11, 2017

Following Iran's ballistic missile tests on January 29, 2017, the Trump administration imposed sanctions on 25 Iranian individuals and entities in February 2017.[677][678][679]Trump reportedly lobbied "dozens" of European officials against doing business with Iran during the May <u>2017 Brussels summit</u>; this likely violated the terms of the JCPOA, under which the U.S. may not pursue "any policy specifically intended to directly and adversely affect the normalization of trade and economic relations with Iran." The Trump administration certified in July 2017 that Iran had upheld its end of the agreement.[680] On May 18, 2018, Trump announced the United States' unilateral departure from the JCPOA.[675]

**Israel**

Trump and Israeli prime minister Benjamin Netanyahu at Yad Vashem, May 2017

Regarding the Israeli–Palestinian conflict, Trump has stated the importance of being a neutral party during potential negotiations, while also having stated that he is "a big fan of Israel".[681] During the campaign he said he would relocate the U.S. embassy in Israel to Jerusalem from its current location, Tel Aviv.[682] On May 22, 2017, Trump was the first U.S. president to visit the Western Wall in Jerusalem, during his first foreign trip, which included Israel, Italy, the Vatican, and Belgium.[683][684] Trump officially recognized Jerusalem as the capital of Israel on December 6, 2017, despite criticism and warnings from world leaders. Trump added that he would initiate the process of establishing a new U.S. embassy in Jerusalem,[685] which was later opened on May 14, 2018.[686] The United Nations General Assembly condemned the move, adopting a resolution that "calls upon all States to refrain from the establishment of diplomatic missions in the Holy City of Jerusalem" in an emergency session on December 21, 2017.[687][688]

## Venezuela

On August 11, 2017, Trump said that he is "not going to rule out a military option" to confront the government of <u>Nicolás Maduro</u>.[689] In September 2018, Trump called "for the restoration of democracy in Venezuela" and said that "socialism has bankrupted the oil-rich nation and driven its people into abject poverty."[690] On January 23, 2019, Maduro announced that <u>Venezuela</u> was <u>breaking ties</u> with the United States following Trump's announcement of recognizing <u>Juan Guaidó</u>, the Venezuelan opposition leader, as the interim president of Venezuela.[691]

**North Korea**

Trump meets <u>Kim Jong-un</u> at <u>the Singapore summit</u> in June 2018.

During the campaign and the early months of his presidency, Trump said he hoped that China would help to rein in North Korea's nuclear ambitions and missile tests.[692]However, North Korea accelerated <u>their missile</u> and <u>nuclear tests</u> leading to increased tension.[692] In July, the country tested two long-range missiles identified by Western observers as <u>intercontinental ballistic missiles</u>, potentially capable of reaching <u>Alaska</u>, <u>Hawaii</u>, and the U.S.

mainland.[693][694] In August, Trump dramatically escalated his rhetoric against North Korea, warning that further provocation against the U.S. would be met with "fire and fury like the world has never seen."[695] North Korean leader Kim Jong-un then threatened to direct the country's next missile test toward Guam.[696]

On June 12, 2018, after several rounds of preliminary staff-level meetings, Trump and Kim held a first nuclear summit.[697] In a joint declaration, both countries vowed to "join their efforts to build a lasting and stable peace regime on the Korean Peninsula", while North Korea repeated its April 2018 promise to "work towards the complete denuclearization of the Korean Peninsula."[698][699] Six months later, North Korea said they would not cease their nuclear weapons program until the U.S. removes its nuclear threat from the Korean peninsula and "all neighboring areas".[700][701]

A a second nuclear summit, announced by Trump in his 2019 State of the Union Address,[702] took place from February 27–28, 2019, in Vietnam's capital Hanoi.[703] It ended abruptly without an agreement, with both sides blaming each other and offering differing accounts of the negotiations.[703][704][705]

**Russia**

*Main article: Russia–United States relations*

Putin and Trump at the **G20 Hamburg summit**, July 2017

During his campaign and as president, Trump repeatedly said that he wants better relations with Russia,[706][707] and he has praised Russian president **Vladimir Putin** as a strong leader.[708][709] Trump had pledged to hold a summit meeting with Putin,[710] stating that Russia could help the U.S. in **fighting ISIS**.[711] According to Putin and some political experts and diplomats, the **U.S.–Russian relations**, which were already at the lowest level since the end of the **Cold War**, have further deteriorated since Trump took office in January 2017.[712][713][714]

Trump and Putin met in a **2018 Russia–United States summit** in Helsinki on July 16, 2018. Trump drew harsh bipartisan criticism in the United States for appearing to side **with Putin's denial** of Russian interference in the 2016 presidential election, rather than accepting the findings of the **United States intelligence community**.[715][716] His comments were strongly criticized by many congressional Republicans and most media commentators, even those who normally support him.[717][718]

**Cuba**

In November 2017, the Trump administration tightened the rules on trade with Cuba and individual visits to the county, undoing the Obama administration's loosening of restrictions. According to an administration official, the new rules were intended to hinder trade with businesses with ties to the Cuban military, intelligence and security services.[719]

## NATO

As a candidate, Trump questioned whether he, as president, would automatically extend security guarantees to NATO members,[720] and suggested that he might leave NATO unless changes are made to the alliance.[721] As president, he reaffirmed the U.S. commitment to NATO in March 2017.[722] However, he has repeatedly accused fellow NATO members of paying less than their fair share of the expenses of the alliance.[723]

In January 2019 *The New York Times* quoted senior administration officials as saying that Trump has privately suggested on multiple occasions that the United States should withdraw from NATO.[724] The next day Trump said the United States is going to "be with NATO 100 percent" but repeated that the other countries have to "step up" and pay more.[725]

## Personnel

*Main article: Political appointments by Donald Trump*

The Trump administration has been characterized by high turnover, particularly among White House staff. By the end of

Trump's first year in office, 34 percent of his original staff had resigned, been fired, or been reassigned.[726] As of early July 2018, 61 percent of Trump's senior aides had left[727] and 141 staffers had left in the past year.[728] Both figures set a record for recent presidents—more change in the first 13 months than his four immediate predecessors saw in their first two years.[729] Notable early departures included National Security Advisor Mike Flynn (after just 25 days in office), Chief of Staff Reince Priebus, replaced by retired Marine General John F. Kelly on July 28, 2017,[730] and Press Secretary Sean Spicer.[729] Close personal aides to Trump such as Steve Bannon, Hope Hicks, John McEntee and Keith Schiller, have quit or been forced out.[731]

Trump has been slow to appoint second-tier officials in the executive branch, saying that many of the positions are unnecessary. As of October 2017, there were hundreds of sub-cabinet positions without a nominee.[732] By January 8, 2019, of 706 key positions, 433 had been filled and Trump had no nominee for 264.[733]

## Cabinet

Main articles: *Cabinet of Donald Trump* and *Formation of Donald Trump's Cabinet*

Cabinet meeting, March 2017

Trump's cabinet nominations included U.S. Senator from Alabama Jeff Sessions as Attorney General,[734] financier Steve Mnuchin as Secretary of the Treasury,[735] retired Marine Corps General James Mattis as Secretary of Defense,[736] and ExxonMobil CEO Rex Tillerson as Secretary of State.[737] Trump also brought on board politicians who had opposed him during the presidential campaign, such as neurosurgeon Ben Carson as Secretary of Housing and Urban Development,[738] and South Carolina Governor Nikki Haley as Ambassador to the United Nations.[739]

Two of Trump's 15 original cabinet members were gone within 15 months: Health and Human Services Secretary Tom Price was forced to resign in September 2017 due to excessive use of private charter jets and military aircraft, and Trump replaced Secretary of State Rex Tillerson with Mike Pompeo in March 2018 over disagreements on foreign policy.[740][731] EPA Administrator Scott Pruitt resigned in July 2018 amidst multiple investigations into his conduct,[741] while Interior Secretary Ryan Zinke resigned five months later as he also faced multiple investigations.[742]

## Investigations

*Further information: Timeline of investigations into Trump and Russia (2017), Timeline of investigations into Trump and Russia (2018), and Timeline of investigations into Trump and Russia (2019)*

An FBI investigation into possible links between Russia and the Trump campaign was launched in mid-2016 during the campaign season. Since he assumed the presidency, Trump has been the subject of increasing Justice Department and congressional scrutiny, with investigations covering his election campaign, transition and inauguration, actions taken during his presidency, along with his private businesses, personal taxes, and charitable foundation.[102]

### Russian interference

*Main articles: Russian interference in the 2016 United States elections, Timeline of Russian interference in the 2016 United States elections, and Links between Trump associates and Russian officials*

In January 2017, American intelligence agencies—the CIA, the FBI, and the NSA, represented by the Director of National Intelligence—jointly stated with "high confidence" that the Russian government interfered in the 2016 presidential election to favor the election of Trump.[743][744] In March 2017, FBI Director James Comey told Congress that "the FBI, as part of our counterintelligence mission, is investigating the Russian government's efforts to interfere in the 2016 presidential election. That includes investigating the nature of any links between individuals associated with the Trump campaign and the Russian government, and whether there was any coordination between the campaign and Russia's efforts."[745] Later, in testimony to the Senate Intelligence Committee on June 8, he affirmed he has "no doubt" that Russia interfered in the 2016 election, adding "they did it with purpose and sophistication".[746]

Trump's connections to Russia have been widely reported by the press.[747][748] One of Trump's campaign managers, Paul Manafort, had worked for several years to help pro-Russian politician Viktor Yanukovych win the Ukrainian presidency.[749] Other Trump associates, including former National Security Advisor Michael T. Flynn and political consultant Roger Stone, have been connected to Russian officials.[750][751] Russian agents were overheard during the campaign saying they could use Manafort and Flynn to influence Trump.[752] Members of Trump's campaign and later his White House staff, particularly Flynn, were in contact with Russian officials both before and after the November election.[753] On December 29, 2016, Flynn talked with Russian Ambassador Sergey Kislyak about sanctions that had been imposed the same day; Trump later fired Flynn for falsely claiming he had not discussed the sanctions.[754]

**Dismissal of James Comey**

*Main article: Dismissal of James Comey*

On May 9, 2017, Trump dismissed FBI Director James Comey. He first attributed this action to recommendations from Attorney General Jeff Sessions and Deputy AG Rod Rosenstein,[755] which criticized Comey's conduct in the investigation about Hillary Clinton's emails.[756] On May 11, Trump stated that he was concerned with the ongoing "Russia thing"[757] and that he had intended to fire Comey earlier, regardless of DoJ advice.[758]

According to a Comey memo of a private conversation on February 14, 2017, Trump said he "hoped" Comey would drop the investigation into Michael Flynn.[759] In March and April, Trump had told Comey that the ongoing suspicions formed a "cloud" impairing his presidency,[760] and asked him to publicly state that he was not personally under investigation.[761] He also asked intelligence chiefs Dan Coats and Michael Rogers to issue statements saying there was no evidence that his campaign colluded with Russia during the 2016 election.[762] Both refused, considering this an inappropriate request, although not illegal.[763] Comey eventually testified on June 8 that while he was director, the FBI investigations did not target Trump himself.[760][764] In a statement on Twitter, Trump implied that he had "tapes" of conversations with Comey, before later stating that he did not in fact have such tapes.[765]

## Special counsel

*Main article: Special Counsel investigation (2017–present)*

On May 17, 2017, Deputy Attorney General Rod Rosenstein appointed Robert Mueller, a former Director of the FBI, to serve as special counsel for the United States Department of Justice (DOJ). In this capacity, Mueller oversees the investigation into "any links and/or coordination between Russian government and individuals associated with the campaign of President Donald Trump, and any matters that arose or may arise directly from the investigation".[766] Trump has repeatedly denied any collusion between the Trump campaign and the Russian government.[767] Mueller is also investigating the Trump campaign's possible ties to Saudi Arabia, the United Arab Emirates, Turkey, Qatar, Israel, and China.[768][769]

The Washington Post reported that days after Comey's dismissal the special counsel started investigating whether Trump had obstructed justice.[770] Trump's lawyer Jay Sekulow stated that he had not been notified of any such investigation.[771][772] ABC News later reported that the special counsel was gathering preliminary information about possible obstruction of justice but had not launched a full-scale investigation.[773]

In January 2018, The New York Times reported that Trump had ordered Mueller to be fired in June 2017, after learning that Mueller was investigating possible obstruction of justice, but backed down after White House Counsel Don McGahn said he would quit;[774] Trump called the report "fake news".[775] The New York Times reported in April 2018 that Trump had again wanted the investigation shut down in early December 2017, but stopped after learning the news reports on which he based his decision were incorrect.[776] In April 2018, following an FBI raid on the office and home of Trump's private attorney Michael Cohen, Trump mused aloud about firing Mueller.[777] In August 2018, Trump wrote that Attorney General Jeff Sessions "should stop" the special counsel investigation "right now"; he also referred to it as a "rigged witch hunt".[778]

In January 2018 it was reported that Mueller wants to interview Trump about the removal of Flynn and Comey.[779] For most of 2018 there was discussion between Mueller's office and White House attorneys about whether Trump would give Mueller an in-person interview or written answers to questions, and what subjects would be covered. Trump himself said publicly he was willing to be interviewed.[780] In November 2018 he said he was preparing written answers to a set of questions, and in late November his legal team said he had submitted answers to the counsel's written questions about "issues regarding the Russia-related topics of the inquiry."[781]

*The New York Times* reported on January 11, 2019, that FBI counterintelligence grew concerned about Trump's ties to Russia during the 2016 campaign but held off opening an investigation because of uncertainty about how to proceed on such a sensitive matter. Trump's behavior during the days immediately before and after Comey's firing caused them to begin investigating whether Trump had been working on behalf of Russia against American interests, knowingly or unknowingly. The FBI merged that counterintelligence investigation with a criminal obstruction of justice investigation related to Comey's firing. Mueller took over that investigation upon his appointment, although it was not immediately clear if he had pursued the counterintelligence angle.[782]

As of February 2019, Trump has publicly criticized people or groups related to the investigations into links between Trump associates and Russia over 1,000 times during his presidency.[783]

## Associates

On August 21, 2018, former Trump campaign chairman Paul Manafort was convicted on eight felony counts of false tax filing and bank fraud.[784] Trump said he felt very badly for Manafort and praised him for resisting the pressure to make a deal with prosecutors, saying "Such respect for a brave man!" According to Giuliani, Trump had sought advice about pardoning Manafort but was counseled against it.[785]

In September Manafort faced a second trial on multiple charges, but reached a plea bargain under which he pleaded guilty to conspiracy and witness tampering and agreed to cooperate fully with investigators.[786] In November, Mueller's office said in a court filing that Manafort had repeatedly lied to investigators, thus violating the terms of the plea agreement.[787] It was also revealed that Manafort, through his attorney, had been briefing White House attorneys about his interactions with the special counsel's office.[788] Trump publicly hinted that he might pardon Manafort,[789] but the incoming chair of the House Judiciary Committee warned that "dangling a pardon in front of Manafort" could lead to charges of obstruction of justice.[790]

On November 29, Trump's former attorney Michael Cohen pleaded guilty to lying to Congress about Trump's 2016 attempts to reach a deal with Russia to build a Trump Tower in Moscow. Cohen said that he had made the false statements on behalf of Trump, who was identified as "Individual-1" in the court documents.[791]

The five Trump associates who have pleaded guilty or have been convicted in Mueller's investigation or related cases include Paul Manafort, Rick Gates, George Papadopoulos, Michael Flynn, and Michael Cohen. The charges against them were not related to collusion with Russia.[792] On January 25, 2019, Trump adviser Roger Stone was arrested at his home in Fort Lauderdale, Florida, and indicted on seven criminal charges.[793]

## Hush payments

Adult film actress Stormy Daniels has alleged that she and Trump had an affair in 2006,[794] which Trump denied.[795] In January 2018, it was reported that just before the 2016 presidential election Daniels was paid $130,000 by Trump's attorney Michael Cohen as part of a non-disclosure agreement (NDA); Cohen later said he paid her with his own money.[796] In February 2018, Daniels sued Cohen's company asking to be released from the NDA and be allowed to tell her story. Cohen obtained a **restraining order** to keep her from discussing the case.[797][798] In March, Daniels claimed in court that the NDA never came into effect because Trump did not sign it personally.[799]

In April 2018, Trump said that he did not know about Cohen paying Daniels, why Cohen had made the payment or where Cohen got the money from.[800] In May, Trump's annual financial disclosure revealed that he reimbursed Cohen in 2017 for payments related to Daniels.[801] In August 2018, in a case brought by the office of the **United States Attorney for the Southern District of New York**,[802] Cohen pleaded guilty in federal court to breaking campaign finance laws, admitting to paying **hush money** of $130,000 to Daniels and $150,000 indirectly to *Playboy* model **Karen McDougal**, and said that he did it at the direction of Trump,[803][804] with the aim of influencing the presidential election.[805] In response, Trump said that he only knew about the payments "later on", and that he paid back Cohen personally, not out of campaign funds.[806] Cohen also said he would cooperate fully with the special counsel investigation.[807]

In a December 7, 2018 sentencing memorandum for Cohen, federal prosecutors implicated Trump in directing Cohen to commit the campaign finance law felonies for which Cohen had pleaded guilty. Shortly after the memorandum court filing, Trump tweeted, "Totally clears the president. Thank you!"[808] Cohen was sentenced to three years in federal prison, stemming from his guilty pleas to five counts of tax evasion and one count each of excessive campaign contribution, unlawful corporate contribution and false statements to a bank.[809] Trump denied directing Cohen to make the payments.[810] That same day, NBC News reported that Trump was present in an August 2015 meeting with Cohen and David Pecker when they discussed how American Media could help counter negative stories about Trump's relationships with women, confirming previous reporting by *The Wall Street Journal*.[811]

## 2019 House investigation

In March 2019 the House Judiciary Committee launched a broad investigation of Trump for possible obstruction of justice, corruption, and abuse of power.[812] The Judiciary Committee chair Jerrold Nadler sent letters demanding documents to 81 individuals and organizations associated with both Trump's presidency, business, and private life, saying it's "very clear that the president obstructed justice."[813][814] Three other committee chairmen wrote the White House and State Department requesting details of Trump's communications with Putin, including any efforts to conceal the content of those communications.[815] According to Senator Mark Warner, vice chairman of the Senate Intelligence Committee, there is "enormous" evidence of the Trump campaign's involvement with Russia. Representative Adam Schiff, chairman of the House Intelligence Committee, stated that there is "direct evidence" of collusion between the Trump campaign and Russia.[816][817]

## Impeachment efforts

*Main article: **Efforts to impeach Donald Trump***

Congressman **Al Green** delivers a speech calling for impeachment of President Trump, June 2017

Formal efforts to start the process of **impeachment** against Trump, who took office in January 2017, have been initiated by **Representatives** **Al Green** and **Brad Sherman**, both **Democrats**.[818][819] Other people and groups have asserted that Trump has engaged in impeachable activity during **his presidency**.[820][821] Talk of impeachment began before Trump took office.[822][823]

Serious proposals to impeach Trump for obstruction of justice were made in May 2017, after Trump fired FBI Director **James Comey**[824][825][826] and allegations surfaced that Trump had asked Comey to drop the investigation against **Michael Flynn**.[827] A December 2017 resolution of impeachment failed in the House by a 58–364 margin.[828] Since the **Republicans** controlled the **Senate**, the likelihood of impeachment during the 2017–2019 **115th Congress** was considered remote.[829][830]

Independently of impeachment, some commentators have speculated that Trump could be stripped of his powers and duties for incapacity under the **25th Amendment of the Constitution**.[831][832]

## 2020 presidential campaign

*Main article: Donald Trump 2020 presidential campaign*

Trump signaled his intention to run for a second term by filing with the FEC within hours of assuming the presidency.[833] This transformed his 2016 election committee into a 2020 reelection one.[834] Trump marked the official start of the campaign with a rally in **Melbourne, Florida**, on February 18, 2017, less than a month after taking office.[835] By January 2018, Trump's reelection committee had $22 million in hand,[836] and it had raised a total amount exceeding $67 million as of December 2018.[837] $23 million were spent in the fourth quarter of 2018, as Trump supported various Republican candidates for the **2018 midterm elections**.[838]

## Notes

^ Jump up to:*a* *b* This estimate is by *Forbes* in their annual ranking. **Bloomberg Billionaires Index** listed Trump's net worth as $2.48 billion on May 31, 2018,[88] and **Wealth-X** listed it as at least $3.8 billion on July 16, 2018.[89]

^ Presidential elections in the United States are decided by the **Electoral College**, in which each state names a number of electors equal to its representation in **Congress**, and all delegates from each state are bound to vote for the winner of the local state vote. Consequently, it is possible for the president-elect to have received fewer votes from the country's total population (the popular vote). This situation has occurred <u>five times since 1824</u>.

^ Some modern sources, including Donald Trump's *The Art of the Deal*, refer to the company as "Elizabeth Trump & Son."[29][30] Contemporary sources, however, refer to it as "E. Trump & Son."[31][32]

^ Records on this matter date from the year 1824. The number "five" includes the elections of 1824, 1876, 1888, 2000, and 2016. Despite their similarities, some of these five elections had peculiar results; e.g. <u>John Quincy Adams</u>trailed in *both* the national popular vote and the electoral college in 1824 (since no one had a majority in the electoral college, Adams was chosen by the House of Representatives), and <u>Samuel Tilden</u> in 1876 remains the only losing candidate to win an actual majority of the popular vote (rather than just a <u>plurality</u>).[490][491]

^ <u>Grover Cleveland</u> was the <u>22nd and 24th president</u>.[501]

**References and recommended further reading**

^ *<u>"Certificate of Birth"</u>. Department of Health – City of New York – Bureau of Records and Statistics. Archived from <u>the original</u> on May 12, 2016. Retrieved October 23, 2018 – via <u>ABC News</u>.*

^ *"Certificate of Birth: Donald John Trump"* (PDF). *The Jamaica Hospital. Archived (PDF) from the original on April 9, 2011. Retrieved October 23, 2018 – via Fox News.*

^ *Rozhon, Tracie (June 26, 1999). "Fred C. Trump, Postwar Master Builder of Housing for Middle Class, Dies at 93". The New York Times. Retrieved October 3, 2018.*

^ **Kranish & Fisher 2017**, p. 32.

^ *Horowitz, Jason (September 22, 2015). "Donald Trump's Old Queens Neighborhood Contrasts With the Diverse Area Around It". The New York Times. Retrieved November 7, 2018.*

^ Jump up to:*a b* **Kranish & Fisher 2017**, p. 45.

^ *The 75th Anniversary Shrapnel. NYMA. Spring 1964. p. 107. Archived from the original on January 22, 2017. Retrieved January 21, 2017.*

^ **Kranish & Fisher 2017**, p. 31, 37.

^ *Schwartzman, Paul; Miller, Michael E. (June 22, 2016). "Confident. Incorrigible. Bully: Little Donny was a lot like candidate Donald Trump". The Washington Post. Retrieved April 2, 2017.*

^ Jump up to:*a b c* *Viser, Matt (August 28, 2015). "Even in college, Donald Trump was brash". The Boston Globe. Retrieved May 28, 2018.*

^ **Blair 2005**, p. 16.

^ Ehrenfreund, Max (September 3, 2015). _"The real reason Donald Trump is so rich"_. **The Washington Post**. Retrieved January 17,2016.

^ _"The Best Known Brand Name in Real Estate"_. **The Wharton School**. Spring 2007. Retrieved April 2, 2017.

^ _"Two Hundred and Twelfth Commencement for the Conferring of Degrees"_ (PDF). **University of Pennsylvania.** May 20, 1968.

^ Lee, Kurtis (August 4, 2016). _"How deferments protected Donald Trump from serving in Vietnam"_. **Los Angeles Times**. Retrieved August 4, 2016.

^ Montopoli, Brian (April 29, 2011). _"Donald Trump avoided Vietnam with deferments, records show"_. **CBS News**. Retrieved July 17,2015.

^ Jump up to:_a_ _b_ **Whitlock, Craig** (July 21, 2015). _"Questions linger about Trump's draft deferments during Vietnam War"_. **The Washington Post**. Retrieved April 2, 2017.

^ Jump up to:_a_ _b_ Eder, Steve; **Philipps, Dave** (August 1, 2016). _"Donald Trump's Draft Deferments: Four for College, One for Bad Feet"_. **The New York Times**. Retrieved August 2, 2016.

^ Goldman, Russell (April 29, 2011). _"Donald Trump's Own Secret: Vietnam Draft Records"_. **ABC News**. Retrieved August 1, 2016.

^ Emery, David (August 2, 2016). *"Donald Trump's Draft Deferments"*. *Snopes.com*. Retrieved October 16, 2018.

^ Selk, Avi (May 20, 2018). *"It's the 50th anniversary of the day Trump left college and (briefly) faced the draft"*. *The Washington Post*. Retrieved March 3, 2019.

^ Brinkley, Colin (February 27, 2019). *"Fordham University confirms Cohen warned it not to disclose Trump's grades"*. *PBS NewsHour*. Retrieved March 3, 2019.

^ Fouhy, Beth. *"Trump: Obama Not Harvard Material"*. *NBC New York*.

^ *"'Grab that record': How Trump's high school transcript was hidden"*. *Washington Post*.

^ **Kranish & Fisher 2017**, p. 19.

^ **Jump up to:**ᵃ ᵇ Panetta, Alexander (September 19, 2015). *"Donald Trump's grandfather ran Canadian brothel during gold rush"*. *CBC News*. Retrieved December 10, 2015.

^ **Kranish & Fisher 2017**, p. 23–25.

^ **Jump up to:**ᵃ ᵇ **Blair 2015a**, p. 5.

^ Trump, Donald; Schwartz, Tony (1987). *The Art of the Deal*. Random House. p. 67. ISBN 978-0-345-47917-4.

^ Knight, Gladys L. (August 11, 2014). *Pop Culture Places: An Encyclopedia of Places in American Popular Culture*. ABC-CLIO. p. 874. ISBN 978-0-313-39883-4.

^ _"Advertisement for E. Trump & Son"_. **_Brooklyn Daily Eagle_**. November 6, 1927. p. D3 – via Newspapers.com.

^ _"Real estate news"_. **_Brooklyn Daily Eagle_**. May 5, 1930. p. 8 – via Newspapers.com.

^ **_Blair, Gwenda_** (December 4, 2001). _The Trumps: Three Generations That Built an Empire_. p. 120. ISBN 978-0-7432-1079-9.

^ **_Blair, Gwenda_** (August 24, 2015). _"The Man Who Made Trump Who He Is"_. **_Politico_**. Retrieved July 24, 2016.

^ Jump up to:_a_ _b_ Hansler, Jennifer (November 28, 2017). _"Trump's family denied German heritage for years"_. **_CNN_**.

^ Carlström, Vilhelm (November 28, 2017). _"Donald Trump claimed he was of Swedish ancestry – but it's a lie"_. **_Business Insider_**.

^ Horowitz, Jason (August 21, 2016). _"For Donald Trump's Family, an Immigrant's Tale With 2 Beginnings"_. **_The New York Times_**.

^ Jump up to:_a_ _b_ **_Pilon, Mary_** (June 24, 2016). _"Donald Trump's Immigrant Mother"_. **_The New Yorker_**. Retrieved April 2, 2017.

^ McGrane, Sally (April 29, 2016). _"The Ancestral German Home of the Trumps"_. **_The New Yorker_**. Retrieved April 2, 2017.

^ Mannion, Cara (February 3, 2017). "3rd Circ. Judge, Trump's Sister, Stops Hearing Cases". Law360. Retrieved April 2, 2017.

^ Puente, Maria (September 12, 2017). "Eric and Lara Trump announce birth of son, POTUS' ninth grandchild". USA Today. Retrieved September 12, 2017.

^ "Trump's daughter, Ivanka, gives birth to third child". Fox News. Associated Press. March 27, 2016. Retrieved March 28, 2016.

^ Brenner, Marie (September 1990). "After The Gold Rush". Vanity Fair. Retrieved January 10, 2016. They were married in New York during Easter of 1977. Mayor Beame attended the wedding at Marble Collegiate Church. Donald had already made his alliance with Roy Cohn, who would become his lawyer and mentor.

^ Jump up to:ᵃ ᵇ Barron, James (September 5, 2016). "Overlooked Influences on Donald Trump: A Famous Minister and His Church". The New York Times. Retrieved October 13, 2016. Mr. Trump married his first wife, Ivana, at Marble, in a ceremony performed by one of America's most famous ministers, the Rev. Norman Vincent Peale.

^ "Ivana Trump becomes U.S. citizen". The Lewiston Journal. Associated Press. May 27, 1988. Retrieved August 21, 2015 – via Google News.

^ _"Ivana Trump to write memoir about raising US president's children"_. **The Guardian**. **Associated Press**. _March 16, 2017. Retrieved May 6, 2017._

^ _Graham, Ruth (July 20, 2016). "Tiffany Trump's Sad, Vague Tribute to Her Distant Father"_. **Slate**. _Retrieved July 24, 2016._

^ _"The Donald Bids Hearts For Marla Trump Wedding Draws 1,100 Friends, But Not Many Stars"_. **The Philadelphia Inquirer**. _December 21, 1993. Archived from the original on December 22, 2015. Retrieved August 21, 2015._

^ _Baylis, Sheila Cosgrove (August 7, 2013). "Marla Maples Still Loves Donald Trump"_. **People**. _Retrieved May 6, 2017._

^ **Stanley, Alessandra** _(October 1, 2016). "The Other Trump"_. **The New York Times**. _Retrieved May 6, 2017._

^ **Waterson, Jim** _(January 26, 2019). "Telegraph apologises and pays damages to Melania Trump"_. **The Guardian**. _Retrieved January 27, 2019._

^ **Brown, Tina** _(January 27, 2005). "Donald Trump, Settling Down"_. **The Washington Post**. _Retrieved May 7, 2017._

^ _Charles, Marissa (August 16, 2015). "Melania Trump would be a first lady for the ages"_. **The New York Post**. _Retrieved May 4, 2017._

^ _Choron, Harry; Choron, Sandy (2011). Money. Chronicle Books. p. 251. ISBN 978-1-4521-0559-8._

^ *"Donald Trump Fast Facts"*. *CNN*. March 7, 2014. Retrieved March 10, 2015.

^ Flegenheimer, Matt; Barbaro, Michael (November 9, 2016). *"Donald Trump Is Elected President in Stunning Repudiation of the Establishment"*. *The New York Times*. Retrieved September 1, 2017.

^ Lipton, Eric; Craig, Susanne (February 12, 2017). *"Trump Sons Forge Ahead Without Father, Expanding and Navigating Conflicts"*. *The New York Times*. Retrieved May 7, 2017.

^ V.v.B (March 31, 2017). *"Ivanka Trump's new job"*. *The Economist*. Retrieved April 3, 2017.

^ Schmidt, Michael S.; Lipton, Eric; Savage, Charlie (January 21, 2017). *"Jared Kushner, Trump's Son-in-Law, Is Cleared to Serve as Adviser"*. *The New York Times*. Retrieved May 7, 2017.

^ Jump up to:[a] [b] Scott, Eugene (July 19, 2015). *"Trump believes in God, but hasn't sought forgiveness"*. *CNN*. Retrieved April 3, 2017.

^ Glueck, Katie (December 7, 2016). *"Trump's religious dealmaking pays dividends"*. *Politico*. Retrieved April 3, 2017. Trump is a Presbyterian, and speculation is already underway over whether, and where, he might go to church regularly in Washington.

^ Mattera, Jason (March 14, 2011). *"Trump Unplugged"*. *Human Events*. Archived from the original on

*March 16, 2011. Retrieved March 16, 2011. I am a Protestant. I am a Presbyterian within the Protestant group and I go to Church as much as I can.*

^ **Blair 2015b**, p. 28–29.

^ Geoghegan, Peter (May 28, 2016). "Few rooting for Donald Trump on his mother's Scottish island". *The Irish Times*. Retrieved April 3,2017.

^ **Kranish & Fisher 2017**, p. 29.

^ Jump up to:ᵃ ᵇ Schwartzman, Paul (January 21, 2016). "How Trump got religion – and why his legendary minister's son now rejects him". *The Washington Post*. Retrieved March 18, 2017.

^ Jump up to:ᵃ ᵇ Blair, Leonardo (August 28, 2015). "Marble Collegiate Church Says Donald Trump Is Not an Active Member". *The Christian Post*. Retrieved October 10, 2018.

^ **Kranish & Fisher 2017**, p. 81.

^ Scott, Eugene (August 28, 2018). "Church says Donald Trump is not an 'active member'". *CNN*. Retrieved October 10, 2018.

^ Weigel, David (August 11, 2015). "In Michigan, Trump attacks China, critiques auto bailout, and judges Bernie Sanders 'weak'". *The Washington Post*. Retrieved August 22, 2015.

^ Haberman, Maggie; Kaplan, Thomas (January 18, 2016). "Evangelicals See Donald Trump as Man of Conviction, if Not Faith". The New York Times. Retrieved April 3, 2017.

^ Burke, Daniel (October 24, 2016). "The guilt-free gospel of Donald Trump". CNN. Retrieved January 17, 2017.

^ "Trump campaign announces evangelical executive advisory board" (Press release). Donald J. Trump for President, Inc. June 21, 2016. Archived from the original on January 18, 2017. Retrieved January 17, 2017.

^ "Who's Who of Trump's 'Tremendous' Faith Advisers". Christianity Today. Retrieved May 10, 2018.

^ Horowitz, Jason (January 2, 2016). "For Donald Trump, Lessons From a Brother's Suffering". The New York Times. Retrieved July 24, 2016.

^ McAfee, Tierney (October 8, 2015). "Donald Trump Opens Up About His Brother's Death from Alcoholism: It Had a "Profound Impact on My Life"". People. [T]here are a few hard and fast principles that he himself lives by: no drugs, no cigarettes and no alcohol. Trump's abstinence from alcohol was largely shaped by the death of his brother, Fred Jr., from alcoholism in 1981.

^ "Part 2: Donald Trump on 'Watters' World'". Watters' World. Fox News. February 6, 2016. Retrieved September 4, 2016. WATTERS: "Have you ever smoked weed?" TRUMP: "No, I have not. I have not. I would tell you 100 percent because everyone else seems to admit it nowadays, so I would actually tell you. This is almost like, it's almost like 'Hey, it's a sign'. No, I have never. I have never smoked a cigarette, either."

^ Herreria, Carla (May 1, 2018). _"Trump's Doctor Says Trump Basically Wrote That Glowing Health Letter: Report"_. _HuffPost_. Retrieved October 10, 2018.

^ Bornstein, Harold (December 4, 2015). _"Statement on Donald J. Trump record of health"_ (PDF). Archived from the original (PDF)on February 4, 2016. Retrieved June 3, 2018.

^ Marquardt, Alex; Crook, Lawrence III (May 1, 2018). _"Bornstein claims Trump dictated the glowing health letter"_. _CNN_. Retrieved May 20, 2018.

^ Frizell, Sam (September 15, 2016). _"Donald Trump's Doctor's Letter Reveals He is Overweight, But 'In Excellent Health'"_. _Time_. Retrieved April 3, 2017.

^ Altman, Lawrence K. (September 18, 2016). _"A Doctor's Assessment of Whether Donald Trump's Health Is 'Excellent'"_. _The New York Times_. Retrieved October 20, 2017.

^ Barclay, Eliza; Belluz, Julia (January 16, 2018). _"Trump's first full presidential physical exam, explained"_. _Vox_. Retrieved January 18,2017.

^ Ducharme, Jamie (January 17, 2018). _"The White House Doctor Called President Trump's Health 'Excellent.' Here's the

_Full Summary of His Physical Exam"_. **Time**. _Retrieved January 18, 2018._

^ **Shear, Michael D.**; **Kolata, Gina** _(January 17, 2018)._ _"Trump's Physical Revealed Serious Heart Concerns, Outside Experts Say"_. **The New York Times**. _Retrieved June 3, 2018._

^ _Howard, Jacqueline; Liptak, Kevin (February 14, 2019)._ _"Trump in 'very good health overall' but obese, according to physical exam results"_. **CNN**. _Retrieved February 15, 2019._

^ **O'Brien, Timothy L.** _(October 23, 2005)._ _"What's He Really Worth?"_. **The New York Times**. _Retrieved February 25, 2016._

^ _"Bloomberg Billionaires Index – Donald Trump"_. **Bloomberg News**. _May 31, 2018. Retrieved July 16, 2018._

^ _"Donald John Trump – Wealth-X Dossiersier"_. **Wealth-X**. _Retrieved July 16, 2018._

^ Jump up to:[a] [b] _"#715 Donald Trump"_. **Forbes**. _2019. Retrieved March 5, 2019._

^ _Walsh, John (October 3, 2018)._ _"Trump has fallen 138 spots on Forbes' wealthiest-Americans list, his net worth down over $1 billion, since he announced his presidential bid in 2015"_. **Business Insider**. _Retrieved October 3, 2018._

^ Jump up to:[a] [b] **Lewandowski, Corey R.**; **Hicks, Hope** _(July 15, 2015)._ _"Donald J. Trump Files Personal Financial Disclosure Statement With Federal Election Commission"_ (PDF). _Archived_ from _the original_ (PDF) on March 9, 2016. Retrieved March 8, 2016.

^ Jump up to:_a_ _b_ _"Donald Trump wealth details released by federal regulators"_. _Yahoo! News_. Archived from _the original_ on August 1, 2015. Retrieved August 9, 2015.

^ Jump up to:_a_ _b_ _c_ _Alesci, Cristina_; Frankel, Laurie; Sahadi, Jeanne (May 19, 2016). _"A peek at Donald Trump's finances"_. _CNN_. Retrieved May 20, 2016.

^ _Harwood, John_ (June 29, 2018). _"Trump's money-making power as unprecedented as his words"_. _CNBC_. Retrieved December 21, 2018.

^ _Fahrenthold, David A._; O'Harrow, Robert Jr. (August 10, 2016). _"Trump: A True Story"_. _The Washington Post_. Retrieved October 14,2018.

^ Greenberg, Jonathan (April 20, 2018). _"Trump lied to me about his wealth to get onto the Forbes 400. Here are the tapes"_. _The Washington Post_.

^ Stump, Scott (October 26, 2015). _"Donald Trump: My dad gave me 'a small loan' of $1 million to get started"_. _CNBC_. Retrieved November 13, 2016.

^ _Barstow, David_; _Craig, Susanne_; Buettner, Russ (October 2, 2018). _"11 Takeaways From The Times's Investigation Into Trump's Wealth"_. _The New York Times_. Retrieved October 3, 2018.

^ _Barstow, David; Craig, Susanne; Buettner, Russ (October 2, 2018). "Trump Engaged in Suspect Tax Schemes as He Reaped Riches From His Father"._ **The New York Times**. Retrieved October 2, 2018.

^ _Campbell, Jon; Spector, Joseph (October 3, 2018). "New York could levy hefty penalties if Trump tax fraud is proven"._ **USA Today**. _Retrieved October 5, 2018._

^ **Jump up to:**_ᵃ ᵇ Woodward, Calvin; Pace, Julie (December 16, 2018). "Scope of investigations into Trump has shaped his presidency". Associated Press. Retrieved December 19, 2018._

^ _"From the Tower to the White House"._ **The Economist**. _February 20, 2016. Retrieved February 29, 2016. Mr Trump's performance has been mediocre compared with the stockmarket and property in New York._

^ _Swanson, Ana (February 29, 2016). "The myth and the reality of Donald Trump's business empire"._ **The Washington Post**.

^ _Breuninger, Kevin (October 2, 2018). "Trump tumbles down the Forbes 400 as his net worth takes major hit"._ **CNBC**. _Retrieved January 4, 2019._

^ **Trump & Schwartz 2009**, p. 46.

^ **Jump up to:**_ᵃ ᵇ Mahler, Jonathan; Eder, Steve (August 27, 2016). "'No Vacancies' for Blacks: How Donald Trump Got His Start, and Was First Accused of Bias"._ **The New York Times**. _Retrieved January 13, 2018._

^ Korte, Gregory (September 1, 2002). "Complex was troubled from beginning". The Cincinnati Enquirer. Retrieved May 20, 2018.

^ Jump up to:ᵃ ᵇ ᶜ Kelly, Meg (February 28, 2018). "The tall tale of President Trump's Cincinnati 'success'". The Washington Post. Retrieved May 19, 2018.

^ Blair 2005, p. 23.

^ Kelly, Conor (July 27, 2015). "Meet Donald Trump: Everything You Need To Know (And Probably Didn't Know) About The 2016 Republican Presidential Candidate". ABC News.

^ Dunlap, David W. (July 30, 2015). "1973: Meet Donald Trump". The New York Times. Trump Management ... was also to allow the league to present qualified applicants for every fifth vacancy ... Trump himself said he was satisfied that the agreement did not 'compel the Trump Organization to accept persons on welfare as tenants unless as qualified as any other tenant.'

^ Kranish, Michael; O'Harrow, Robert Jr. (January 23, 2016). "Inside the government's racial bias case against Donald Trump's company, and how he fought it". The Washington Post. Civil rights groups in the city viewed the Trump company as just one example of a nationwide problem of housing discrimination. But targeting the Trumps provided a chance to have an impact, said Eleanor Holmes Norton, who was then chairwoman of the city's human rights commission. 'They were big names.'

^ **Kranish & Fisher 2017**, p. 64–69, 104.

^ *Kessler, Glenn (March 3, 2016). "Trump's false claim he built his empire with a 'small loan' from his father". The Washington Post.*

^ **Kranish & Fisher 2017**, p. 84.

^ **Wooten 2009**, p. 32–35.

^ *Geist, William (April 8, 1984). "The Expanding Empire of Donald Trump". The New York Times.*

^ *Dohan, William C. (September 28, 2015). "Decades-Old Questions Over Trump's Wealth and Education". The New York Times. Retrieved June 9, 2018.*

^ **Kranish & Fisher 2017**, p. 86–88.

^ *Flegenheimer, Matt; Haberman, Maggie (March 29, 2016). "With the New York Presidential Primary, the Circus Is Coming Home". The New York Times. Retrieved March 29, 2016.*

^ *Burns, Alexander (December 9, 2016). "Donald Trump Loves New York. But It Doesn't Love Him Back". The New York Times. Retrieved December 9, 2016.*

^ **Kranish & Fisher 2017**, p. 95.

^ _Goldberger, Paul (April 4, 1983). "Architecture: Atrium of Trump Tower is a Pleasant Surprise". The New York Times._

^ _Freedlander, David (September 29, 2015). "A 1980s New York City Battle Explains Donald Trump's Candidacy". Bloomberg News. Retrieved October 23, 2016._

^ _Lyman, Rick (November 1, 1986). "Faster and cheaper, Trump finishes N.Y.C. ice rink". The Philadelphia Inquirer. Archived from the original on November 4, 2014. Retrieved February 27, 2014._

^ _Fahrenthold, David A. (October 29, 2016). "Trump boasts about his philanthropy. But his giving falls short of his words". The Washington Post. Retrieved July 3, 2018._

^ _Purnick, Joyce (May 1, 2011). "The Donald Trump we know (and don't love): He's riding high in polls, but NYC's seen his bad side". New York Daily News. Retrieved May 10, 2018._

^ Wooten 2009, p. 65–66.

^ Kranish & Fisher 2017, p. 190.

^ _Stout, David; Gilpin, Kenneth (April 12, 1995). "Trump Is Selling Plaza Hotel To Saudi and Asian Investors". The New York Times. Retrieved May 6, 2017._

^ _Dunlap, David W. (July 17, 1994). "For a Troubled Building, a New Twist". The New York Times. Retrieved November 18, 2016._

^ *Muschamp, Herbert (June 21, 1995). "Trump Tries to Convert 50's Style into 90's Gold; Makeover Starts on Columbus Circle Hotel". The New York Times. Retrieved January 18, 2017.*

^ Wooten 2009, p. 108.

^ Wooten 2009, p. 81–82.

^ *Bagli, Charles V. (June 1, 2005). "Trump Group Selling West Side Parcel for $1.8 billion". The New York Times. Retrieved May 17, 2016.*

^ *Elstein, Aaron (April 17, 2016). "Trump's lost Empire: The deal that marked the Donald's turn from New York real estate". Crain's New York Business.*

^ Pacelle 2001, p. 18.

^ *"Trump World Tower". Emporis. Retrieved May 22, 2008.*

^ Wooten 2009, p. 86–87.

^ *Peterson-Withorn, Chase (April 23, 2018). "Donald Trump Has Gained More Than $100 Million On Mar-a-Lago". Forbes. Retrieved July 4, 2018.*

^ *"Trump Fights Property Taxes". Associated Press. March 29, 1988. Retrieved July 4, 2018.*

^ *Dangremond, Sam (December 22, 2017). "A History of Mar-a-Lago, Donald Trump's American Castle". townandcountrymag.com. Retrieved July 3, 2018.*

^ Jump up to:<u>_a_</u> <u>_b_</u> Luongo, Michael (November 2017). _"The Ironic History of Mar-a-Lago"_. **Smithsonian**. Retrieved December 9, 2017.

^ Jordan, Mary; Helderman, Rosalind S. (October 14, 2015). _"Inside Trump's Palm Beach castle and his 30-year fight to win over the locals"_. **The Washington Post**. Retrieved July 4, 2018.

^ Lee, Robert. _"How Do Golf Initiation Fees Work?"_. **Golfweek**. Retrieved July 4, 2018.

^ Kranish & Fisher 2017, p. 161.

^ Dangremond, Sam (October 9, 2017). _"Here's What We Know About the Membership of Mar-a-Lago"_. **Town&Country**. Retrieved July 4,2018.

^ Frank, Robert (January 25, 2017). _"Mar-a-Lago membership fee doubles to $200,000"_. **CNBC**. Retrieved July 4, 2018.

^ Wooten 2009, p. 57–58.

^ Kranish & Fisher 2017, p. 128.

^ _"Trump Stake in Holiday"_. **The New York Times**. September 5, 1986. Retrieved May 31, 2017.

^ Crudele, John (November 13, 1986). _"Holiday Corp. Plans Restructuring"_. **The New York Times**. Retrieved May 31, 2017.

^ Wooten 2009, p. 59–60.

^ **Kranish & Fisher 2017**, p. 137.

^ *Cuff, Daniel (December 18, 1988). "Seven Acquisitive Executives Who Made Business News in 1988: Donald Trump – Trump Organization; The Artist of the Deal Turns Sour into Sweet". The New York Times. Retrieved May 27, 2011.*

^ *Glynn, Lenny (April 8, 1990). "Trump's Taj – Open at Last, With a Scary Appetite". The New York Times. Retrieved August 14, 2016.*

^ *Parry, Wayne (May 20, 2016). "New owner wants to make Trump's Taj Mahal casino great again". PBS NewsHour. Associated Press. Retrieved August 14, 2016.*

^ *"Trump reaches agreement with bondholders on Taj Mahal". United Press International. April 9, 1991. Retrieved March 21, 2016.*

^ **Kranish & Fisher 2017**, p. 135.

^ *Bingham, Amy (April 21, 2011). "Donald Trump's Companies Filed for Bankruptcy 4 Times". ABC News. Retrieved February 20, 2015.*

^ *"Taj Mahal is out of Bankruptcy". The New York Times. October 5, 1991. Retrieved May 22, 2008.*

^ *Hylton, Richard (May 11, 1990). "Trump Is Reportedly Selling Yacht". The New York Times. Retrieved July 3, 2018.*

^ Schneider, Karen S. (May 19, 1997). _"The Donald Ducks Out"_. _People_. Retrieved September 10, 2015.

^ Kranish & Fisher 2017, p. 132–133.

^ Norris, Floyd (June 7, 1995). _"Trump Plaza casino stock trades today on Big Board"_. _The New York Times_. Retrieved December 14, 2014.

^ McQuade, Dan (August 16, 2015). _"The Truth About the Rise and Fall of Donald Trump's Atlantic City Empire"_. _Philadelphia_. Retrieved March 21, 2016.

^ _"How Donald Trump Made Millions Off His Biggest Business Failure"_. _Fortune_. Retrieved May 6, 2018.

^ Garcia, Ahiza (December 29, 2016). _"Trump's 17 golf courses teed up: Everything you need to know"_. _CNNMoney_. Retrieved January 21, 2018.

^ _"Donald Trump Personal Financial Disclosure Form 2015"_ (PDF). _The Washington Post_. July 15, 2015.

^ Melby, Caleb (July 19, 2016). _"Trump Is Richer in Property and Deeper in Debt in New Valuation"_. _Bloomberg News_. In the year that Donald Trump was transformed ... into the presumptive Republican nominee, the value of his golf courses and his namesake Manhattan tower soared ... His net worth rose to $3 billion on the Bloomberg Billionaires Index ...

^ Jump up to:_a b_ _"Donald Trump: King of Clubs"_. _Golf_. February 21, 2007. Retrieved August 5, 2018.

^ DiMeglio, Steve (March 3, 2015). *"Donald Trump brings new life to world of golf"*. *USA Today*. Retrieved July 21, 2018.

^ Beall, Joel (March 20, 2017). *"President Trump appears to still really like golf, makes 11th trip to course in eight weeks in office"*. Retrieved July 21, 2018.

^ *Cillizza, Chris* (January 3, 2018). *"Donald Trump's huge golf hypocrisy"*. *CNN*. Retrieved July 21, 2018.

^ Wang, Jennifer (March 20, 2017). *"From Manila to Hawaii, Meet The Licensing Partners Who Paid Trump The Most"*. *Forbes*. Retrieved May 6, 2017.

^ Blankfeld, Keren. *"Donald Trump on His Brand Value: Forbes' Numbers Are Ridiculous"*. *Forbes*.

^ Williams, Aaron; Narayanswamy, Anu (January 25, 2017). *"How Trump has made millions by selling his name"*. Retrieved December 12, 2017.

^ Anthony, Zane; Sanders, Kathryn; *Fahrenthold, David A.* (April 13, 2018). *"Whatever happened to Trump neckties? They're over. So is most of Trump's merchandising empire"*. *The Washington Post*.

^ *"Dive into Donald Trump's thousands of lawsuits"*. *USA Today*. Retrieved April 17, 2018.

^ Penzenstadler, Nick; *Page, Susan* (June 2, 2016). *"Exclusive: Trump's 3,500 lawsuits unprecedented for a presidential nominee"*. *USA Today*. Retrieved June 2, 2016. About 100 additional disputes centered on other issues at the casinos. Trump and his enterprises have been named in almost 700 personal-injury claims and about 165 court disputes with government agencies ... Due to his branding value, Trump is determined to defend his name and reputation.

^ Savransky, Rebecca (June 2, 2016). "Trump brags about winning record in lawsuits". The Hill.

^ Hylton, Richard D. (June 27, 1990). "Banks Approve Loans for Trump, But Take Control of His Finances". The New York Times. Retrieved October 13, 2018.

^ Jump up to:ᵃ ᵇ Flitter, Emily (July 17, 2016). "Art of the spin: Trump bankers question his portrayal of financial comeback". Reuters. Retrieved October 14, 2018.

^ Hood, Bryan (June 29, 2015). "4 Times Donald Trump's Companies Declared Bankruptcy". Vanity Fair. Retrieved January 17, 2016.

^ Li, Hao (April 12, 2011). "Donald Trump Questioned on His Bankruptcies". International Business Times. Retrieved February 19,2015.

^ Stone, Peter (May 5, 2011). "Donald Trump's lawsuits could turn off conservatives who embrace tort reform". The Center for Public Integrity. Retrieved March 14, 2016.

^ Kurtz, Howard (April 24, 2011). "Kurtz: The Trump Backlash". Newsweek. Retrieved March 14, 2016.

^ Winter, Tom. _"Trump Bankruptcy Math Doesn't Add Up"_. __NBC News__. Retrieved October 8, 2016.

^ O'Connor, Clare (April 29, 2011). _"Fourth Time's A Charm: How Donald Trump Made Bankruptcy Work For Him"_. __Forbes__. Retrieved February 19, 2015.

^ Smith, Allan (December 8, 2017). _"Trump's long and winding history with Deutsche Bank could now be at the center of Robert Mueller's investigation"_. __Business Insider__. Retrieved October 14, 2018.

^ Zurcher, Anthony (July 23, 2015). _"Five take-aways from Donald Trump's financial disclosure"_. __BBC Online__. Retrieved January 17, 2016.

^ Jump up to:_a b_ __Markazi, Arash__ (July 14, 2015). _"5 things to know about Donald Trump's foray into doomed USFL"_. __ESPN__.

^ Morris, David (September 24, 2017). _"Donald Trump Fought the NFL Once Before. He Got Crushed"_. __Fortune__. Retrieved June 22, 2018.

^ _"Trump Gets Tyson Fight"_. __The New York Times__. February 25, 1988. Retrieved February 11, 2011.

^ __Anderson, Dave__ (July 12, 1988). _"Sports of The Times; Trump: Promoter Or Adviser?"_. __The New York Times__. Retrieved February 11, 2011.

^ Hogan, Kevin (April 10, 2016). *"The Strange Tale of Donald Trump's 1989 Biking Extravaganza"*. **Politico**. Retrieved April 12, 2016.

^ Hylton, Richard D. (April 16, 1991). *"NWA-Trump Shuttle Deal Seen as Near"*. **The New York Times**. Retrieved March 14, 2019.

^ Andino, Gabe (July 9, 2015). *"Remember That One Time Donald Trump Owned an Airline"*. **NYCAviation**. Retrieved March 13, 2019.

^ Jump up to:[a] [b] **Kessler, Glenn** (August 11, 2016). *"Too good to check: Sean Hannity's tale of a Trump rescue"*. **The Washington Post**. Retrieved March 14, 2019.

^ *"Special Friday Flashback: When Trump Ran 'The Shuttle'"*. Airways Magazine. January 20, 2017. Retrieved March 14, 2019.

^ Binkowski, Brooke (October 22, 2016). *"Did Donald Trump Transport Stranded Troops on His Own Airplane?"*. **Snopes**. Retrieved March 14, 2019.

^ *"Trump Sells Miss Universe Organization to WME-IMG Talent Agency"*. **The New York Times**. September 15, 2015. Retrieved January 9, 2016.

^ *"Donald Trump just sold off the entire Miss Universe Organization"*. **Business Insider**. September 14, 2015. Retrieved May 6, 2016.

^ Kranish & Fisher 2017, p. 164.

^ *Rutenberg, Jim (June 22, 2002). "Three Beauty Pageants Leaving CBS for NBC". The New York Times. Retrieved August 14, 2016.*

^ *De Moraes, Lisa (June 22, 2002). "There She Goes: Pageants Move to NBC". The Washington Post. Retrieved August 14, 2016.*

^ *Zara, Christopher (October 29, 2016). "Why the heck does Donald Trump have a Walk of Fame star, anyway? It's not the reason you think". Fast Company. Retrieved June 16, 2018.*

^ *Stanhope, Kate (June 29, 2015). "NBC Cuts Ties With Donald Trump Over "Derogatory Statements," Pulls Miss USA and Miss Universe Pageants". The Hollywood Reporter. Retrieved June 30, 2015.*

^ *"Trump Sells Miss Universe Organization to WME-IMG Talent Agency". The New York Times. September 15, 2015. Retrieved February 5, 2016.*

^ *Gitell, Seth (March 8, 2016). "I Survived Trump University". Politico. Retrieved March 18, 2016.*

^ *Cohan, William D. "Big Hair on Campus: Did Donald Trump Defraud Thousands of Real-Estate Students?". Vanity Fair. Retrieved March 6, 2016.*

^ Barbaro, Michael (May 19, 2011). _"New York Attorney General Is Investigating Trump's For-Profit School"_. **The New York Times.**

^ Jump up to:_a b_ Halperin, David (March 1, 2016). _"NY Court Refuses to Dismiss Trump University Case, Describes Fraud Allegations"_. **The Huffington Post.**

^ Freifeld, Karen (October 16, 2014). _"New York judge finds Donald Trump liable for unlicensed school"_. **Reuters.** Retrieved February 20,2015.

^ Jump up to:_a b_ Barbaro, Michael; Eder, Steve (May 31, 2016). _"Former Trump University Workers Call the School a 'Lie' and a 'Scheme' in Testimony"_. **The New York Times.** Retrieved March 24, 2018.

^ Lee, Michelle Ye Hee (February 27, 2016). _"Donald Trump's misleading claim that he's 'won most of' lawsuits over Trump University"_. **The Washington Post.** Retrieved February 27, 2016.

^ McCoy, Kevin (August 26, 2013). _"Trump faces two-front legal fight over 'university'"_. **USA Today.**

^ Rappeport, Alan (June 3, 2016). _"That Judge Attacked by Donald Trump? He's Faced a Lot Worse"_. **The New York Times.** Retrieved June 4, 2016.

^ Ford, Matt (June 3, 2016). _"Why Is Donald Trump So Angry at Judge Gonzalo Curiel?"_. The Atlantic. Retrieved June 3, 2016.

^ Eder, Steve (November 18, 2016). _"Donald Trump Agrees to Pay $25 Million in Trump University Settlement"_. **The New York Times**. Retrieved November 18, 2016.

^ _"Donald Trump Agrees to Pay $25 Million in Trump University Settlement"_. **New York Daily News**. November 18, 2016. Retrieved November 18, 2016.

^ Tigas, Mike; Wei, Sisi. _"Nonprofit Explorer – ProPublica"_. **ProPublica**. Retrieved September 9, 2016.

^ _"Donald J Trump Foundation Inc – GuideStar Profile"_. **GuideStar**. Retrieved September 9, 2016.

^ Fahrenthold, David A. (September 1, 2016). _"Trump pays IRS a penalty for his foundation violating rules with gift to aid Florida attorney general"_. **The Washington Post**.

^ Jump up to:[a] [b] [c] Fahrenthold, David A.; Helderman, Rosalind S. (April 10, 2016). _"Missing from Trump's list of charitable giving: His own personal cash"_. **The Washington Post**.

^ Solnik, Claude. "Taking a peek at Trump's (foundation) tax returns", **Long Island Business News** (September 15, 2016): "charitable giving to conservative political groups, healthcare and sports-related charities."

^ Fahrenthold, David A.; Rindler, Danielle (August 18, 2016). _"Searching for evidence of Trump's personal giving"_. **The Washington Post**.

^ Qiu, Linda. _"Yes, Donald Trump has given to the Clinton Foundation"_. **PolitiFact**. Retrieved October 17, 2018.

^ Cillizza, Chris; Fahrenthold, David A. _(September 15, 2016). "Meet the reporter who's giving Donald Trump fits"_. **The Washington Post**.

^ Jump up to:_a b_ Bradner, Eric; Frehse, Rob (September 14, 2016). _"NY attorney general is investigating Trump Foundation practices"_. **CNN**. Retrieved September 25, 2016. The Post had reported that the recipients of five charitable contributions listed by the Trump Foundation had no record of receiving those donations. But the newspaper updated its report after CNN questioned the accuracy of three of the five donations it had cited.

^ Toh, Michelle (September 14, 2016). _"Trump Foundation Falls Under Investigation By New York Attorney General"_. **Fortune**. Retrieved September 27, 2016.

^ Fahrenthold, David A. _(October 3, 2016). "Trump Foundation ordered to stop fundraising by N.Y. attorney general's office"_. **The Washington Post**.

^ Jacobs, Ben _(December 24, 2016). "Donald Trump to dissolve his charitable foundation after mounting complaints"_. **The Guardian**. Retrieved December 25, 2016.

^ _"Donald Trump is shutting down his charitable foundation"_. **NBC News**. November 20, 2017. Retrieved November 28, 2017.

^ Isidore, Chris; Schuman, Melanie (June 14, 2018). *"New York attorney general sues Trump Foundation"*. *CNN*. Retrieved June 15,2018.

^ Thomsen, Jacqueline (June 14, 2018). *"Five things to know about the lawsuit against the Trump Foundation"*. *The Hill*. Retrieved June 15,2018.

^ Jump up to:*a b* Geewax, Marilyn (January 20, 2018). *"Trump Has Revealed Assumptions About Handling Presidential Wealth, Businesses"*. *NPR*.

^ Jump up to:*a b* *"A list of Trump's potential conflicts"*. *BBC Online*. April 18, 2017.

^ Jump up to:*a b c* Venook, Jeremy (August 9, 2017). *"Trump's Interests vs. America's, Dubai Edition"*. *The Atlantic*.

^ Jump up to:*a b* LaFraniere, Sharon (January 25, 2018). *"Lawsuit on Trump Emoluments Violations Gains Traction in Court"*. *The New York Times*. Retrieved January 25, 2018.

^ LaFraniere, Sharon (March 28, 2018). *"Lawsuit Over Trump's Ties to His Businesses Is Allowed to Advance"*. *The New York Times*. Retrieved January 3, 2019.

^ LaFraniere, Sharon (July 25, 2018). *"In Ruling Against Trump, Judge Defines Anticorruption Clauses in Constitution for First Time"*. *The New York Times*. Retrieved January 3, 2019.

^ LaFraniere, Sharon (November 2, 2018). "Judge Orders Evidence to Be Gathered in Emoluments Case Against Trump". The New York Times. Retrieved January 3, 2019.

^ O'Connell, Jonathan; Marimow, Ann E.; Fahrenthold, David A. "2 attorneys general issue subpoenas to Trump entities in Washington hotel case". Chicago Tribune. Retrieved January 4, 2019.

^ LaFraniere, Sharon (December 17, 2018). "Justice Department Asks Court to Halt Emoluments Case Against Trump". The New York Times. Retrieved January 4, 2019.

^ Wolfe, Jan (December 21, 2018). "U.S. appeals court grants Trump request for halt to emoluments case". Reuters. Retrieved January 3,2019.

^ Jump up to:a b Kruse, Michael (June 1, 2018). "He Pretty Much Gave In to Whatever They Asked For". Politico. Retrieved June 11, 2018.

^ Jump up to:a b c Mayer, Jane (July 25, 2016). "Donald Trump's Ghostwriter Tells All". The New Yorker. Retrieved June 19, 2017.

^ Mayer, Jane (July 20, 2016). "Donald Trump Threatens the Ghostwriter of "The Art of the Deal"". The New Yorker. Retrieved June 11, 2018.

^ Lozada, Carlos (July 30, 2015). "I just binge-read eight books by Donald Trump. Here's what I learned". The Washington Post. Retrieved June 18, 2017.

^ "Donald Trump bio". WWE. Retrieved March 14, 2015.

^ Jump up to:*a b c* Kelly, Chris; Wetherbee, Brandon (December 9, 2016). "Heel in Chief". Slate. Retrieved March 5, 2019.

^ Graser, Marc (February 25, 2013). "Donald Trump Enters WWE's Hall of Fame". Variety. Retrieved March 5, 2019.

^ Jump up to:*a b* Koffler, Jacob (August 7, 2015). "Donald Trump's 16 Biggest Business Failures and Successes". Time.

^ Jump up to:*a b* Grynbaum, Michael M.; Parker, Ashley (July 16, 2016). "Donald Trump the Political Showman, Born on 'The Apprentice'". The New York Times. Retrieved July 8, 2018.

^ Nussbaum, Emily (July 31, 2017). "The TV That Created Donald Trump". The New Yorker. Retrieved July 8, 2018.

^ Feely, Paul (February 27, 2015). "Trump won't renew 'Apprentice' so that he might focus on a presidential run". New Hampshire Union Leader. Archived from the original on July 10, 2015. Retrieved July 28, 2015.

^ Byers, Dylan (March 18, 2015). "NBC still planning for 'Apprentice,' despite Donald Trump's presidential claims". Politico. Retrieved July 28, 2015.

^ Siegel, Jacob (June 29, 2015). "NBC Just Fired Presidential Hopeful Donald Trump from 'The Apprentice'". Boy Genius Report. Retrieved July 28, 2015.

^ Fischer, Russ (November 30, 2009). "Casting Notes: Donald Trump Cameos in Wall Street 2; Jeremy Piven and Kate Walsh go to Canada". Slashfilm.com. Retrieved September 18, 2018.

^ LaFrance, Adrienne (December 21, 2015). "Three Decades of Donald Trump Film and TV Cameos". The Atlantic.

^ Lockett, Dee (June 21, 2016). "Yes, Donald Trump Did Actually Play a Spoiled Rich Kid's Dad in The Little Rascals". Vulture. Retrieved July 14, 2018.

^ Shanley, Patrick (September 15, 2016). "Emmys Flashback: When Trump Sang the 'Green Acres' Theme in Overalls". The Hollywood Reporter. Retrieved July 14, 2018.

^ Nededog, Jethro (December 15, 2016). "Megan Mullally regrets helping Trump with a 'landslide' win: 'I'm not giving him any points'". Business Insider. Retrieved July 14, 2018.

^ Jump up to:a b Handel, Jonathan (July 22, 2015). "How Did Donald Trump Get a $110K SAG Pension?". The Hollywood Reporter. Retrieved January 17, 2016.

^ Palmeri, Christopher (July 22, 2015). "Inside Donald Trump's $110,000 Hollywood Pension Disclosure". Bloomberg News. Retrieved January 17, 2016.

^ Handler, Jonathan (June 16, 2017). "Trump Ethics Filing Reveals SAG Pension, Entertainment Income". The Hollywood Reporter. Retrieved July 14, 2018.

^ Kranish & Fisher 2017, p. 166.

^ Massie, Christopher; Kaczynski, Andrew (March 16, 2016). "There Are Hours Of Audio Of Donald Trump's Nationally Syndicated Radio Show In The 2000s". BuzzFeed News. Retrieved October 21, 2018.

^ Silverman, Stephen M. (April 29, 2004). "The Donald to Get New Wife, Radio Show". People. Retrieved November 19, 2013.

^ Tedeschi, Bob (February 6, 2006). "Now for Sale Online, the Art of the Vacation". The New York Times. Retrieved October 21, 2018.

^ Grynbaum, Michael M. (July 1, 2018). "Fox News Once Gave Trump a Perch. Now It's His Bullhorn". The New York Times. Retrieved July 7, 2018.

^ Gertz, Matthew (January 5, 2018). "I've Studied the Trump-Fox Feedback Loop for Months. It's Crazier Than You Think". Politico. Retrieved July 8, 2018.

^ Montopoli, Brian (April 1, 2011). "Donald Trump gets regular Fox News spot". CBS News. Retrieved July 7, 2018.

^ Grossman, Matt; Hopkins, David A. (September 9, 2016). "How the conservative media is taking over the Republican Party". The Washington Post. Retrieved October 19, 2018.

^ Langer, Gary (November 5, 2017). "ABC News/Washington Post Poll: A year after his surprise election, 65 percent say

Trump's achieved little" (PDF). Langer Research Associates. Retrieved November 5,2017.

^ Jones, Jeffrey M. (October 20, 2017). "Trump Job Approval Slips to 36.9% in His Third Quarter". Gallup. Retrieved October 20, 2017.

^ Balz, Dan; Clement, Scott (November 5, 2017). "Poll: Trump's performance lags behind even tepid public expectations". The Washington Post.

^ Wike, Richard; Stokes, Bruce; Poushter, Jacob; Fetterolf, Janell (June 26, 2017). "U.S. Image Suffers as Publics Around World Question Trump's Leadership". Pew Research Center. Retrieved January 11, 2018.

^ "Poll: Trump hits new low after Charlottesville". Politico. August 23, 2017.

^ Silver, Nate (December 20, 2018). "How popular is Donald Trump? – How Trump compares with past presidents". FiveThirtyEight. Retrieved December 21, 2018.

^ Kwong, Jessica (January 16, 2019). "Donald Trump Approval Rating Average in First Two Years is Lowest For Any President Since World War II". Newsweek. Retrieved January 25, 2019.

^ Bach, Natasha (December 28, 2017). "Trump Is the Only Elected U.S. President Not to Be Named America's Most Admired Man In His First Year". Fortune. Retrieved June 11, 2018.

^ Jump up to:_a_ _b_ _"Most Admired Man and Woman"_. _Gallup_. Retrieved June 12,2018.

^ Shamsian, Jacob. _"Barack and Michelle Obama top Gallup's list of most-admired men and women in the world, trouncing the Trumps"_. _Business Insider_. Retrieved January 2, 2019.

^ Jump up to:_a_ _b_ Qiu, Linda (April 29, 2017). _"Fact-Checking President Trump Through His First 100 Days"_. _The New York Times_.

^ Kessler, Glenn; Lee, Michelle Ye Hee (May 1, 2017). _"President Trump's first 100 days: The fact check tally"_. _The Washington Post_.

^ Qiu, Linda (June 22, 2017). _"In One Rally, 12 Inaccurate Claims From Trump"_. _The New York Times_.

^ McGranahan, Carole (May 2017). _"An anthropology of lying: Trump and the political sociality of moral outrage"_. _American Ethnologist_. 44(2): 243–248. doi:10.1111/amet.12475.

^ Kessler, Glenn (December 30, 2018). _"A year of unprecedented deception: Trump averaged 15 false claims a day in 2018"_. _The Washington Post_. Retrieved January 10, 2019.

^ Jump up to:_a_ _b_ Glasser, Susan (August 3, 2018). _"It's True: Trump Is Lying More, and He's Doing It on Purpose"_. _The New Yorker_. Retrieved January 10, 2019.

^ **Jump up to:** [a] [b] **Konnikova, Maria** *(January 20, 2017).* *"Trump's Lies vs. Your Brain".* **Politico.** *Retrieved March 31, 2018.*

^ **Stolberg, Sheryl Gay** *(August 7, 2017).* *"Many Politicians Lie. But Trump Has Elevated the Art of Fabrication".* **The New York Times.** *Retrieved February 19, 2019.*

^ Lee, Michelle Ye Hee; **Kessler, Glenn**; Kelly, Meg *(October 10, 2017).* *"President Trump has made 1,318 false or misleading claims over 263 days".* **The Washington Post.** *Retrieved November 5, 2017.*

^ **Kessler, Glenn**; Rizzo, Salvador; Kelly, Meg *(March 4, 2019).* *"President Trump has made 9,014 false or misleading claims over 773 days".* **The Washington Post.** *Retrieved March 4, 2019.*

^ **Kessler, Glenn**; Rizzo, Salvador; Kelly, Meg *(November 2, 2018).* *"President Trump has made 6,420 false or misleading claims over 649 days".* **The Washington Post.** *Retrieved November 2, 2018.*

^ **Kessler, Glenn**; Rizzo, Salvador; Kelly, Meg *(September 13, 2018).* *"President Trump has made more than 5,000 false or misleading claims".* **The Washington Post.** *Retrieved October 16, 2018.*

^ Feldman, Josh *(December 31, 2018).* *"'Unprecedented Deception': Washington Post Analysis Finds Trump Averaged*

15 False Claims a Day in 2018". *Mediaite*. Retrieved December 31, 2018.

^ * *Baker, Peter* (January 12, 2018). *"A President Who Fans, Rather Than Douses, the Nation's Racial Fires"*. *The New York Times*.

Warren, Dorian (January 11, 2018). *"We Must Denounce Trump's Racist Actions, Not Just His Racist Words"*. *The Nation*. Retrieved January 12, 2018.

*D'Antonio, Michael* (June 7, 2016). *"Is Donald Trump Racist? Here's What the Record Shows"*. *Fortune*. Retrieved January 12,2018.

Berney, Jesse (August 15, 2017). *"Trump's Long History of Racism"*. *Rolling Stone*. Retrieved January 12, 2018.

^ **Jump up to:**_a b_ *"Every moment in Trump's charged relationship with race"*. *PBS NewsHour*. January 12, 2018. Retrieved January 13, 2018.

^ Lopez, German (January 14, 2018). *"Donald Trump's long history of racism, from the 1970s to 2018"*. *Vox*.

^ Sarlin, Benjy (October 7, 2016). *"Donald Trump Says Central Park Five Are Guilty, Despite DNA Evidence"*. *NBC News*. Retrieved January 13, 2018.

^ *Parker, Ashley*; Eder, Steve (July 2, 2016). *"Inside the Six Weeks Donald Trump Was a Nonstop 'Birther'"*. *The New York Times*.

^ Abramson, Alana (September 16, 2016). _"How Donald Trump Perpetuated the 'Birther' Movement for Years"_. **ABC News**.

^ Shear, Michael D. (April 27, 2011). _"With Document, Obama Seeks to End 'Birther' Issue"_. **The New York Times**. Retrieved August 27,2016.

^ Madison, Lucy (April 27, 2011). _"Trump takes credit for Obama birth certificate release, but wonders 'is it real?'"_. **CBS News**. Retrieved May 9, 2011.

^ _"Donald J. Trump – Biography"_. **The Trump Organization**. _Archived_ from the original on August 28, 2016. Retrieved August 27,2016. In 2011, after failed attempts by both Senator McCain and Hillary Clinton, Mr. Trump single handedly forced President Obama to release his birth certificate, which was lauded by large segments of the political community.

^ Keneally, Meghan (September 18, 2015). _"Donald Trump's History of Raising Birther Questions About President Obama"_. **ABC News**. Retrieved August 27, 2016.

^ Haberman, Maggie; Rappeport, Alan (September 16, 2016). _"Trump Drops False 'Birther' Theory, but Floats a New One: Clinton Started It"_. **The New York Times**.

^ Schaffner, Brian F.; Macwilliams, Matthew; Nteta, Tatishe (March 2018). "Understanding White Polarization in the 2016 Vote for President: The Sobering Role of Racism and

Sexism". *Political Science Quarterly*. 133 (1): 9–34. *doi*:10.1002/polq.12737.

^ Jump up to:*a b* *"Donald Trump Presidential Campaign Announcement Full Speech (C-SPAN)"* (Video). YouTube. C-SPAN. June 16, 2015. Retrieved June 2, 2018.

^ Jump up to:*a b* Trump, Donald (June 16, 2015). *Here's Donald Trump's Presidential Announcement Speech* (Speech). Trump Tower, New York City – via *Time*. Transcript of full speech

^ *"Here Are All the Times Donald Trump Insulted Mexico"*. *Time*. August 31, 2016. Retrieved January 13, 2018.

^ *"Five Insults Donald Trump Has Fired At Mexicans In The Presidential Race"*. *Sky News*. September 1, 2016. Retrieved January 13, 2018.

^ Steinhauer, Jennifer; Martin, Jonathan; Herszenhorn, David M. (June 7, 2016). *"Paul Ryan Calls Donald Trump's Attack on Judge 'Racist,' but Still Backs Him"*. *The New York Times*. Retrieved January 13,2018.

^ Merica, Dan (August 26, 2017). *"Trump: 'Both sides' to blame for Charlottesville"*. *CNN*. Retrieved January 13, 2018.

^ Kiely, Eugene (January 16, 2018). *"What Did Trump Say at Immigration Meeting?"*. *FactCheck.org*. Retrieved February 19, 2018. Durbin quoted the president as saying of African nations, 'Those shitholes send us the people that they don't want.'

^ Beauchamp, Zack (January 11, 2018). _"Trump's "shithole countries" comment exposes the core of Trumpism"_. _Vox_. Retrieved January 11, 2018.

^ _Dawsey, Josh_ (January 11, 2018). _"Trump's history of making offensive comments about nonwhite immigrants"_. _The Washington Post_. Retrieved January 11, 2018.

^ Weaver, Aubree Eliza (January 12, 2018). _"Trump's 'shithole' comment denounced across the globe"_. _Politico_. Retrieved January 13, 2018.

^ Pace, Julie (January 12, 2018). _"Trump's own words revive debate over whether he's racist"_. _Associated Press_.

^ _"Donald Trump denies being a racist after 'shithole' row"_. _BBC Online_. January 15, 2018. Retrieved January 15, 2018.

^ _Wintour, Patrick_; _Burke, Jason_; Livsey, Anna (January 13, 2018). _"'There's no other word but racist': Trump's global rebuke for 'shithole' remark"_. _The Guardian_. Retrieved January 13, 2018.

^ Raymond, Adam K. (November 30, 2017). _"British MPs Condemn 'Racist,' 'Incompetent' Trump for Endorsing 'Vile Fascist' Group"_. _New York_. Retrieved January 13, 2018.

^ Salama, Vivian (January 12, 2018). _"Trump's history of breaking decorum with remarks on race, ethnicity"_. _NBC News_. Retrieved January 13, 2018.

^ Nichols, Laura (June 29, 2017). *"Poll: Majority of Trump Voters Say His Political Correctness Is 'About Right'"*. *Morning Consult*. Retrieved January 13, 2018.

^ *"Trump's 'shithole' comment is his new rock bottom"*. *CNN*. January 12, 2018. Retrieved January 13, 2018.

^ Jump up to:*a b* McElwee, Sean; McDaniel, Jason (May 8, 2017). *"Economic Anxiety Didn't Make People Vote Trump, Racism Did"*. *The Nation*. Retrieved January 13, 2018.

^ Lopez, German (December 15, 2017). *"The past year of research has made it very clear: Trump won because of racial resentment"*. *Vox*. Retrieved January 14, 2018.

^ *"Harsh Words For U.S. Family Separation Policy, Quinnipiac University National Poll Finds; Voters Have Dim View Of Trump, Dems On Immigration"*. *Quinnipiac University Polling Institute*. July 3, 2018. Retrieved July 5, 2018.

^ Marcin, Tim (July 5, 2018). *"44 Percent Of White Americans Think Donald Trump Is Racist, New Poll Finds"*. *Newsweek*. Retrieved July 5, 2018.

^ Parnes, Amy (April 28, 2018). *"Trump's love-hate relationship with the press"*. *The Hill*. Retrieved July 4, 2018.

^ Ingram, Mathew (March 1, 2016). *"Love and Hate: The Media's Co-Dependent Relationship With Donald Trump"*. *Fortune*. Retrieved July 4, 2018.

^ "Trump's love-hate relationship with media intensifies". *Arab News*. January 24, 2017. Retrieved July 4, 2018.

^ D'Antonio, Michael (July 10, 2016). "Who is Donald Trump?"(Interview). *CNN*. Retrieved July 4, 2018.

^ Jump up to:*a b* Walsh, Kenneth T. (August 15, 2016). "Trump: Media Is 'Dishonest and Corrupt'". *U.S. News & World Report*. 'If the disgusting and corrupt media covered me honestly and didn't put false meaning into the words I say, I would be beating Hillary by 20 percent,' Trump also tweeted Sunday.

^ Bondarenko, Veronika. "Trump keeps saying 'enemy of the people' — but the phrase has a very ugly history". *Business Insider*. Retrieved October 25, 2017.

^ Jump up to:*a b* Cillizza, Chris (June 14, 2016). "This Harvard study is a powerful indictment of the media's role in Donald Trump's rise". *The Washington Post*.

^ Thomsen, Jacqueline. "'60 Minutes' correspondent: Trump said he attacks the press so no one believes negative coverage". *The Hill*. Retrieved May 23, 2018.

^ Bump, Philip (May 9, 2018). "Trump makes it explicit: Negative coverage of him is fake coverage". *The Washington Post*. Retrieved May 9, 2018.

^ _"Trump Calls Media 'Enemy Of The American People' In Latest Attack"_. San Francisco, California: KPIX-TV. _Associated Press_. February 17, 2017. Retrieved February 17, 2017.

^ Stelter, Brian; Collins, Kaitlan. _"Trump's latest shot at the press corps: 'Take away credentials?'"_. _CNNMoney_. Retrieved May 9, 2018.

^ Guess, Andrew; Nyhan, Brendan; Reifler, Jason (January 9, 2018). _"Selective Exposure to Misinformation: Evidence from the consumption of fake news during the 2016 U.S. presidential campaign"_ (PDF). Dartmouth.edu. Retrieved February 4, 2018.

^ H. Allcott; M.Gentzkow (2017). _"Social Media and Fake News in the 2016 election"_ (PDF). Journal of Economic Perspectives. 31 (2): 211–236. doi:10.1257/jep.31.2.211. Retrieved May 3, 2017.

^ Sarlin, Benjy (January 14, 2018). _"'Fake news' went viral in 2016. This professor studied who clicked"_. NBC News. Retrieved February 4, 2018.

^ Garber, Megan (April 3, 2017). _"'Donald Trump' Gets a Comedy Central Series"_. The Atlantic. Retrieved April 4, 2017.

^ Jump up to:_a b_ McCann, Allison (July 14, 2016). _"Hip-Hop Is Turning On Donald Trump"_. FiveThirtyEight.

^ mantolius (February 25, 2016). _25 years of Donald Trump mentions in hip hop_. Retrieved November 15, 2016 – via YouTube.

^ Beaumont-Thomas, Ben (December 20, 2017). "Eminem attacks Donald Trump: 'He's got people brainwashed'". *The Guardian*. Retrieved August 27, 2018.

^ Zaru, Deena (July 28, 2018). "Why top protest songs in hip-hop don't mention Donald Trump: 'He's irrelevant to the movement'". *ABC News*. Retrieved August 27, 2018.

^ Steeve, Dustin (January 23, 2017). "Donald Trump's Social Media Use Is Key To Sidelining The Press". *The Federalist*. Retrieved May 31, 2017.

^ Qui, Linda (April 27, 2017). "Fact-Checking President Trump Through His First 100 Days". *The New York Times*. Retrieved June 25, 2017.

^ Kessler, Glenn; Lee, Michelle Ye Hee (May 1, 2017). "Fact Checker Analysis – President Trump's first 100 days: The fact check tally". *The Washington Post*. Retrieved June 25, 2017.

^ Drinkard, Jim; Woodward, Calvin (June 24, 2017). "Fact check: Trump's missions unaccomplished despite his claims". *Chicago Tribune*. Retrieved June 25, 2017.

^ "Donald Trump: Robert Gordon University strips honorary degree". *BBC Online*. May 3, 2018. Retrieved December 9, 2015.

^ Gibbs, Nancy (December 7, 2016). "Why Donald Trump is TIME's Person of the Year". *Time*. Retrieved December 7, 2016.

^ Kim, Eun Kyung (December 7, 2016). _"Donald Trump: Mitt Romney is still in the running for secretary of state"_. _Today_. Retrieved December 7, 2016.

^ Davis, Julie Hirschfeld (December 7, 2016). _"Mitt Romney Still in the Running for Secretary of State, Trump Says"_. _The New York Times_. Retrieved December 7, 2016.

^ Luce, Edward (December 12, 2016). _"FT Person of the Year: Donald Trump"_. _Financial Times_. Retrieved December 17, 2017.

^ _"The World's Most Powerful People"_. _Forbes_. December 2016. Retrieved December 14, 2016.

^ Jump up to:_a_ _b_ Gillin, Joshua (August 24, 2015). _"Bush says Trump was a Democrat longer than a Republican 'in the last decade'"_. _PolitiFact_. Retrieved March 18, 2017.

^ Kurtzleben, Danielle (July 28, 2015). _"Most of Donald Trump's Political Money Went To Democrats — Until 5 Years Ago"_. _NPR_. Retrieved September 5, 2018.

^ Oreskes, Michael (September 2, 1987). _"Trump Gives a Vague Hint of Candidacy"_. _The New York Times_. Retrieved February 17, 2016.

^ Jump up to:_a_ _b_ Butterfield, Fox (November 18, 1987). _"Trump Urged To Head Gala Of Democrats"_. _The New York Times_.

^ Kranish & Fisher 2017, p. 3.

^ Gallup 1990, p. 3.

^ Jump up to:<sup>a b</sup> Trump, Donald J. (February 19, 2000). "What I Saw at the Revolution". The New York Times.

^ Jump up to:<sup>a b</sup> Winger, Richard (December 25, 2011). "Donald Trump Ran For President in 2000 in Several Reform Party Presidential Primaries". Ballot Access News.

^ Johnson, Glen. "Donald Trump eyeing a run at the White House". Standard-Speaker. Hazelton, Pennsylvania.

^ "CA Secretary of State – Primary 2000 – Statewide Totals". ca.gov. Archived from the original on February 16, 2015. Retrieved July 1,2015.

^ Travis, Shannon (May 17, 2011). "Was he ever serious? How Trump strung the country along, again". CNN. Retrieved June 7, 2015.

^ "Donald Trump in the No Spin Zone". Fox News. September 22, 2005. Retrieved June 17, 2018.

^ "Trump endorses McCain". CNN. September 18, 2008. Retrieved July 12, 2016.

^ "GOProud Leads 'Trump in 2012' Movement at CPAC". Towleroad.com. February 10, 2011.

^ Jump up to:<sup>a b</sup> CNN Political Unit (May 16, 2011). "Trump not running for president". CNN. Retrieved May 16, 2011.

^ *"Trump endorses Romney, cites tough China position and electability"*. **Fox News**. February 2, 2012.

^ **MacAskill, Ewen** (May 16, 2011). *"Donald Trump bows out of 2012 US presidential election race"*. **The Guardian**. Few US political commentators took his campaign seriously and many suggested he was only in it for the publicity.

^ Grier, Peter (February 10, 2011). *"Donald Trump says he might run for president. Three reasons he won't"*. **The Christian Science Monitor**. Retrieved April 21, 2011.

^ Linkins, Jason (February 11, 2011). *"Donald Trump Brings His 'Pretend To Run For President' Act To CPAC"*. **The Huffington Post**. Retrieved April 21, 2011.

^ **Haberman, Maggie**; Burns, Alexander (March 12, 2016). *"Donald Trump's Presidential Run Began in an Effort to Gain Stature"*. **The New York Times**. Retrieved April 13, 2018.

^ Moody, Chris (March 5, 2013). *"Donald Trump to address CPAC"*. **Yahoo! News**. Retrieved March 6, 2013.

^ Madison, Lucy (March 15, 2013). *"Trump: Immigration reform a "suicide mission" for GOP"*. **CBS News**.

^ Amira, Dan (March 15, 2013). *"Photos of Donald Trump Delivering His Self-Aggrandizing CPAC Speech to a Half-Empty Ballroom"*. **New York** (magazine).

^ *"Trump researching 2016 run"*. **Page Six**. May 27, 2013.

^ Spector, Joseph (October 14, 2013). _"N.Y. Republicans want Donald Trump to run for governor"_. _USA Today_. Retrieved October 31, 2013.

^ Miller, Jake (February 13, 2014). _"Trump trumped by Cuomo in N.Y. governor race, poll finds"_. _CBS News_. Retrieved February 9, 2017.

^ Feely, Paul (February 27, 2015). _"Trump won't renew 'Apprentice' so that he might focus on a presidential run"_. _New Hampshire Union Leader_. Archived from _the original_ on July 12, 2018. Retrieved July 22, 2018.

^ Lerner, Adam B. (June 16, 2015). _"The 10 best lines from Donald Trump's announcement speech"_. _Politico_. Retrieved June 7, 2018.

^ Donald Trump [@realDonaldTrump] (September 5, 2015). _"By self-funding my campaign, I am not controlled by my donors, special interests or lobbyists. I am only working for the people of the U.S.!"_(Tweet). Retrieved June 7, 2018 – via _Twitter_.

^ Graham, David A. (May 13, 2016). _"The Lie of Trump's 'Self-Funding' Campaign"_. _The Atlantic_. Retrieved June 7, 2018.

^ Linshi, Jack (July 7, 2015). _"More People Are Running for Presidential Nomination Than Ever"_. _Time_. Retrieved February 14,2016.

^ Reeve, Elspeth (October 27, 2015). _"How Donald Trump Evolved From a Joke to an Almost Serious Candidate"_. _The New Republic_. Retrieved July 23, 2018.

^ Bump, Philip (March 23, 2016). _"Why Donald Trump is poised to win the nomination and lose the general election, in one poll"_. _The Washington Post_.

^ Nussbaum, Matthew (May 3, 2016). _"RNC Chairman: Trump is our nominee"_. _Politico_. Retrieved May 4, 2016.

^ Hartig, Hannah; Lapinski, John; Psyllos, Stephanie (July 19, 2016). _"Poll: Clinton and Trump Now Tied as GOP Convention Kicks Off"_. _NBC News_.

^ _"2016 General Election: Trump vs. Clinton"_. _The Huffington Post_. Retrieved October 3, 2016.

^ _"General Election: Trump vs. Clinton"_. RealClearPolitics. Retrieved October 3, 2016.

^ Levingston, Ivan (July 15, 2016). _"Donald Trump officially names Mike Pence for VP"_. _CNBC_.

^ _"Trump closes the deal, becomes Republican nominee for president"_. _Fox News_. July 19, 2016.

^ Timm, Jane C. (July 17, 2016). _"9 Elephants in the Room at RNC: Who's Missing From the Speakers List"_. _NBC News_. Retrieved August 16, 2016.

^ Raju, Manu (May 5, 2016). "Flake, McCain split over backing Trump". CNN. Retrieved May 7, 2016.

^ Battaglio, Stephen (July 22, 2016). "35 million TV viewers watch Donald Trump's acceptance speech at GOP convention". Los Angeles Times. Retrieved July 23, 2016.

^ Agiesta, Jennifer. "Trump bounces into the lead". CNN. Retrieved August 3, 2016.

^ Newport, Frank (July 26, 2016). "For First Time, Trump's Image on Par With Clinton's". Gallup News. Retrieved August 3, 2016.

^ "2016 Presidential Debate Schedule". September 23, 2015. Retrieved September 30, 2016.

^ Stelter, Brian (September 27, 2016). "Debate breaks record as most-watched in U.S. history". CNNMoney. Retrieved September 30, 2016.

^ "US presidential debate: Trump won't commit to accept election result". BBC News. October 20, 2016. Retrieved October 27, 2016.

^ "How US media reacted to the third presidential debate". Australian Broadcasting Corporation. October 20, 2016. Retrieved October 27, 2016.

^ "Trump's promises before and after election". BBC Online. September 19, 2017.

^ Edwards, Jason A. (2018). "Make America Great Again: Donald Trump and Redefining the U.S. Role in the World". *Communication Quarterly*. 66 (2): 176. doi:10.1080/01463373.2018.1438485. ISSN 0146-3373. On the campaign trail, Trump repeatedly called North Atlantic Treaty Organization (NATO) 'obsolete,'

^ Muller, Jan-Werner (2016). What Is Populism?. *University of Pennsylvania Press*. p. 101. ISBN 978-0-8122-9378-4.

^ Kazin, Michael (March 22, 2016). "How Can Donald Trump and Bernie Sanders Both Be 'Populist'?". *The New York Times Magazine*.

^ Becker, Bernie (February 13, 2016). "Trump's 6 populist positions". *Politico*.

^ "Tax Reform | Donald J Trump for President". Donaldjtrump.com. Archived from the original on January 4, 2016. Retrieved January 6,2016.

^ Ehrenfreund, Max (December 16, 2015). "Liberals will love something Donald Trump said last night". *The Washington Post*.

^ Sharman, Jon (December 21, 2016). "Democrats can finally agree with Donald Trump on something". *The Independent*. Retrieved December 21, 2016.

^ Williams, Mason B. (January 7, 2017). "Would Trump's Infrastructure Plan Fix America's Cities?". *The Atlantic*.

^ *Shafer, Jack (May 2016). "Did We Create Trump?". Politico. ... Trump's outrageous comments about John McCain, Muslims, the 14th Amendment and all the rest ...*

^ Trump & Schwartz 2009, p. 56.

^ *Fahrenthold, David A. (August 17, 2015). "20 times Donald Trump has changed his mind since June". The Washington Post.*

^ *Hensch, Mark (July 12, 2015). "'Meet the Press' tracks Trump's flip-flops". The Hill.*

^ **Jump up to:**ᵃ ᵇ *Noah, Timothy (July 26, 2015). "Will the real Donald Trump please stand up?". Politico.*

^ *Timm, Jane C. "A Full List of Donald Trump's Rapidly Changing Policy Positions". NBC News. Retrieved July 12, 2016.*

^ *Koppel, Ted (July 24, 2016). "Trump: "I feel I'm an honest person"". CBS News. 'Well, I think that I'm an honest person,' Trump said. 'I feel I'm an honest person. And I don't mind being criticized at all by the media, but I do wanna — you know, I do want them to be straight about it.'*

^ *Blake, Aaron (July 6, 2015). "Donald Trump is waging war on political correctness. And he's losing". The Washington Post.*

^ *"The 'King of Whoppers': Donald Trump". FactCheck.org. December 21, 2015.*

^ *Holan, Angie Drobnic*; Qiu, Linda (December 21, 2015). *"2015 Lie of the Year: the campaign misstatements of Donald Trump"*. *PolitiFact*.

^ *Farhi, Paul* (February 26, 2016). *"Think Trump's wrong? Fact checkers can tell you how often. (Hint: A lot.)"*. *The Washington Post*.

^ *Stelter, Brian* (September 26, 2016). *"The weekend America's newspapers called Donald Trump a liar"*. *CNN*.

^ *McCammon, Sarah* (August 10, 2016). "Donald Trump's controversial speech often walks the line". *NPR*. *Many of Trump's opaque statements seem to rely on suggestion and innuendo.*

^ Jump up to:*a b* Flitter, Emily; Oliphant, James (August 28, 2015). *"Best president ever! How Trump's love of hyperbole could backfire"*. *Reuters*.

^ *Barkun, Michael* (2017). "President Trump and the Fringe". *Terrorism and Political Violence*. 29 (3): 437. *doi*:10.1080/09546553.2017.1313649. *ISSN* 1556-1836.

^ *Lopez, German* (August 14, 2017). *"We need to stop acting like Trump isn't pandering to white supremacists"*. *Vox*. Retrieved January 2, 2018.

^ *Blow, Charles M.* (September 18, 2017). *"Is Trump a White Supremacist?"*. *The New York Times*.

^ Kharakh, Ben; Primack, Dan (March 22, 2016). *"Donald Trump's Social Media Ties to White Supremacists"*. *Fortune*.

^ White, Daniel (January 26, 2016). *"Trump Criticized for Retweeting Racist Account"*. *Time*.

^ *"White Nationalists and the Alt-Right Celebrate Trump's Victory"*. *Southern Poverty Law Center*. Retrieved November 10, 2016.

^ Chan, Melissa (February 28, 2016). *"Donald Trump Refuses to Condemn KKK, Disavow David Duke Endorsement"*. *Time*. Retrieved January 20, 2018.

^ Lozada, Carlos (December 30, 2016). *"Donald Trump and the alt-right: A marriage of convenience"*. *The Washington Post*. Retrieved March 18, 2017.

^ Nelson, Libby (August 12, 2017). *""Why we voted for Donald Trump": David Duke explains the white supremacist Charlottesville protests"*. *Vox*. Retrieved August 18, 2018.

^ Cummings, William (August 15, 2017). *"Former KKK leader David Duke praises Trump for his 'courage'"*. *USA Today*. Retrieved August 18, 2018.

^ Haberman, Maggie (May 5, 2016). *"Donald Trump 'Disavows' David Duke's Remarks on 'Jewish Extremists'"*. *The New York Times*.

^ Jump up to:_a b_ *"Trump disavows 'alt-right' supporters"*. *BBC Online*. November 23, 2016.

^ Jump up to:<sup>a</sup> <sup>b</sup> Scott, Eugene (March 3, 2016). "Trump denounces David Duke, KKK". CNN.

^ Ohlheiser, Abby (June 3, 2016). "Anti-Semitic Trump supporters made a giant list of people to target with a racist meme". The Washington Post.

^ Weigel, David (August 20, 2016). "'Racialists' are cheered by Trump's latest strategy". The Washington Post. Retrieved June 23,2018.

^ Krieg, Gregory (August 25, 2016). "Clinton is attacking the 'Alt-Right' – What is it?". CNN. Retrieved August 25, 2016.

^ Sevastopulo, Demetri. "'Alt-right' movement makes mark on US presidential election". Financial Times.

^ Hawley, George (2017). Making Sense of the Alt-Right. Columbia University Press. ISBN 978-0-231-54600-3.

^ Wilson, Jason (November 15, 2016). "Clickbait scoops and an engaged alt-right: everything to know about Breitbart News". The Guardian. Retrieved November 18, 2016.

^ "Donald Trump's New York Times Interview: Full Transcript". The New York Times. November 23, 2016.

^ "Executive Branch Personnel Public Financial Disclosure Report (U.S. OGE Form 278e)" (PDF). U.S. Office of Government Ethics. July 15, 2015. Archived from the original (PDF) on July 23, 2015 – via Bloomberg Businessweek.

^ "Romney calls decision by Trump not to release tax returns 'disqualifying'". Fox News. May 11, 2016. Retrieved July 18, 2016.

^ Cillizza, Chris (April 17, 2018). "Happy Tax Day! Donald Trump still has never released his tax returns!". CNN. Retrieved June 9, 2018.

^ Rappeport, Alan (May 11, 2016). "Donald Trump Breaks With Recent History by Not Releasing Tax Returns". The New York Times. Retrieved July 19, 2016.

^ Disis, Jill (January 26, 2017). "Presidential tax returns: It started with Nixon. Will it end with Trump?". CNN. Retrieved June 9, 2018.

^ Erb, Kelly Phillips (August 12, 2016). "Trump Won't Release Tax Returns, Citing IRS Audit: Is It A Legitimate Excuse?". Forbes. Retrieved June 9, 2018.

^ Collinson, Stephen; Diamond, Jeremy; Khan, Hasan (February 25, 2016). "Donald Trump rejects Mitt Romney's ironic tax attack". CNN. Retrieved February 25, 2016.

^ Isidore, Chris; Sahadi, Jeanne (February 26, 2016). "Trump says he can't release tax returns because of audits". CNN. Retrieved February 26, 2016.

^ Browning, Lynnley (February 26, 2016). "Trump's 12 Years of Audits 'Very Unusual,' Ex-IRS Agent Says". Bloomberg News. Retrieved February 26, 2016.

^ *Kopan, Tal* (May 13, 2016). *"Trump on his tax rate: 'None of your business'"*. *CNN*.

^ *Wilhelm, Colin* (January 24, 2016). *"Trump vows to release his tax returns"*. *Politico*. Retrieved February 22, 2016. It's a little tax

^ *Zarroli, Jim* (February 26, 2016). *"Fact-Check: Donald Trump Can't Release His Taxes While Being Audited?"*. *NPR*.

^ *Eder, Steve; Twohey, Megan* (October 10, 2016). *"Donald Trump Acknowledges Not Paying Federal Income Taxes for Years"*. *The New York Times*.

^ *Politico Staff* (October 10, 2016). *"Full transcript: Second 2016 presidential debate"*. *Politico*.

^ *"Pages From Donald Trump's 1995 Income Tax Records"*. *The New York Times*. October 1, 2016.

^ *Barstow, David; Craig, Susanne;* Buettner, Russ; *Twohey, Megan*(October 1, 2016). *"Donald Trump Tax Records Show He Could Have Avoided Taxes for Nearly Two Decades, The Times Found"*. *The New York Times*.

^ *Baker, Peter;* Drucker, Jesse; *Craig, Susanne; Barstow, David* (March 15, 2017). *"Trump Wrote Off $100 Million in Business Losses in 2005"*. *The New York Times*. Retrieved March 15, 2017.

^ Jagoda, Naomi. _"WH releases Trump tax info ahead of MSNBC report: He paid $38M in federal taxes in '05"_. **The Hill**. Retrieved March 15, 2017.

^ Ford, Matt (December 7, 2017). _"What About the 19 Women Who Accused Trump of Sexual Misconduct?"_. **The Atlantic**.

^ **Byers, Dylan** (October 12, 2016). _"Donald Trump threatens to sue New York Times over sexual harassment report"_. **CNNMoney**. Retrieved October 13, 2016.

^ _"Trump demands NYT retracts 'libelous article' about alleged assault as new claims emerge"_. **Fox News**. October 13, 2016. Retrieved October 13, 2016.

^ Healy, Patrick; **Rappeport, Alan** (October 13, 2016). _"Donald Trump Calls Allegations by Women 'False Smears'"_. **The New York Times**. Retrieved October 13, 2016.

^ Sakuma, Amanda (October 26, 2016). _"Donald Trump Surrogates Have Their Own Baggage With Women Voters"_. **NBC News**. ... _newly unearthed audio recordings showed Trump bragging about forcibly kissing women and grabbing them by the genitals._

^ Jan, Tracy (October 14, 2016). _"More women accuse Trump of aggressive sexual behavior"_. **The Boston Globe**. _Trump has been confronted with a slew of allegations of sexual misconduct over the past week, starting with a report in The Washington Post of a 2005 tape featuring him bragging about forcibly kissing women and grabbing them by the genitals._

^ Lawler, David; Henderson, Barney; Allen, Nick; Sherlock, Ruth (October 13, 2016). _"US presidential debate recap: Polls split on whether Donald Trump or Hillary Clinton won poisonous argument"_. _The Daily Telegraph_. ... it was a matter of minutes before the lewd tape, in which Mr. Trump brags about 'grabbing p----' and forcibly kissing women, was brought up.

^ Jump up to:_a b_ Timm, Jane C. (October 7, 2016). _"Trump caught on hot mic making lewd comments about women in 2005"_. _NBC News_. Retrieved June 10, 2018.

^ Burns, Alexander; Haberman, Maggie; Martin, Jonathan (October 7, 2016). _"Donald Trump Apology Caps Day of Outrage Over Lewd Tape"_. _The New York Times_. Retrieved October 8, 2016.

^ Jensen, Salvatore (October 8, 2016). _"Donald Trump's vulgar conversation about women caught on hot mic"_. _Cosumnes Connection_. Archived from _the original_ on October 9, 2016. Retrieved October 8, 2016.

^ Hagen, Lisa (October 7, 2016). _"Kaine on lewd Trump tapes: 'Makes me sick to my stomach'"_. _The Hill_. Retrieved October 8, 2016.

^ Stacey, Madison (October 8, 2016). _"Pence to fill in for Donald Trump Saturday following video leak"_. Indianapolis, Indiana: _WXIN-TV_. Retrieved October 8, 2016.

^ Blake, Aaron (October 8, 2016). "Here's the fast-growing list of Republicans calling for Donald Trump to drop out". *The Washington Post*. Retrieved October 8, 2016.

^ Nelson, Libby; Frostenson, Sarah (October 20, 2016). "A brief guide to the 17 women Trump has allegedly assaulted, groped or harassed". *Vox*. Retrieved October 21, 2016.

^ Helderman, Rosalind S. "The growing list of women who have stepped forward to accuse Trump of touching them inappropriately". *The Washington Post*. Retrieved October 16, 2016.

^ Stableford, Dylan (October 17, 2016). "The women who have accused Donald Trump". *Yahoo! News*. Retrieved October 18, 2016.

^ ""I never said I'm a perfect person," Trump says about lewd comments". *CBS News*. *Associated Press*. October 7, 2016. Retrieved December 11, 2016.

^ Schmidt, Kiersten; Andrews, Wilson (December 19, 2016). "A Historic Number of Electors Defected, and Most Were Supposed to Vote for Clinton". *The New York Times*. Retrieved January 31, 2017.

^ Desilver, Drew (December 20, 2017). "Trump's victory another example of how Electoral College wins are bigger than popular vote ones". *Pew Research Center*.

^ Thomas, G. Scott (2015). _Counting the Votes: A New Way to Analyze America's Presidential Elections_. ABC-CLIO. p. 125. ISBN 978-1-4408-3883-5.

^ Cheney, Kyle (December 14, 2016). _"Trump lawyer cites 1876 crisis to rebuke Electoral College suit"_. **Politico**.

^ _"Official 2016 Presidential General Election Results"_ (PDF). **Federal Election Commission**. December 2017. Retrieved February 12,2018.

^ Tani, Maxwell (November 9, 2016). _"Trump pulls off biggest upset in U.S. history"_. **Politico**. Retrieved November 9, 2016.

^ Cohn, Nate (November 9, 2016). _"Why Trump Won: Working-Class Whites"_. **The New York Times**. Retrieved November 9, 2016.

^ **Silver, Nate** (January 17, 2017). _"Can You Trust Trump's Approval Rating Polls?"_. **FiveThirtyEight**.

^ **Silver, Nate** (September 21, 2017). _"The Media Has A Probability Problem"_. **FiveThirtyEight**.

^ Martin, Emmie (January 23, 2017). _"Donald Trump is officially the richest US president in history"_. **Business Insider**. Retrieved September 9, 2017.

^ Weber, Peter (November 9, 2016). _"Donald Trump will be the first U.S. president with no government or military experience"_. **The Week**.

^ Yomtov, Jesse (November 8, 2016). *"Where Trump ranks among least experienced presidents"*. *USA Today*.

^ Jump up to:*a b* Crockett, Zachary (November 11, 2016). *"Donald Trump will be the only US president ever with no political or military experience"*. *Vox*. Retrieved January 3, 2017.

^ *"Will Trump Be The 44th Or 45th President? Yes And Yes NPR Ethics Handbook"*. *NPR*. Retrieved June 4, 2017.

^ Moyer, Justin Wm.; Starrs, Jenny; Larimer, Sarah (March 11, 2016). *"Trump supporter charged after sucker-punching protester at North Carolina rally"*. *The Washington Post*. Retrieved August 31, 2016.

^ Sullivan, Sean; Miller, Michael E. (June 3, 2016). *"Ugly, bloody scenes in San Jose as protesters attack Trump supporters outside rally"*. *The Washington Post*. Retrieved August 31, 2016.

^ Diamond, Jeremy (May 28, 2016). *"Pro-Trump, anti-Trump groups clash in San Diego"*. *CNN*. Retrieved August 31, 2016.

^ Cummings, William (November 11, 2016). *"Trump calls protests 'unfair' in first controversial tweet as president-elect"*. *USA Today*. Retrieved November 27, 2016.

^ Colson, Thomas (November 11, 2016). *"Trump says protesters have 'passion for our great country' after calling demonstrations 'very unfair'"*. *Business Insider*. Retrieved November 14, 2016.

^ Przybyla, Heidi M.; Schouten, Fredreka (January 22, 2017). "At 2.6 million strong, Women's Marches crush expectations". *USA Today* (online ed.). Retrieved January 22, 2017.

^ Buncombe, Andrew (January 22, 2017). "We asked ten people why they felt empowered wearing a pink 'pussy' hat". *The Independent*. Retrieved January 15, 2017.

^ "Here's your list of all the protests happening against the Muslim Ban – ThinkProgress". Thinkprogress.org. Retrieved September 18,2018.

^ Quigley, Aidan (January 25, 2017). "All of Trump's executive actions so far". *Politico*. Retrieved January 28, 2017.

^ Barnes, Robert (January 31, 2017). "Trump picks Colo. appeals court judge Neil Gorsuch for Supreme Court". *The Washington Post*. Retrieved February 1, 2017.

^ Andrews, Wilson; Parlapiano, Alicia (December 15, 2017). "What's in the Final Republican Tax Bill". *The New York Times*. Retrieved December 22, 2017.

^ Sherman, Natalie; Palumbo, Daniele (January 26, 2018). "Can Trump claim credit for bonus rush?". *BBC Online*.

^ Kurtzleben, Danielle. "CHARTS: See How Much Of GOP Tax Cuts Will Go To The Middle Class". *NPR*.

^ Seipel, Arnie; Kurtzleben, Danielle (December 20, 2017). "Trump Celebrates Legislative Win After Congress Passes $1.5 Trillion Tax Cut Bill". *NPR*.

^ Berman, Russell (December 12, 2017). "What's in—and Out of—the Final Republican Tax Bill". *The Atlantic*.

^ Schlesinger, Jacob M. (November 15, 2018). "Trump Forged His Ideas on Trade in the 1980s—And Never Deviated". *The Wall Street Journal*. Retrieved November 15, 2018.

^ "Lawrence Solomon: Donald Trump's protectionism fits right in with Republicans". Retrieved July 22, 2016.

^ Epstein, Reid J.; Nelson, Colleen McCain (June 28, 2016). "Donald Trump Lays Out Protectionist Views in Trade Speech". *The Wall Street Journal* (subscription required). Retrieved July 22, 2016.

^ Appelbaum, Binyamin (March 10, 2016). "On Trade, Donald Trump Breaks With 200 Years of Economic Orthodoxy". *The New York Times*. Retrieved July 22, 2016.

^ "Trump calls NAFTA a "disaster"". *CBS News*. September 25, 2015.

^ "Election 2016: Your money, your vote. Yes, 'President Trump' really could kill NAFTA – but it wouldn't be pretty". *CNN*. July 6, 2016. Retrieved September 1, 2016.

^ Bradner, Eric (January 23, 2017). "Trump's TPP withdrawal: 5 things to know". *CNN*. Retrieved March 12, 2018.

^ Turak, Natasha (March 2, 2018). *"'Straight up stupid,' 'incompetent' and 'misguided': Economist Adam Posen rips Trump's tariffs"*. **CNBC**. Retrieved March 15, 2018.

^ Inman, Phillip (March 10, 2018). *"The war over steel: Trump tips global trade into new turmoil"*. **The Guardian**. Retrieved March 15,2018.

^ Lane, Charles (October 21, 2015). *"Donald Trump's contempt for the free market"*. **The Washington Post**. Retrieved July 22, 2016.

^ **Haberman, Maggie** (January 7, 2016). *"Donald Trump Says He Favors Big Tariffs on Chinese Exports"*. **The New York Times**. Retrieved July 22, 2016.

^ Dann, Carrie (July 23, 2016). *"Trump: I'm Running Against Clinton, Not 'Rest of the World'"*. **NBC News**. Retrieved July 31, 2016.

^ Needham, Vicki (July 24, 2016). *"Trump suggests leaving WTO over import tax proposal"*. **The Hill**. Retrieved July 31, 2016.

^ *"Trump tariffs: US President imposes levy on steel and aluminium"*. **BBC Online**. March 8, 2018. Retrieved March 9, 2018.

^ *"EU's retaliatory tariffs on US products come into effect"*. **Deutsche Welle**. June 22, 2018. Retrieved June 24, 2018.

^ Ewing, Jack (June 21, 2018). *"Europe Retaliates Against Trump Tariffs"*. **The New York Times**. Retrieved June 24, 2018.

^ Boudreau, Catherine (July 6, 2018). *"Trump country hit hard by Chinese tariffs"*. **Politico**. Retrieved July 6, 2018.

^ Hjelmgaard, Kim (July 6, 2018). *"Trump launches $34 billion trade war and China 'immediately' fires back"*. **USA Today**. Retrieved July 6, 2018.

^ Wei, Han; Qi, Zhang (June 15, 2018). *"Trade War Back on Stage With New U.S. Tariffs - Caixin Global"*. *Caixin*. Retrieved August 9, 2018.

^ Jump up to:*a b* Chen, Yawen; Lawder, David (September 18, 2018). *"China says Trump forces its hand, will retaliate against new U.S. tariffs"*. **Reuters**. Retrieved September 23, 2018.

^ Kim, Tae (September 18, 2018). *"China hits back: It will impose tariffs on $60 billion worth of US goods effective Sept. 24"*. **CNBC**.

^ Zaharia, Marius (July 6, 2018). *"How trade war with US can hurt China and economies including Australia"*. **Sydney Morning Herald**. Retrieved July 6, 2018.

^ Kool, Tom (July 6, 2018). *"Analysis: Tariffs from China, US have potential for $2 trillion trade war fallout"*. **USA Today**. Retrieved July 6, 2018.

^ Chang, Sue (July 3, 2018). _"Fitch warns President Trump's trade fight could cost the world $2 trillion in global trade"_. _Market Watch_. Retrieved December 31, 2018.

^ _"An America first energy plan"_ (Press release). May 26, 2016. Archived from _the original_ on December 3, 2016. Retrieved December 3, 2016.

^ Tabuchi, Hiroko (March 3, 2017). _"Trump Got Nearly $1 Million in Energy-Efficiency Subsidies in 2012"_. _The New York Times_. Retrieved May 27, 2018.

^ _"Trump proposes cuts to climate and clean-energy programs"_. _National Geographic Society_. February 12, 2018. Retrieved May 27, 2018.

^ Parker, Ashley; Davenport, Coral (May 26, 2016). _"Donald Trump's Energy Plan: More Fossil Fuels and Fewer Rules"_. _The New York Times_.

^ Samenow, Jason (March 22, 2016). _"Donald Trump's unsettling nonsense on weather and climate"_. _The Washington Post_.

^ Embury-Dennis, Tom. _"Trump's environment chief Scott Pruitt suggests climate change could be good for humanity"_. _The Independent_. Retrieved February 27, 2018.

^ Bacon, John. _"Scientists rebuff EPA chief's claim that global warming may be good"_. _USA Today_. Retrieved May 28, 2018.

^ *"In Their Own Words: 2016 Presidential Candidates on Climate Change"* (PDF). *League of Conservation Voters*. Archived from the original (PDF) on October 18, 2016. Retrieved July 12, 2016.

^ Liptak, Kevin; Acosta, Jim (June 1, 2017). *"Trump on Paris accord: 'We're getting out'"*. *CNN*. Retrieved June 1, 2017.

^ Dennis, Brandy. *"As Syria embraces Paris climate deal, it's the United States against the world"*. *The Washington Post*. Retrieved May 28, 2018.

^ Adriance, Sam (February 16, 2017). *"President Trump Signs First Congressional Review Act Disapproval Resolution in 16 Years"*. *The National Law Review*. Retrieved March 8, 2017.

^ Farand, Chloe (March 6, 2017). *"Donald Trump Disassembles 90 Federal State Regulations in Just Over a Month in White House"*. *The Independent*. Retrieved March 7, 2017.

^ *"Trump-Era Trend: Industries Protest. Regulations Rolled Back. A Dozen Examples"*. *The New York Times*. March 5, 2017. Retrieved March 7, 2017 – via DocumentCloud. More than 90 Obama-era federal regulations have been revoked or delayed or enforcement has been suspended, in many cases based on requests from the industries the rules target.

^ Shear, Michael D. (January 23, 2017). *"Trump Orders Broad Hiring Freeze for Federal Government"*. *The New York Times*. Retrieved January 23, 2017.

^ "Trump Orders Hiring Freeze for Much of Federal Government". Fox News. January 24, 2017. Retrieved March 6, 2017.

^ Jump up to:a b Yoder, Eric (February 16, 2017). "Hiring freeze could add to government's risk, GAO chief warns". The Washington Post. 'We've looked at hiring freezes in the past by prior administrations and they haven't proven to be effective in reducing costs and they cause some problems if they're in effect for a long period of time', Comptroller General Gene Dodaro told a House Oversight and Government Reform Committee hearing.

^ Rappeport, Alan (April 11, 2017). "Trump's Directive Will Lift Hiring Freeze, as It Asks Agencies for Cuts". The New York Times. Retrieved January 3, 2019.

^ "Trump Signs Executive Order to Drastically Cut Federal Regs". Fox News. January 30, 2017. Retrieved March 6, 2017.

^ The White House, Office of the Press Secretary (January 30, 2017). "Presidential Executive Order on Reducing Regulation and Controlling Regulatory Costs". Retrieved May 16, 2017.

^ Calabresi, Massimo (March 9, 2017). "Inside Donald Trump's War against the State". Time. Staffed by experts who oversee an open governmental process, they say, the federal bureaucracy exists to protect those who would otherwise be at the mercy of better-organized, better-funded interests.

^ Jump up to:_a_ _b_ Kertscher, Tom (September 11, 2015). _"Donald Trump wants to replace Obamacare with a single-payer health care system, GOP congressman says"_. **Politifact** Wisconsin. Retrieved January 12,2017.

^ Trump, Donald (2000). _The America We Deserve_. Los Angeles: Renaissance Books. pp. 258–278. **ISBN** **978-1-58063-131-0**. Retrieved January 12, 2017.

^ Millward, David (August 7, 2015). _"Trump under attack as he praises NHS care"_. **The Daily Telegraph**. Retrieved January 25, 2017.

^ Learmonth, Andrew (August 8, 2015). _"US presidential hope Donald Trump hails the NHS in Scotland"_. **The National**. Retrieved January 25, 2017.

^ Kodjak, Alison (November 9, 2016). _"Trump Can Kill Obamacare With Or Without Help From Congress"_. **All Things Considered**. **NPR**. Retrieved January 12, 2017.

^ Walsh, Deirdre; Lee, MJ (January 10, 2017). _"Trump wants Obamacare repeal 'quickly,' but Republicans aren't ready"_. **CNN**. Retrieved January 12, 2017.

^ Sullivan, Peter (May 4, 2017). _"House passes Obamacare repeal"_. **The Hill**. Retrieved July 31, 2017.

^ _"GOP Obamacare repeal bill fails in dramatic late-night vote"_. **CNN**. July 28, 2017. Retrieved July 31, 2017.

^ Nelson, Louis (July 18, 2017). _"Trump says he plans to 'let Obamacare fail'"_. **Politico**. Retrieved September 29, 2017.

^ Young, Jeffrey (August 31, 2017). _"Trump Ramps Up Obamacare Sabotage With Huge Cuts To Enrollment Programs"_. **HuffPost**. Retrieved September 29, 2017.

^ Pradhan, Rachana (August 31, 2017). _"Trump administration slashes Obamacare outreach"_. **Politico**. Retrieved September 29, 2017.

^ Pear, Robert (December 18, 2017). _"Without the Insurance Mandate, Health Care's Future May Be in Doubt"_. **The New York Times**.

^ Sullivan, Peter (December 2, 2017). _"Senate GOP repeals ObamaCare mandate"_. **The Hill**.

^ Jost, Timothy (December 20, 2017). _"The Tax Bill And The Individual Mandate: What Happened, And What Does It Mean?"_. **Health Affairs**. doi:10.1377/hblog20171220.323429 (inactive 2018-12-14).

^ Wright, David (April 21, 2016). _"Trump: I would change GOP platform on abortion"_. **CNN**.

^ Jump up to:_a b_ De Vogue, Ariane (November 15, 2016). _"Trump: Same-sex marriage is 'settled,' but Roe v Wade can be changed"_. **CNN**. Retrieved November 30, 2016.

^ Ehrenfreund, Max (July 22, 2015). _"Here's what Donald Trump really believes"_. **The Washington Post**.

^ Peters, Jeremy W. (January 30, 2017). _"Obama's Protections for L.G.B.T. Workers Will Remain Under Trump"_. **The New York Times**. Retrieved February 2, 2017.

^ O'Hara, Mary Emily. _"LGBTQ Advocates Say Trump's New Executive Order Makes Them Vulnerable to Discrimination"_. **NBC News**. Retrieved July 30, 2017.

^ Gorman, Michele (May 20, 2016). _"A brief history of Donald Trump's stance on gun rights"_. **Newsweek**.

^ _"Second Amendment Rights"_. Donald J. Trump for President. Archived from the original on January 7, 2016. Retrieved May 22, 2017. There has been a national background check system in place since 1998 ... Too many states are failing to put criminal and mental health records into the system ... What we need to do is fix the system we have and make it work as intended.

^ Krieg, Gregory (June 20, 2016). _"The times Trump changed his positions on guns"_. **CNN**.

^ _"Donald Trump on Marijuana"_. **C-SPAN**. Retrieved October 17, 2018.

^ Diamond, Jeremy (December 11, 2015). _"Trump: Death penalty for cop killers"_. **CNN**. Retrieved March 15, 2016.

^ Foderaro, Lisa (May 1, 1989). *"Angered by Attack, Trump Urges Return of the Death Penalty"*. **The New York Times**. Retrieved March 15, 2016.

^ McCarthy, Tom. *"Donald Trump: I'd bring back 'a hell of a lot worse than waterboarding'"*. **The Guardian**. Retrieved February 8, 2016.

^ *"Ted Cruz, Donald Trump Advocate Bringing Back Waterboarding"*. **ABC News**. February 6, 2016. Retrieved February 9, 2016.

^ *"Who pays for Donald Trump's wall?"*. **BBC Online**. February 6, 2017. Retrieved December 9, 2017.

^ *"Donald Trump emphasizes plans to build 'real' wall at Mexico border"*. **Canadian Broadcasting Corporation**. August 19, 2015. Retrieved September 29, 2015.

^ Oh, Inae (August 19, 2015). *"Donald Trump: The 14th Amendment is Unconstitutional"*. **Mother Jones**. Retrieved November 22, 2015.

^ *"Trump retreats on deportations, vows no amnesty"*. Houston, Texas: **KTRK-TV**. **Associated Press**. September 1, 2016. Retrieved September 2, 2016.

^ Scott, Eugene (December 13, 2015). *"Trump: My Muslim friends don't support my immigration ban"*. **CNN**.

^ Barro, Josh (December 15, 2015). *"How Unpopular Is Trump's Muslim Ban? Depends How You Ask"*. **The New York**

*Times*. Donald J. Trump's proposal to bar Muslim noncitizens from entering the United States ...

^ Colvin, Jill; Barrow, Bill (December 14, 2015). "Donald Trump's supporters see plenty of sense in views that his critics denounce". **U.S. News & World Report**. He said American citizens, including Muslim members of the military, would be exempt, as would certain world leaders and athletes coming to the U.S. to compete.

^ Johnson, Jenna (June 25, 2016). "Trump now says Muslim ban only applies to those from terrorism-heavy countries". **Chicago Tribune**. [A] reporter asked Trump if [he] would be OK with a Muslim from Scotland coming into the United States and he said it 'wouldn't bother me.' Afterward, [spokeswoman] Hicks said in an email that Trump's ban would now just apply to Muslims in terror states ...

^ Detrow, Scott (June 13, 2016). "Trump Calls To Ban Immigration From Countries With 'Proven History Of Terrorism'". **NPR**. I will suspend immigration from areas of the world where there's a proven history of terrorism against the United States, Europe or our allies until we fully understand how to end these threats.

^ Park, Haeyoun (July 22, 2016). "Trump Vows to Stop Immigration From Nations 'Compromised' by Terrorism. How Could It Work?". **The New York Times**. Retrieved July 25, 2016.

^ Jump up to:ᵃ ᵇ "Trump signs new travel ban directive". **BBC News**. March 6, 2017. Retrieved March 18, 2017.

^ Grinberg, Emanuella; Park, Madison (January 30, 2017). _"2nd day of protests over Trump's immigration policies"_. _CNN_. Retrieved March 18, 2017.

^ _"US airports on frontline as Donald Trump's travel ban causes chaos and protests"_. _The Guardian_. January 28, 2017. Retrieved July 19, 2017.

^ Shear, Michael D.; Cooper, Helene (January 27, 2017). _"Trump Bars Refugees and Citizens of 7 Muslim Countries"_. _The New York Times_. Retrieved January 28, 2017.

^ Baker, Peter (January 29, 2017). _"Travelers Stranded and Protests Swell Over Trump Order"_. _The New York Times_. Retrieved November 12, 2018.

^ Perez, Evan; Diamond, Jeremy (January 30, 2017). _"Trump fires acting AG after she declines to defend travel ban"_. _CNN_. Retrieved March 12, 2018.

^ _"Statement on the Appointment of Dana Boente as Acting Attorney General"_. The White House. January 30, 2017. Retrieved August 29, 2017.

^ Shear, Michael D.; Landler, Mark; Apuzzo, Matt; Lichtblau, Eric (January 30, 2017). _"Trump Fires Acting Attorney General Who Defied Him"_. _The New York Times_. Retrieved August 29, 2017.

^ Barrett, Devlin; Frosch, Dan (February 4, 2017). _"Federal Judge Temporarily Halts Trump Order on Immigration, Refugees"_. _The Wall Street Journal_.

^ **Liptak, Adam** (February 5, 2017). *"Where Trump's Travel Ban Stands"*. *The New York Times*.

^ **Chakraborty, Barnini** (March 6, 2017). *"Trump Signs New Immigration Order, Narrows Scope of Travel Ban"*. **Fox News**. Retrieved March 6,2017.

^ **Levine, Dan; Rosenberg, Mica** (March 15, 2017). *"Hawaii judge halts Trump's new travel ban before it can go into effect"*. **Reuters**.

^ **Sherman, Mark** (June 26, 2017). *"Trump says Supreme Court decision on travel ban a 'clear victory for our national security'"*. **Chicago Tribune**. **Associated Press**. Retrieved June 27, 2017.

^ **Laughland, Oliver** (September 25, 2017). *"Trump travel ban extended to blocks on North Korea, Venezuela and Chad"*. **The Guardian**. Retrieved October 13, 2017.

^ **Hurley, Lawrence** (December 4, 2017). *"Supreme Court lets Trump's latest travel ban go into full effect"*. **Reuters**.

^ Jump up to:[a] [b] **Liptak, Adam** (January 19, 2018). *"Supreme Court to Consider Challenge to Trump's Latest Travel Ban"*. **The New York Times**. Retrieved January 26, 2017.

^ **Biskupic, Joan** (April 25, 2018). *"Key moments from the Supreme Court travel ban hearing"*. **CNN**. Retrieved May 24, 2018.

^ Wagner, Meg; Ries, Brian (June 26, 2018). _"Supreme Court upholds Trump's travel ban"_. _CNN_. Retrieved June 26, 2018.

^ Bennett, Brian; Memoli, Michael A. (February 16, 2017). _"The White House has found ways to end protection for 'Dreamers' while shielding Trump from blowback"_. _Los Angeles Times_. Retrieved February 22, 2017.

^ Shear, Michael D.; Davis, Julie Hirschfeld (September 5, 2017). _"Trump Moves to End DACA and Calls on Congress to Act"_. _The New York Times_. Retrieved September 6, 2017.

^ Kopan, Tal (September 5, 2017). _"Trump ends DACA, but gives Congress window to save it"_. _CNN_.

^ Kopan, Tal (March 5, 2018). _"DACA's March 5 'deadline' marks only inaction"_. _CNN_.

^ Kopan, Tal (September 6, 2017). _"Blue states sue Trump over DACA"_. _CNN_. Retrieved September 6, 2017.

^ Jordan, Miriam (April 24, 2018). _"U.S. Must Resume DACA and Accept New Applications, Federal Judge Rules"_. _The New York Times_.

^ Vergano, Dan (June 15, 2018). _"Immigrant Children Who Are Forcibly Separated From Their Parents Face Long-Term Trauma"_. _BuzzFeed News_. Retrieved June 20, 2018.

^ Bachega, Hugo (June 7, 2018), _Separation of migrant families: What other countries do_, _BBC Online_

^ Burke, Garance; Mendoza, Martha (June 20, 2018). *"Toddlers Separated From Parents at the Border Are Being Detained in 'Tender Age' Shelters"*. *Time*. Archived from the original on June 20, 2018. Retrieved July 24, 2018.

^ Colvin, Jill (June 18, 2018). *"President Trump's Family Separation Policy Is Dividing Republicans"*. *Time*. Archived from the original on June 18, 2018. Retrieved June 18, 2018.

^ Davis, Julie (June 15, 2018). *"Separated at the Border From Their Parents: In Six Weeks, 1,995 Children"*. *The New York Times*. Retrieved June 18, 2018.

^ Mcardle, Maiead (June 15, 2018). *"White House Blames Democrats for Separation of Families at Border"*. *National Review*. Retrieved June 18, 2018.

^ Sarlin, Benjy (June 15, 2018). *"Despite claims, GOP immigration bill would not end family separation, experts say"*. *NBC News*. Retrieved June 18, 2018.

^ Shear, Michael D.; Goodnough, Abby; Haberman, Maggie (June 20, 2018). *"Trump Retreats on Separating Families, but Thousands May Remain Apart"*. *The New York Times*. Retrieved June 20, 2018.

^ Jarrett, Laura (June 27, 2018). *"Federal judge orders reunification of parents and children, end to most family separations at border"*. *CNN*. Retrieved June 28, 2018.

^ Davis, Julie Hirschfeld; Tackett, Michael (January 2, 2019). *"Trump and Democrats Dig In After Talks to Reopen*

Government Go Nowhere". *The New York Times*.
Retrieved January 3, 2019.

^ Wamsley, Laurel (January 9, 2019). *"How Is The Shutdown Affecting America? Let Us Count The Ways"*. *NPR*.

^ Paletta, Damian; Werner, Erica (January 2, 2019). *"Trump falsely claims Mexico is paying for wall, demands taxpayer money for wall in meeting with Democrats"*. *The Washington Post*. Retrieved January 3, 2019.

^ Nakamura, David; Kim, Seung Min (January 9, 2019). *"'He's a gut politician': Trump's go-to negotiating tactics aren't working in shutdown standoff"*. *The Washington Post*. Retrieved January 10, 2019.

^ Pramuk, Jacob (January 4, 2019). *"Democrats face off with Trump (again) over border wall as government shutdown enters 14th day"*. *CNBC*. Retrieved January 10, 2019.

^ Everett, Burgess; Ferris, Sarah; Oprysko, Caitlin (December 11, 2018). *"Trump says he's 'proud' to shut down government during fight with Pelosi and Schumer"*. *Politico*. Retrieved January 10, 2019.

^ Fandos, Nicholas; Stolberg, Sheryl Gay; Baker, Peter (January 25, 2019). *"Trump Signs Bill Reopening Government for 3 Weeks in Surprise Retreat From Wall"*. *The New York Times*. Retrieved January 27, 2019.

^ Seipel, Arnie (January 12, 2019). _"It's Official: The Partial Government Shutdown Is The Longest In U.S. History"_. **NPR**. Retrieved January 12, 2019.

^ Pramuk, Jacob; Wilkie, Christina (January 15, 2019). _"Trump declares national emergency to build border wall, setting up massive legal fight"_. **CNBC**. Retrieved February 16, 2019.

^ Owen, Paul (5 March 2019). _"Senate set to reject Trump's national emergency declaration"_. The Guardian. Retrieved 5 March 2019.

^ Cassidy, John (February 29, 2016). _"Donald Trump Is Transforming the G.O.P. Into a Populist, Nativist Party"_. **The New Yorker**. Retrieved March 5, 2016.

^ Jump up to:[a] [b] **Rucker, Philip**; **Costa, Robert** (March 21, 2016). _"Trump questions need for NATO, outlines noninterventionist foreign policy"_. **The Washington Post**.

^ Jump up to:[a] [b] Dueck, Colin (November 3, 2015). _"Donald Trump, American Nationalist"_. **The National Interest**.

^ **Amanpour, Christiane** (July 22, 2016). _"Donald Trump's speech: 'America first,' but an America absent from the world"_. **CNN**.

^ _"Donald Trump reveals his isolationist foreign-policy instincts"_. **The Economist**. May 22, 2016.

^ _"US President Donald Trump praises China's Xi Jinping for consolidating grip on power"_. **Deutsche Welle**. March 4, 2018.

^ Lemire, Jonathan; Colvin, Jill (November 13, 2017). _"Donald Trump repeatedly praises Philippines' President Duterte during Asia trip"_. **Global News**.

^ Revesz, Rachael (May 21, 2017). _"Donald Trump praises Egypt President al-Sisi and plans trip to Cairo"_. **The Independent**.

^ Talev, Margaret; Jacobs, Jennifer (September 21, 2017). _"Trump Praises Erdogan for 'High Marks' Amid Crackdown Concerns"_. **Bloomberg News**.

^ LaVito, Angelica (November 6, 2017). _"Trump praises Saudi king after crackdown"_. **CNBC**.

^ Spinaci, Di Gianluigi (June 15, 2018). _"Donal Trump elogia il premier italiano Giuseppe Conte: "È fantastico" – Video"_ (in Italian). TPI News.

^ _"Trump praises Brazil's new President Bolsonaro after he vowed to 'strengthen democracy'"_. **CNBC**. Reuters. January 1, 2019.

^ Gera, Vanessa (July 24, 2017). _"Amid protests, Polish leader puts brakes on judicial shakeup"_. **Associated Press**.

^ Maizland, Lindsay (July 20, 2017). _"Trump praised Poland as a defender of the West. But their democracy is unraveling"_. **Vox**.

^ Corn, David (November 2, 2016). _"Trump Once Called for Sending US Ground Troops to Fight ISIS and "Take That Oil""_. _Mother Jones_.

^ Gaouette, Nicole (March 11, 2016). _"Trump wants 30,000 troops. Would that defeat ISIS?"_. _CNN_. Retrieved July 12, 2016.

^ Sanger, David E.; Haberman, Maggie (March 22, 2016). _"Presidential Candidates Walking a Tightrope Over the Fight on Terrorism"_. _The New York Times_. Retrieved December 20, 2018.

^ _"Syria war: Trump's missile strike attracts US praise – and barbs"_. _BBC News_. April 7, 2017. Retrieved April 8, 2017.

^ _"Trump denies he wanted Syria leader killed"_. _BBC Online_. September 5, 2018. Retrieved December 20, 2018.

^ Joyce, Kathleen (April 14, 2018). _"US strikes Syria after suspected chemical attack by Assad regime"_. _Fox News_. Retrieved April 14, 2018.

^ Landler, Mark; Cooper, Helene; Schmitt, Eric (December 19, 2018). _"Trump withdraws U.S. Forces From Syria, Declaring 'We Have Won Against ISIS'"_. _The New York Times_. Retrieved December 31, 2018.

^ _"Syria conflict: Trump's withdrawal plan shocks allies"_. _BBC Online_. Retrieved December 20, 2018.

^ _Borger, Julian_; Chulov, Martin (December 20, 2018). _"Trump shocks allies and advisers with plan to pull US troops out of Syria"_. _The Guardian_. Retrieved December 20, 2018.

^ _Cooper, Helene_ (December 20, 2018). _"Jim Mattis, Defense Secretary, Resigns in Rebuke of Trump's Worldview"_. _The New York Times_. Retrieved December 21, 2018.

^ _Demirjian, Karoun_ (January 6, 2019). _"Contradicting Trump, Bolton says no withdrawal from Syria until ISIS destroyed, Kurds' safety guaranteed"_. _The Washington Post_. Retrieved January 6, 2019.

^ _Sanger, David E._; Weiland, Noah; _Schmitt, Eric_ (January 6, 2019). _"Bolton Puts Conditions on Syria Withdrawal, Suggesting a Delay of Months or Years"_. _The New York Times_. Retrieved January 6, 2019.

^ Jump up to:_a_ _b_ _"Trump praises arms sales as he meets Saudi crown prince"_. _Financial Times_. March 20, 2018.

^ _"Senate Votes Down Ending Trump's Support for Saudi-led War in Yemen"_. _Haaretz_. May 21, 2018.

^ _Phelps, Jordyn_; Struyk, Ryan (May 20, 2017). _"Trump signs $110 billion arms deal with Saudi Arabia on 'a tremendous day'"_. _ABC News_. Retrieved July 6, 2018.

^ _Jaffe, Greg_; _Ryan, Missy_ (January 21, 2018). _"Up to 1,000 more U.S. troops could be headed to Afghanistan this spring"_. _The Washington Post_.

^ _Gordon, Michael R.; Schmitt, Eric; Haberman, Maggie_ (August 20, 2017). _"Trump Settles on Afghan Strategy Expected to Raise Troop Levels"_. _The New York Times_.

^ Rampton, Roberta; Landay, Jonathan (January 29, 2018). _"Trump rejects peace talks with Taliban in departure from Afghan strategy"_. _Reuters_.

^ Weiler, Yuram Abdullah (December 2, 2017). _"What is Basij and how does it function against U.S. and Zionism?"_. Khamenei.ir. Retrieved February 6, 2019.

^ _Tur, Katy_ (July 14, 2015). _"Donald Trump Weighs in on Iran Deal"_. _NBC News_.

^ Jump up to:_ᵃ ᵇ_ Lederman, Josh (May 8, 2018). "Trump declares US leaving 'horrible' Iran nuclear accord". _Associated Press_. Retrieved May 8,2018.

^ Bobic, Igor (August 16, 2015). _"Donald Trump Would Not Rip Up The Iran Deal"_. _The Huffington Post_.

^ _Borger, Julian; Smith, David_ (February 2, 2017). _"Trump administration 'officially putting Iran on notice', says Michael Flynn"_. _The Guardian_. Retrieved November 9, 2018.

^ _"Trump administration tightens Iran sanctions, Tehran hits back"_. _Reuters_. February 3, 2016.

^ _Borger, Julian; Smith, David_ (February 3, 2017). _"Trump administration imposes new sanctions on Iran"_. _The Guardian_. Retrieved November 9, 2018.

^ Aleem, Zeeshan (July 21, 2017). "Iran says the US is violating the nuclear deal. It has a point". *Vox*. Retrieved July 22, 2017.

^ "Would Donald Trump be 'neutral' between Israel and its enemies?". *PolitiFact*. Retrieved October 17, 2018.

^ "Moving US embassy to Jerusalem may be slipping down Trump's agenda". *The Guardian*. Reuters. January 23, 2017. Retrieved February 4, 2017.

^ Landler, Mark; Horowitz, Jason (May 24, 2017). "With Gift and in Conversation, Vatican Presses Trump on Climate Change". *The New York Times*. Retrieved May 14, 2018.

^ Rafferty, Andrew (May 23, 2017). "Trump Becomes First Sitting U.S. President to Visit Western Wall". *NBC News*. Retrieved May 24, 2017.
Baker, Luke; Holland, Steve (May 23, 2017). "In U.S. presidential first, Trump prays at Jerusalem's Western Wall". London, England: *Reuters*. Retrieved May 24, 2017.
Diamond, Jeremy (May 23, 2017). "Trump makes historic visit to Western Wall". *CNN*. Retrieved May 24, 2017.

^ Nelson, Louis; Nussbaum, Matthew (December 6, 2017). "Trump says U.S. recognizes Jerusalem as Israel's capital, despite global condemnation". *Politico*. Retrieved December 6, 2017.

^ "US Embassy opens in Jerusalem: 'When Trump makes a promise, he keeps it'". *Ynetnews*. May 14, 2018. Retrieved July 25, 2018.

^ "*Illegal Israeli actions in Occupied East Jerusalem and the rest of the Occupied Palestinian Territory – Turkey and Yemen: draft resolution – Status of Jerusalem*". *United Nations General Assembly*. December 19, 2017. Retrieved December 21, 2017.

^ Gladstone, Rick (December 21, 2017). "*Defying Trump, U.N. General Assembly Condemns U.S. Decree on Jerusalem*". *The New York Times*. Retrieved December 21, 2017.

^ Johnson, Jenna; Wagner, John (August 11, 2017). "*Trump won't 'rule out a military option' in Venezuela*". *The Washington Post*.

^ Wroughton, Lesley; Ellsworth, Brian (September 25, 2018). "*U.S. sanctions Venezuela officials, Trump slams Maduro*". *Reuters*.

^ "*Venezuela's President breaks diplomatic relations with US over Donald Trump's support of Opposition Leader*". *Australian Broadcasting Corporation*. *Reuters/AP*. January 24, 2019.

^ Jump up to:*ᵃ ᵇ* Kennedy, Merrit (April 17, 2017). "*Pence Tells North Korea: 'The Era Of Strategic Patience Is Over'*". *NPR*. Retrieved April 19, 2017.

^ Lendon, Brad (July 30, 2017). "*US slams North Korea missile test as Kim claims 'whole US mainland' in reach*". *CNN*. Retrieved August 11, 2017.

^ Wright, David (July 28, 2017). "North Korean ICBM Appears Able to Reach Major US Cities". All Things Nuclear. Union of Concerned Scientists. Retrieved July 28, 2017.

^ Rucker, Philip; DeYoung, Karen (August 10, 2017). "Trump reiterates warning to N. Korea: 'Fire and fury' may not have been 'tough enough'". The Washington Post. Retrieved December 21, 2018.

^ Talmadge, Eric; Lemire, Jonathan (August 11, 2017). "Trump doubles down on 'fire and fury' vow as wargames near". U.S. News & World Report. Associated Press. Retrieved September 30, 2017.

^ Yong, Jeremy Au; Wei, Tan Dawn (June 12, 2018). "Trump-Kim summit: Kim Jong Un gave unwavering commitment to denuclearisation, says Trump". The Straits Times. Retrieved June 13, 2018.

^ "Joint Statement of President Donald J. Trump of the United States of America and Chairman Kim Jong Un of the Democratic People's Republic of Korea at the Singapore Summit". The White House. Retrieved June 12, 2018.

^ Rosenfeld, Everett (June 12, 2018). "Document signed by Trump and Kim includes four main elements related to 'peace regime'". CNBC. Retrieved June 12, 2018.

^ Kim, Tong-Hyung (December 20, 2018). "North Korea Says It Won't Give Up Nuclear Weapons Unless the U.S. Removes Nuclear Threat". Time. Retrieved December 26, 2018.

^ McArdle, Mairead (December 20, 2018). "North Korea Refuses Nuclear Disarmament until U.S. Eliminates 'Nuclear Threat'". National Review. Retrieved December 26, 2018.

^ "Trump announces second North Korea summit". BBC Online. February 6, 2019. Retrieved February 6, 2019.

^ Jump up to:[a] [b] Rucker, Philip; Denyer, Simon; Nakamura, David (February 28, 2019). "North Korea's foreign minister says country seeks only partial sanctions relief". The Washington Post. Retrieved March 4, 2019.

^ Wong, Edward (February 28, 2019). "Trump's Talks With Kim Jong-un Collapse, and Both Sides Point Fingers". The New York Times. Retrieved March 1, 2019.

^ Diamond, Jeremy (February 28, 2019). "Takeaways from the Trump-Kim Hanoi summit". CNN. Retrieved March 1, 2019.

^ Flores, Reena (January 7, 2017). "Donald Trump urges 'good relationship' with Russia in tweets". CBS News. Retrieved May 2, 2017.

^ Berry, Lynn (January 29, 2017). "GOP warns Trump not to lift Russia sanctions after call with Putin". PBS NewsHour. Associated Press. Retrieved May 2, 2017.

^ Viebeck, Elise; Markon, Jerry; DeYoung, Karen (November 14, 2016). "Trump, Putin agree in phone call to improve 'unsatisfactory' relations between their countries, Kremlin says". The Washington Post. Retrieved March 14, 2017.

^ Conrad, Peter (January 13, 2017). *"Trump and Putin's Bromance Could Change the World"*. **GQ**. Retrieved May 29, 2017.

^ Oliphant, Roland; Millward, David (January 28, 2017). *"Donald Trump and Vladimir Putin ready to hold summit following historic phone call"*. **The Daily Telegraph**. Retrieved May 31, 2017.

^ *"Trump suggests U.S. accept Russia's annexation of Crimea"*. **PBS NewsHour**. **Associated Press**. August 1, 2016. Retrieved February 19, 2017.

^ Carroll, Oliver (January 19, 2018). *"US-Russia relations fail to improve in Trump's first year and they are likely to get worse"*. **The Independent**.

^ Osborne, Samuel (April 12, 2017). *"Vladimir Putin says US-Russia relations are worse since Donald Trump took office"*. **The Independent**.

^ Smith, Alexander (March 30, 2018). *"U.S.-Russian relations worst Ambassador Antonov can remember"*. **NBC News**.

^ Zurcher, Anthony (July 16, 2018). *"Trump-Putin summit: After Helsinki, the fallout at home"*. **BBC Online**. Retrieved July 18, 2018.

^ Calamur, Krishnadev (July 16, 2018). *"Trump Sides With the Kremlin, Against the U.S. Government"*. **The Atlantic**. Retrieved July 18, 2018.

^ Fox, Lauren (July 16, 2018). _"Top Republicans in Congress break with Trump over Putin comments"_. __CNN__. Retrieved July 18, 2018.

^ Relman, Eliza (July 18, 2018). _"Trump's staunchest media allies are facing their biggest test yet — and some of them are finally abandoning him"_. __Business Insider__. Retrieved July 18, 2018.

^ __DeYoung, Karen__ (November 8, 2017). _"White House implements new Cuba policy restricting travel and trade"_. __The Washington Post__.

^ __Sanger, David E.__; __Haberman, Maggie__ (July 20, 2016). _"Donald Trump Sets Conditions for Defending NATO Allies Against Attack"_. __The New York Times__. Retrieved July 31, 2016.

^ _"What's Trump's Position on NATO?"_. __FactCheck.org__. Retrieved July 31, 2016.

^ _"Trump supports NATO, but Senate holds up expansion"_. __Newsweek__. Reuters. March 1, 2017. Retrieved May 2, 2017.

^ __Baker, Peter__ (May 26, 2018). _"Trump Says NATO Allies Don't Pay Their Share. Is That True?"_. __The New York Times__. Retrieved July 12, 2018.

^ Barnes, Julian E.; __Cooper, Helene__ (January 14, 2019). _"Trump Discussed Pulling U.S. From NATO, Aides Say Amid New_

_Concerns Over Russia"_. _The New York Times._
Retrieved January 19, 2019.

^ Morin, Rebecca (January 17, 2019). _"Trump: We will be with NATO '100 percent'"_. **Politico**. Retrieved January 19, 2019.

^ Trimble, Megan (December 28, 2017). _"Trump White House Has Highest Turnover in 40 Years"_. **U.S. News & World Report**. Retrieved March 16, 2018.

^ Wise, Justin (July 2, 2018). _"AP: Trump admin sets record for White House turnover"_. **The Hill**. Retrieved July 3, 2018.

^ _"Trump White House sets turnover records, analysis shows"_. **NBC News**. **Associated Press**. July 2, 2018. Retrieved July 3, 2018.

^ Jump up to:_a b_ Keith, Tamara. _"White House Staff Turnover Was Already Record-Setting. Then More Advisers Left"_. **NPR**. Retrieved March 16, 2018.

^ **Baker, Peter; Haberman, Maggie**. _"Reince Priebus Pushed Out After Rocky Tenure as Trump Chief of Staff"_. **The New York Times**.

^ Jump up to:_a b_ _"Tracking Turnover in the Trump Administration"_. **Brookings Institution**. March 16, 2018. Retrieved March 16, 2018.

^ Keith, Tamara (October 12, 2017). _"Trump Leaves Top Administration Positions Unfilled, Says Hollow Government By Design"_. **NPR**. Retrieved March 16, 2018.

^ "Tracking how many key positions Trump has filled so far". *The Washington Post*. January 8, 2019. Archived from the original on January 9, 2019.

^ "President Donald J. Trump Selects U.S. Senator Jeff Sessions for Attorney General, Lt. Gen. Michael Flynn as Assistant to the President for National Security Affairs and U.S. Rep. Mike Pompeo as Director of the Central Intelligence Agency" (Press release). New York City: Office of the President Elect and of the Vice President Elect. November 18, 2016. Retrieved November 18, 2016.

^ "Former US banker Steve Mnuchin confirms he will be US treasury secretary". *BBC News*. November 30, 2016. Retrieved November 30, 2016.

^ Lamothe, Dan. "Trump has chosen retired Marine Gen. James Mattis for secretary of defense". *The Washington Post*. Retrieved December 1, 2016.

^ Shear, Michael D.; Haberman, Maggie (December 12, 2016). "Rex Tillerson, Exxon C.E.O., chosen as Secretary of State". *The New York Times*. Retrieved December 26, 2016.

^ Gabriel, Trip (December 5, 2016). "Trump Chooses Ben Carson to Lead HUD". *The New York Times*. Retrieved December 5, 2016.

^ Costa, Robert (November 23, 2016). "Gov. Nikki Haley tapped to be Trump's U.N. ambassador". *The Washington Post*. Retrieved November 23, 2016.

^ Jones-Rooy, Andrea (November 29, 2017). _"The Incredibly And Historically Unstable First Year Of Trump's Cabinet"_. _FiveThirtyEight_. Retrieved March 16, 2018.

^ Hersher, Rebecca; Neelyin, Brett (July 5, 2018). _"Scott Pruitt Out At EPA"_. _NPR_. Retrieved July 5, 2018.

^ Eilperin, Juliet; Dawsey, Josh. _"Ryan Zinke resigns as interior secretary amid multiple investigations"_. _Chicago Tribune_. Retrieved January 3, 2019.

^ Rosenberg, Matthew (July 6, 2017). _"Trump Misleads on Russian Meddling: Why 17 Intelligence Agencies Don't Need to Agree"_. _The New York Times_.

^ _"Intelligence Report on Russian Hacking"_. _The New York Times_. January 6, 2017. p. ii. Retrieved January 8, 2017. _We assess Russian President Vladimir Putin ordered an influence campaign in 2016 aimed at the US presidential election. Russia's goals were to undermine public faith in the US democratic process, denigrate Secretary Clinton, and harm her electability and potential presidency. We further assess Putin and the Russian Government developed a clear preference for President-elect Trump. We have high confidence in these judgments._

^ Berman, Russell (March 20, 2017). _"It's Official: The FBI Is Investigating Trump's Links to Russia"_. _The Atlantic_. Retrieved June 7, 2017.

^ "James Comey: "No doubt" Russia interfered in 2016 election". *CBS News*. June 8, 2017. Retrieved June 8, 2017.

^ McCarthy, Tom (December 13, 2016). "Trump's relationship with Russia – what we know and what comes next". *The Guardian*. Retrieved March 11, 2017.

^ Bump, Philip (March 3, 2017). "The web of relationships between Team Trump and Russia". *The Washington Post*. Retrieved March 11, 2017.

^ Phillips, Amber (August 19, 2016). "Paul Manafort's complicated ties to Ukraine, explained". *The Washington Post*. Retrieved June 14,2017.

^ Nesbit, Jeff (August 15, 2016). "Donald Trump's Many, Many, Many, Many Ties to Russia". *Time*. Retrieved February 28, 2017.

^ Haberman, Maggie (March 21, 2017). "Roger Stone, the 'Trickster' on Trump's Side, Is Under F.B.I. Scrutiny". *The New York Times*.

^ Williams, Katie Bo (May 24, 2017). "NYT: Russians discussed using Manafort, Flynn to influence Trump". *The Hill*. Retrieved May 28,2017.

^ Parker, Ned; Landay, Jonathan; Strobel, Warren (May 18, 2017). "Exclusive: Trump campaign had at least 18 undisclosed contacts with Russians: sources". *Reuters*. Retrieved May 19, 2017.

^ Murray, Sara; Borger, Gloria; Diamond, Jeremy (February 14, 2017). _"Flynn resigns amid controversy over Russia contacts"_. _CNN_. Retrieved March 2, 2017.

^ Shear, Michael D.; Apuzzo, Matt (May 10, 2017). _"F.B.I. Director James Comey Is Fired by Trump"_. _The New York Times_. Retrieved May 10, 2017.

^ Smith, David (May 9, 2017). _"Donald Trump fires FBI director Comey over handling of Clinton investigation"_. _The Guardian_. Retrieved May 9, 2017.

^ Barrett, Devlin; Rucker, Philip (May 11, 2017). _"Trump said he was thinking of Russia controversy when he decided to fire Comey"_. _The Washington Post_. Retrieved May 12, 2017.

^ Stanek, Becca (May 11, 2017). _"President Trump just completely contradicted the official White House account of the Comey firing"_. _The Week_. Retrieved May 11, 2017.

^ Wilber, Del Quentin; Viswanatha, Aruna (May 16, 2017). _"Trump Asked Comey to Drop Flynn Investigation, According to Memo Written by Former FBI Director"_. _The Wall Street Journal_ (subscription required). Retrieved May 16, 2017.

^ Jump up to:_a b_ Comey, James (June 8, 2017). _"Statement for the Record Senate Select Committee on Intelligence"_ (PDF). United States Senate Select Committee on Intelligence. United States Government. p. 7. Retrieved June 7, 2017.

^ Schmidt, Michael S.; Goldman, Adam (June 7, 2017). "Comey to Testify Trump Pressured Him to Say He Wasn't Under Investigation". *The New York Times*. Retrieved June 7, 2017.

^ Sciutto, Jim; Watkins, Eli (May 23, 2017). "Trump asked DNI, NSA to deny evidence of Russia collusion". *CNN*.

^ Dilanian, Ken; Windrem, Robert (May 22, 2017). "Trump Asked Top Intel Officials to Push Back Publicly on Russia Probe". *NBC News*.

^ Thrush, Glenn; Haberman, Maggie (June 8, 2017). "'I Was Right': As Trump Watches Comey on TV, Anxiety Yields to Relief". *The New York Times*. Retrieved June 9, 2017.

^ Landler, Mark; Haberman, Maggie (June 22, 2017). "Trump Says He Did Not Tape Comey Conversations". *The New York Times*.

^ Rosenstein, Rod (May 17, 2017). "Rod Rosenstein's Letter Appointing Mueller Special Counsel". *The New York Times*. Retrieved May 18, 2017.

^ Bump, Philip (January 11, 2018). "Analysis | Trump and the White House have denied Russian collusion more than 140 times". *The Washington Post*.

^ Mazzetti, Mark; Bergman, Ronen; Kirkpatrick, David D. (May 19, 2018). "Trump Jr. and Other Aides Met With Gulf Emissary Offering Help to Win Election". *The New York Times*.

^ *Keating, Joshua (March 8, 2018). "It's Not Just a "Russia" Investigation Anymore". Slate.*

^ *Vitkovskaya, Julie (June 16, 2017). "Trump Is Officially under Investigation. How Did We Get Here?". The Washington Post. Retrieved June 16, 2017. Trump is officially under investigation... Special counsel investigating Trump for possible obstruction of justice... The president is being investigated...*

^ *Sekulow, Jay (June 18, 2017). "Transcript: Jay Sekulow on "Face the Nation," June 18, 2017". Face the Nation (Interview). Interviewed by John Dickerson. CBS News. Retrieved June 19, 2017. SEKULOW: The president is not and has not been under investigation.*
*DICKERSON: How do you know?*
*SEKULOW: Because we've received no notice of investigation. There has been no notification from the special counsel's office that the president is under investigation.*

^ *Niquette, Mark; Krasny, Ros; Smialek, Jeanna (June 18, 2017). "Trump Not Under Investigation for Obstruction, Lawyer Says". Bloomberg News.*

^ *Thomas, Pierre (June 19, 2017). "Where things stand with special counsel Mueller's Russia probe". ABC News. According to sources familiar with the process ... [a]n assessment of evidence and circumstances will be completed before a final decision is made to launch an investigation of the president of the United States regarding potential obstruction of justice.*

^ *Schmidt, Michael S.; Haberman, Maggie (January 25, 2018). "Trump Ordered Mueller Fired, but Backed Off When White House Counsel Threatened to Quit". The New York Times.*

^ *Helderman, Rosalind S.; Dawsey, Josh (January 26, 2018). "Trump moved to fire Mueller in June, bringing White House counsel to the brink of leaving". The Washington Post. Retrieved January 26, 2018.*

^ *Haberman, Maggie; Schmidt, Michael S. (April 10, 2018). "Trump Sought to Fire Mueller in December". The New York Times.*

^ *Salama, Vivian (April 10, 2018). "White House: President Trump 'certainly believes he has the power' to fire Mueller". NBC News. Retrieved April 11, 2018.*

^ *Keneally, Meghan; Mallin, Alexander (August 1, 2018). "Trump to Sessions: Shut down Russia probe". ABC News. Retrieved August 1,2018.*

^ *Leonnig, Carol D.; Horwitz, Sari; Dawsey, Josh (January 23, 2018). "Mueller seeks to question Trump about Flynn and Comey departures". The Washington Post.*

^ *"Trump's lawyers want him to refuse Mueller interview request: NY Times". Reuters. February 6, 2018.*

^ *Smith, Allan (November 20, 2018). "Trump submits written answers to Robert Mueller's questions". NBC News. Retrieved December 12,2018.*

^ _Goldman, Adam; Schmidt, Michael S.;_ Fandos, Nicholas (January 11, 2019). _"F.B.I. Opened Inquiry Into Whether Trump Was Secretly Working on Behalf of Russia"_. **_The New York Times_**.

^ Buchanan, Larry; Yourish, Karen (February 19, 2019). _"Trump Has Publicly Attacked the Russia Investigation More Than 1,100 Times"_. **_The New York Times_**. _Retrieved February 22, 2019._

^ Zapotosky, Matt; Bui, Lynh; Jackman, Tom; Barrett, Devlin (August 21, 2018). _"Manafort convicted on 8 counts; mistrial declared on 10 others"_. **_The Washington Post_**. _Retrieved August 21, 2018._

^ _Leonnig, Carol D.; Dawsey, Josh_ (August 23, 2018). _"Trump sought his lawyers' advice weeks ago on possibility of pardoning Manafort, Giuliani says"_. **_The Washington Post_**. _Retrieved August 23, 2018._

^ Polantz, Katelyn (September 14, 2018). _"Paul Manafort pleads guilty and agrees to cooperate with Mueller investigation"_. **_CNN_**. _Retrieved September 16, 2018._

^ _LaFraniere, Sharon_ (November 26, 2018). _"Manafort Breached Plea Deal by Repeatedly Lying, Mueller Says"_. **_The New York Times_**. _Retrieved November 27, 2018._

^ _"Manafort's Lawyers Brief Trump's Team On Mueller Talks, Giuliani Tells AP"_. **_NPR_**. _November 28, 2018. Retrieved December 12, 2018._

^ Deng, Boer (November 29, 2018). _"Trump hints at a pardon for Paul Manafort"_. _The Times_. Retrieved December 12, 2018.

^ Sullivan, Kate (November 27, 2018). _"Nadler warns Trump 'dangling a pardon' for Manafort is 'close to obstruction of justice'"_. _CNN_. Retrieved December 12, 2018.

^ Barrett, Devlin; Zapotosky, Matt; _Helderman, Rosalind S._ (November 29, 2018). _"Michael Cohen, Trump's former lawyer, pleads guilty to lying to Congress about Moscow project"_. _The Washington Post_. Retrieved December 12, 2018.

^
—

For a list of persons who have been charged, see _Vitkovskaya, Julie; Granados, Samuel; Uhrmacher, Kevin; Williams, Aaron_ (December 12, 2018). _"Who's been charged in Mueller-linked probes, and why"_. _The Washington Post_. Retrieved December 20, 2018. _Four former Trump campaign officials have pleaded guilty in Mueller's investigation, though none were charged with colluding with Russians to affect the 2016 election._

For charges against Michael Flynn, Rick Gates, and George Papadopoulos, see _Mangan, Dan (July 30, 2018)_. _"Trump and Giuliani are right that 'collusion is not a crime.' But that doesn't matter for Mueller's probe"_. _CNBC_.

For charges against Michael Flynn, Rick Gates, Paul Manafort, and Michael Cohen, see _"Mueller investigation: No jail time sought for Trump ex-adviser Michael Flynn"_. _BBC Online_. December 5, 2018.

^ Mazzetti, Mark; Sullivan, Eileen; Haberman, Maggie (January 25, 2019). "Indicting Roger Stone, Mueller Shows Link Between Trump Campaign and WikiLeaks". The New York Times. Retrieved January 25, 2019.

^ Luckhurst, Toby. "The Stormy Daniels-Donald Trump story explained". BBC Online. Retrieved March 11, 2018.

^ Nelson, Louis (March 7, 2018). "White House on Stormy Daniels: Trump 'denied all these allegations'". Politico. Retrieved March 16,2018.

^ Tatum, Sophie; Cuomo, Chris (February 14, 2018). "Trump's lawyer says he paid $130,000 to porn star ahead of election". CNN. Retrieved March 16, 2018.

^ Fitzpatrick, Sarah (March 8, 2018). "Trump lawyer Michael Cohen tries to silence adult-film star Stormy Daniels". NBC News. Retrieved March 16, 2018.

^ Fitzpatrick, Sarah; Connor, Tracy (March 16, 2018). "Trump tries to move Stormy Daniels lawsuit to federal court, claims she owes him $20 million". NBC News. Retrieved March 17, 2018.

^ Carter, Brandon (March 6, 2018). "Stormy Daniels files lawsuit against Trump". The Hill. Daniels, whose legal name is Stephanie Clifford, claims in her suit filed Tuesday that the nondisclosure agreement is not valid because Trump never signed the deal, according to documents revealed publicly by her attorney, Michael Avenatti.

^ "Trump breaks his silence on payment to porn star Stormy Daniels". Australian Broadcasting Corporation. April 6, 2018. Retrieved May 3, 2018.

^ "Trump Acknowledges Financial 'Liability' For Stormy Daniels Payment". NPR. Retrieved May 16, 2018.

^ Blumenthal, Paul (September 2, 2018). "It's Not Just Robert Mueller. President Donald Trump Faces Six Separate Investigations And Lawsuits". HuffPost. Retrieved September 3, 2018.

^ Neumeister, Larry; Hays, Tom (August 22, 2018). "Cohen pleads guilty, implicates Trump in hush-money scheme". Associated Press.

^ "Trump accused of directing hush money". BBC Online. August 22, 2018.

^ Wise, Justin (August 24, 2018). "Shep Smith: Trump's 'hush money' wasn't about sex but about influencing election". The Hill. Retrieved August 25, 2018.

^ Singman, Brooke. "Trump insists he learned of Michael Cohen payments 'later on,' in 'Fox & Friends' exclusive". Fox News. Retrieved August 23, 2018.

^ "Trump ex-lawyer 'happy' to aid Russia probe". BBC Online. August 22, 2018.

^ Barrett, Devlin; Zapotosky, Matt (December 7, 2018). "Court filings directly implicate Trump in efforts to buy women's silence, reveal new contact between inner circle and Russian". *The Washington Post*. Retrieved December 7, 2018.

^ Cone, Allen; Adamczyk, Ed (December 13, 2018). *"Michael Cohen sentenced to 3 years in prison stemming from plea deal"*. *United Press International*. Retrieved December 21, 2018.

^ Wagner, John (December 13, 2018). *"Trump denies directing Michael Cohen to break the law to buy the silence of Playboy playmate and porn star"*. *The Washington Post*. Retrieved December 21, 2018.

^ *"Trump was in the room during hush money discussions with tabloid publisher"*. *NBC News*. Retrieved December 14, 2018.

^ *"House Judiciary Committee launches probe into possible obstruction by Trump"*. *Yahoo! News*. March 3, 2019. Retrieved March 3, 2019.

^ *"US: House panel to widen Trump probe, request documents"*. *Al Jazeera*. March 3, 2019. Retrieved March 3, 2019.

^ Fandos, Nicholas (March 4, 2019). *"With Sweeping Document Request, Democrats Launch Broad Trump Corruption Inquiry"*. *The New York Times*. Retrieved March 6, 2019.

^ Fandos, Nicholas (March 4, 2019). *"With Sweeping Document Request, Democrats Launch Broad Trump Corruption Inquiry"* – via NYTimes.com.

^ Darrah, Nicole (March 3, 2019). "Mark Warner says there's 'enormous' evidence of Russia-Trump collusion". *Fox News*. Retrieved March 4, 2019.

^ Tamborrino, Kelsey (March 3, 2019). "Warner: 'Enormous amounts of evidence' of possible Russia collusion". *Politico*. Retrieved March 4,2019.

^ See:

Singman, Brooke (June 7, 2017). "Reps. Green and Sherman announce plan to file articles of impeachment". *Fox News*. Retrieved June 7, 2017.

For the draft resolutions, see: Sherman, Brad (June 12, 2017), *Impeaching Donald John Trump, President of the United States, for high crimes and misdemeanors* (PDF), United States House of Representatives, retrieved June 12, 2017 and Green, Al (May 17, 2017), "Calling for Impeachment of the President" (PDF), *Congressional Record*, United States House of Representatives, 63(85), pp. H4227–H4228, retrieved May 17, 2017 (video at YouTube Archived June 9, 2017, at the Wayback Machine)

^ "Democratic Rep. Sherman Drafts Article of Impeachment Against Trump". *Roll Call*. June 12, 2017. Retrieved June 12, 2017.

^ Revesz, Rachael (January 20, 2017). "Website aiming to impeach Donald Trump so popular it crashed". *The Independent*. Retrieved January 20, 2017.

^ Gold, Matea (January 20, 2017). _"The campaign to impeach President Trump has begun"_. **The Washington Post**. Retrieved January 20, 2017.

^ Fox, Emily Jane (December 15, 2016). _"Democrats Are Paving the Way to Impeach Donald Trump"_. **Vanity Fair**. Retrieved December 15, 2016.

^ **Teachout, Zephyr** (November 17, 2016). _"Trump's Foreign Business Ties May Violate the Constitution"_. **The New York Times**. Retrieved November 17, 2016.

^ Hamedy, Saba (May 11, 2017). _"Blumenthal: Comey firing 'may well produce impeachment proceedings'"_. **CNN**. Retrieved May 11, 2017.

^ Roarty, Alex (May 10, 2017). _"Democrats talk of an 'impeachment clock' for Trump"_. **The McClatchy Company**. Retrieved May 10,2017.

^ Easley, Jonathan (May 10, 2017). _"Dem reps: Trump is 'moving' toward impeachment"_. **The Hill**. Retrieved May 10, 2017.

^ _"CNN's Wolf Blitzer: "Are We Getting Closer" To Impeachment Of Donald Trump?"_. **RealClearPolitics**. May 16, 2017. Retrieved May 16, 2017.

^ DeBonis, Mike (December 6, 2017). _"House votes to kill Texas lawmaker's Trump impeachment effort"_. **The Washington Post**.

^ Bump, Philip (July 14, 2017). _"No matter how bad it gets for him, here's why Trump isn't getting impeached this year [analysis]"_. **The Washington Post**. Retrieved July 14, 2017.

^ Burns, Alexander (October 11, 2018). _"Pledge to Impeach Trump, a Key Donor Demands of Democrats"_. **The New York Times**. Retrieved October 17, 2018.

^ Cain, Patrick (May 16, 2017). _"There's a process to remove incapable presidents, but it probably won't be used on Trump – yet"_. **Global News**. Retrieved May 16, 2017.

^ Prokop, Andrew (January 12, 2018). _"The 25th Amendment, explained: how a president can be declared unfit to serve"_. **Vox**. Retrieved January 12, 2018.

^ Westwood, Sarah (January 22, 2017). _"Trump hints at re-election bid, vowing 'eight years' of 'great things'"_. **The Washington Examiner**. Retrieved February 19, 2017.

^ _"Trump breaks precedent, files as candidate for re-election on first day"_. Azfamily.com. January 31, 2017. Archived from the original on February 2, 2017. Retrieved February 19, 2017.

^ Graham, David A. (February 15, 2017). _"Trump Kicks Off His 2020 Reelection Campaign on Saturday"_. **The Atlantic**. Retrieved February 19, 2017.

^ McCormick, John; Jacobs, Jennifer (January 31, 2018). _"Trump's 2020 Re-Election Committee Has $22.1 Million in the Bank"_. **Bloomberg News**. Retrieved March 24, 2018.

^ *"Donald J. Trump for President, Inc. / Presidential – Principal campaign committee / Financial summary"*. www.fec.gov. **Federal Election Commission**. December 31, 2018. Retrieved February 5,2019.

^ Donald J. Trump for President, Inc. (January 31, 2019). *"FEC Form 3P – Report of receipts and disbursements – Filing FEC-1312481"*. **Federal Election Commission**. Retrieved February 5, 2019.

## Further reading

*Blair, Gwenda* (2005). *Donald Trump: Master Apprentice*. **Simon & Schuster**. **ISBN** **978-0-7432-7510-1**.

*Blair, Gwenda* (2015a). *Donald Trump: The Candidate*. Simon & Schuster. **ISBN** **978-1-4391-2937-1**.

*Blair, Gwenda* (2015b) [First published 2001]. *The Trumps: Three Generations That Built an Empire*. Simon & Schuster. *ISBN* *978-1-5011-3936-9*.

*Gallup, George Jr.* (1990). *The Gallup Poll: Public Opinion 1989*. **Rowman & Littlefield**. **ISBN** **978-0-8420-2344-3**.

*Pacelle, Mitchell* (2001). *Empire: A Tale of Obsession, Betrayal, and the Battle for an American Icon*. **John Wiley & Sons**. **ISBN** **978-0-471-23865-2**.

*Kranish, Michael*; *Fisher, Marc* (2017) [First published 2016]. *Trump Revealed: The Definitive Biography of the 45th President*. Simon & Schuster. **ISBN** **978-1-5011-5652-6**.

Light, Larry (2012). *Taming the Beast: Wall Street's Imperfect Answers to Making Money*. John Wiley & Sons. ISBN 978-1-118-08420-5.

Trump, Donald J.; Schwartz, Tony (2009) [First published 1987]. *Trump: The Art of the Deal*. Random House. ISBN 978-0-446-35325-0.

Wooten, Sara (2009). *Donald Trump: From Real Estate to Reality TV*. Enslow Publishers. ISBN 978-0-7660-2890-6.

| Presidency | Election |
|---|---|
| | Reactions |
| | Transition |
| | Inauguration |
| | Timeline |
| | first 100 days |
| | 2017 Q1 |
| | 2017 Q2 |
| | 2017 Q3 |

2017 Q4

2018 Q1

2018 Q2

2018 Q3

2018 Q4

2019 Q1

domestic trips

| Timelines | | |
|---|---|---|
| Personnel | | |
| Direct indictments (list of charges) | | |

2017

2018

2019

## In Conclusion: Repeated from Chapter 2-For effect to Bring the Truth Home

I agree with those that we at times have to break from tribal politics. The voting a strict political line regardless of the candidate's history and moral aptitude is a mistake. Voters who support Donald Trump generally do not believe in climate change, have a stronger need for closer, dislike novelty, are more comforted by structure and hierarchy, more readily perceive circumstances as threatening, and are more parochial in their empathy. As a result of system justification allows Trump followers to rationalize and be less discomfited by inequality.

Many of Donald Trump's followers view our best days are behind us, in familiar circumstances that should be returned to, to "Makes Things Great Again "or "Make America Great Again". Your author believes America was great before, now & will be great going forward, despite Donald Trump. Donald Trump has persuaded impoverished white Americans to so often vote against their own economic self-interest. Donald Trump depends on the psychological issues of needing structured familiarity show that for poor whites, voting Trump constitutes an implicit act of system justification and risk aversion. Better to resist change and deal with the devil you know. Another words Donald Trump takes advantage of those who do not do their research and are attracted to a side show. It is your authors contention that the lower and middle class are more likely to win a million dollars in the lottery than obtain help from Donald Trump's policies and tax breaks.  .